Lean Production for the Small Company

Mike Elbert

CRC Press
Taylor & Francis Group
Boca Raton London New York

CRC Press is an imprint of the
Taylor & Francis Group, an **informa** business

A PRODUCTIVITY PRESS BOOK

CRC Press
Taylor & Francis Group
6000 Broken Sound Parkway NW, Suite 300
Boca Raton, FL 33487-2742

© 2013 by Taylor & Francis Group, LLC
CRC Press is an imprint of Taylor & Francis Group, an Informa business

Printed in the United States of America on acid-free paper
Version Date: 20120611

International Standard Book Number: 978-1-4398-7779-1 (Paperback)

Visit the Taylor & Francis Web site at
http://www.taylorandfrancis.com

and the CRC Press Web site at
http://www.crcpress.com

This book is dedicated to my wife Suretta and daughters Michelle and Danielle, without whom this book would not have been possible. I cannot express enough my love and gratitude for all their help and understanding, and all their support throughout the years.

Contents

Preface

This book is designed to walk companies through the implementation of Lean manufacturing within their companies. We start with the fundamentals and build upon them to teach all the tools and processes needed to implement Lean manufacturing based on the Toyota Production System (TPS). We teach how to determine and calculate the waste in business and manufacturing systems, as well as how to use continuous improvement to implement the changes needed to eliminate wasteful steps and processes. We explain how to remove variations within business and manufacturing processes to achieve a steady continuous flow of product through a system that more efficiently delivers product on time to customers. Time is spent on how to design factories for Lean manufacturing, emphasizing how to use customer order demands to schedule the production floor rather than using estimated production schedules, which can lead to excess inventory and inflexibility in meeting customer demand. New methods and tools are discussed that focus on reducing inventory, improving inventory turns, and improving raw material flow through the factory. Companies are taught how to work and partner with suppliers and customers. One chapter is dedicated to the accounting process and how to improve your cash-to-cash cycle time. All the chapters in this book, when implemented, will result in a culture change within your company that will improve business and turn your company into a continuously improving and learning organization that never stops eliminating waste and improving processes.

All of this allows companies to grow, without adding the cost of additional space or hiring more people, to become more competitive in the markets they serve. Think about how exciting it is to achieve new levels of success with very little or no outlay of cash. Many small- to mid-sized manufacturing firms see significant improvements in the following areas:

- Productivity improvements   20% to 30%
- Improved inventory turns   100% to 200%
- Facility space savings   20% to 30%
- Lead time reductions   10% to 50%
- Product cost reductions   5% to 15%

I began thinking about this book in 2005 when I started to realize that unlike many of the large corporations I had worked for, many small companies were not being given the opportunity to utilize the significant advantages of Lean manufacturing as described and documented by James Womack, Jeffery Liker, PhD, and others who had studied the TPS in depth. As I grew more knowledgeable about the advantages of the system and studied more about small business, I became convinced there was an application for TPS within these types of companies.

After leaving a career spent at companies of varying sizes, I decided to focus on consulting for small business. I wanted to teach and help them transform their organizations into cultures of continuous improvement and learning by using TPS, which would result in improved profits and growth for the company. What I found was that companies were very interested in improving their business and manufacturing processes but were without the financial resources to hire consulting help to achieve the transformation. It is important to remember that these tools, methods, and ideals can be used in any industry and although the process is typically called Lean manufacturing, it can be used in any part of your business—from manufacturing to sales to human resources.

In today's business atmosphere, competition is fierce and the cost of doing business is high! Companies need to differentiate their product from the rest of the field but need to have a business structure that is extremely cost efficient, quick to respond to customer demand, and an efficient producer of high-quality products. After spending many years working in manufacturing, I began to notice that the same issues were being revisited with surprising regularity. Some of the issues were cyclical in nature while others would manifest themselves based on who the new managers were, and where they placed their emphasis in trying to improve the business. Everyone had an idea on how to fix the problems!

The problem was that everyone was learning from their previous experiences, as well as what was being taught in business or engineering schools. They were not looking and listening with an open mind or seeking new and creative ways to improve their companies. In the 1980s, the University of Michigan embarked on a study of the U.S.–Japan automobile industry; what they found was a company in Japan called Toyota. Toyota had taken many of the manufacturing and management processes developed over the years and combined them with new concepts into an outstanding management and production system dedicated to the elimination of waste. American automobile manufacturers were the first to take advantage of this new-found system.

I became fascinated by what I was learning about the Toyota Production System and began applying some of the methods and strategies to manufacturing in the early 1990s while working at Graco, Inc., a manufacturer of spray painting systems for the automotive industry. When I moved on to Sanofi Diagnostics Pasteur, a manufacturer of specialized medical equipment, I implemented some of these same strategies within the instrument manufacturing group and found the same amazing results.

I am not aware of any other book that has focused its efforts to consolidate the TPS/Lean manufacturing systems into one concise location where you can go to see, learn, and use the actual tools and procedures that make up the fundamental processes that have made Toyota and other companies so successful.

I would like to thank the people who provide me with support as I continue my journey of learning with TPS. They are Jennifer Klettheimer and Chuck Streeter of Harris Lean Systems, and Dennis Edwards of the Allsteel division of Hon Industries. I would also like to thank my friend Dennis Strand for his help and support in preparing this book.

As your company becomes a learning organization focused on people, process, and flow, I am certain you will find your Lean journey as exciting and fulfilling as I have. Assuredly, it is one of continuous learning that never ends as your company continues to perfect its knowledge and skills with the Toyota Production System.

Michael J. Elbert
Elbert Lean Business Systems, LLC

About The Author

Mike Elbert is president of Elbert Lean Business Systems, LLC, a consulting service that helps businesses eliminate waste.

A qualified Lean Practitioner, Mike is a leader in business and manufacturing processes and systems with an MBA in manufacturing systems from the University of St. Thomas.

Industries that Mike has worked in include electronic components, consumer electronics, heavy metal fabrication, precision machining, plastic and rubber molding, and medical device manufacturing. He spent more than twenty-five years as a manager of engineering, quality, product, and process design, and he understands the importance of planning, teamwork, and accountability.

During his thirty-plus years in manufacturing, Mike has worked in a diverse range of organizations, including small-, mid-, and large-sized corporations. For the past twenty-five years, he has worked with Lean manufacturing systems and its predecessors, focusing on improving manufacturing processes and equipment.

Mike believes that any business, including start-ups, can improve efficiency and income by identifying and eliminating waste from processes, including the extended supply chain. He offers a range of programs and services that include teaching Lean business systems, facilitating improvement meetings, and directing the overall transformation of your company to a Lean organization. Drawing on decades of experience in low- and high-volume production, he now focuses mainly on the implementation of Lean business and manufacturing systems while also providing many classical industrial engineering products.

After a career spent reducing costs and improving manufacturing efficiency, Mike now teaches and coaches others on how to achieve the same success. He is passionate about Lean business and manufacturing systems and their ability to improve your company, products, and customer satisfaction.

Mike has published articles and has been quoted in *Industrial Engineering* magazine, and was a columnist for the Minnesota Manufacturers Alliance's monthly newsletter. He has taught seminars for the Minnesota Manufacturers Alliance, Minnesota Employers Association, and nationally for the Institute of Industrial Engineers. He is a life member of the Institute of Industrial Engineers and a member of its Twin Cities Chapter 38.

Mike Elbert is available for private consultations on Lean Enterprise Systems, operations management, industrial engineering, and facility design. For more information, please visit his website at www.elbertleansystems.com.

Chapter 1

Introduction

Who Should Use This Book

As a small business owner, you have many responsibilities and wear many hats on a day-to-day basis. One day you are the chief accountant, while the next day you are the marketing manager and salesman, perhaps the production scheduler, chief engineer, or even the human resources manager, just to name a few. Your time is at a premium and your management staff's time is also precious. As a business consultant, I have met with small business owners and small factory managers who have a desire to improve their operations. They know that to stay competitive in today's market, they must eliminate waste and keep costs down. They have an interest in improving their operations; consequently, due to a lack of financial resources, available time, or higher priorities, they have found the availability of consulting services out of their reach. For these reasons, this book has been prepared to aid you and your company in continuous improvement efforts.

Toyota Corporation has made Lean manufacturing a wonderful success, and its concepts have been copied worldwide by major corporations. However, many small companies have been unable to take advantage of these concepts for many reasons. This book was created for small businesses as a tool and workbook to help incorporate Lean manufacturing concepts and its tools into your operations. While I still believe the use of on-site trained consultants is helpful to teach and guide your transformation, it is important that they understand the needs of small business.

Having implemented Lean manufacturing and its predecessor's principles and concepts into all types and sizes of corporations, I believe this book will provide you with the basic elements for successful implementation.

Guidance: Can I Use This Book if I Am Not a Manufacturer of Metal Parts?

 One constant misconception is that Lean manufacturing can only be used by the manufacturing department within your company. This is entirely incorrect. The methodology and tools can be used in any department—from marketing, to sales, administration, field service, shipping, etc. The reason it is called *Lean manufacturing* is because manufacturing is the easiest and most visible place to start.

Also, many books use the auto industry as examples in their books. However, any industry—medical device, hospitals, medical clinics, retail sales, government, etc.—can use this book, and all of the discussions and examples can be directly applied to their industries. All you have to do is substitute your processes in place of the ones in this book.

This book is for every small company that wants to improve its business and manufacturing processes.

How to Use This Book

I have designed this book to be a hands-on workbook-type tool that you can use as a teaching reference and a source for visual aids and forms. I have not attempted to give you all the fine details of Lean manufacturing because we know that time and resources are limited within the small company, but I have tried to provide you with a basic understanding of Lean and how to use the tools of Lean. You will find this book is structured around specific topics that are all elements of Lean manufacturing and business systems.

I recommend that you and your immediate staff read this book together and discuss how these tools and concepts can be used in or adapted to your organization. As we progress through the book, each topic and chapter build upon the other, so knowing and understanding each one are important before moving on. Be sure to take the time to completely discuss the book with your staff because all of you will be responsible for the final success of your transformation to a Lean organization. Many of the terms used in Lean manufacturing are Japanese in origin and may be unfamiliar to you. I have used standard English-language terms where I could; however, in some cases it is important to learn a new term. When a new term in another language is needed, I explain the term and its origin.

Brief History of Lean Manufacturing

Many people have heard of "Lean manufacturing" and have some understanding of it. You may be aware of the Toyota Corporation as being the father of the modern Lean movement and, without a doubt, they have taken the philosophy, discipline, and tools used to a level no one else has ever done. But, did they create all of this on their own? It is my belief that without significant steps in manufacturing prior to Toyota's use of these tools, someone else may have achieved the same success.

As a foundation for understanding Lean manufacturing, we must have a fundamental understanding of how we got to where we are today. Let us take a look at what needed to happen to create the roots of Lean manufacturing; see Table 1.1

As you can see from Table 1.1, each advance in manufacturing helped spur the next paradigm-shifting advance. In 1950, after World War II, Mr. Toyoda and Mr. Ohno began to rebuild the Toyota Corporation. This rebuilding effort came as a whole new philosophy of manufacturing in how to strategize and manage corporations. Certainly the Japanese culture played a significant part in the success of their efforts, but their success is built on visiting and learning from some of the greatest manufacturing and process industries in the United States.

As we have moved through each paradigm shift in manufacturing and business, we have achieved additional advantages in the world market; however, each step was met with enthusiasm by early adopters and scorn by naysayers who do not accept change easily. Those of us in the middle who wait to see which way the wind is blowing may be left behind. If we do not openly adopt new and current manufacturing techniques, our businesses may not reach the success level we desire.

From my personal experience watching my father run his small business, I watched as technology passed him by. I remember talking with him and

Table 1.1   The Roots of Lean Manufacturing

Interchangeable parts	Eli Whitney	1850s
Modern machine tools begin to emerge		1860–1875
Drafting and drawing standards are created Standardized tolerance system is developed	Henry Ford	1860–1875
Time study is developed and introduced Work standard methodology created Standardized work instituted	Fredrick Taylor	1890–1910
Time and motion studies Process charts	Frank and Lillian Gilbreth	1890–1910
Assembly line Ford develops his modern management philosophy Vertical integration Flow manufacturing	Henry Ford	1912–1926
Statistical process control Total quality management	Joseph Juran Edward Demming	1942–1948
Just-in-time manufacturing Toyota production system Stockless production Work teams 5S housekeeping Quality circles Empowered employees Value stream management (focused factories)	Eiji Toyoda Taiichi Ohno	1950–1985

Source: Courtesy of Strategos, Inc., www.strategosinc.com; modified by Mike Elbert.

suggesting he get a computer for his office; that was back in 1985. At that time, he could see no need for changing the way his business operated. Although his business was a success and still exists today, he could have made his life so much easier and afforded himself more time to grow his business rather than do paperwork. He was proud of the fact that he had kept his main machine tool running for more than forty years. But imagine if he had updated the equipment, how much more efficient and productive he would have been. However, I understood that having done things the same way for more than forty years, it would have been difficult for him to change.

Also, if you have a niche market and are comfortable with your profitability, you will not look for ways to improve your business operations. My father had a niche market in which he was the only player in the immediate geographical area; because he was not willing to be progressive in his approach to business, competition entered the area, which made him less profitable because competitors were taking market share. Although he did things very well and was known for quality work and high integrity, which were some of his core competencies and values, he failed to adjust to current times. He should have asked himself regularly, "In the business in which I want to compete, what should I do on a regular basis to separate and distinguish myself from my competition so that customers want to buy from me?" Why do I tell you this story? It is to show you that you can become stagnant doing the same thing year-to-year; and by not accepting new methods and technologies, you will fall behind your competition.

The Philosophy of Lean Manufacturing and Business Systems

The basic philosophy of Lean manufacturing is to eliminate wasteful steps found in all processes used by a company to provide a product for its customers. The expenditure of any resource that does not create value for the customer is wasteful and should be removed. How is this done? You do this by improving the manufacturing and business processes used in your company. In the book *The Toyota Way* (Liker, 2004), this is referred to as "The Toyota Production System (TPS) and Lean Production," a true systems approach to achieving the high level of success that Toyota has enjoyed. This systems approach uses the same basic approach and tools to eliminate wasteful steps and processes in product development, sales and marketing, manufacturing, logistics, and management, thus becoming so cost efficient and productive at producing and providing quality product on time to your customers that your competition is not considered a possible supplier by your customer.

Many companies have superficially applied Lean concepts and, if asked, they will say, "We are doing Lean manufacturing." The fact is that about 75% of companies in the United States say they are Lean; however, only about 3%

to 5% have achieved the level of success and deployment of Lean that Toyota has achieved. The remainder are using "Lean tools" but have not achieved the systems approach and use of personnel that truly identifies them as a Lean manufacturer/producer.

A survey by the Aberdeen Group in 2004 indicated that most companies are in catch-up mode and need to rethink their tactics and tools to improve their Lean effectiveness. More than 50% of the companies in the survey said they sporadically use Lean techniques, while more than 85% had Lean knowledge in only a few people. The vast majority, more than 90%, said they still use paper-based systems for production planning (Aberdeen Group, 2004). This reaffirms that most companies have only used a fraction of Toyota's Lean production tools and techniques.

Taiichi Ohno was the creator and founder of the Toyota Production System (TPS). In his book *Toyota Production System: Beyond Large-Scale Production,* he states,

> All we are doing is looking at the time line, from the moment the customer gives us an order to the point when we collect the cash. And we are reducing that time line by removing the non-value-added wastes.

There are two types of costs related to your business: value-added and non-value-added costs. A value-added cost is one that the customer expects to pay for, for example, fastening two pieces of material together, paint on the exterior of a product to protect it from rust, etc. Non-value-added cost is what the customer will not pay for, for example, time to move material within your shop to the next operation, cost of excess inventory sitting between processes, inefficient staff and processes, and even final inspection. OK, final inspection, you have to be kidding, no? If you eliminate wasteful steps in the process, you improve your process time; if you have more time, you can have your assembly personnel check their own work or the work of their predecessor, thus eliminating the need for final inspection because no errors should ever reach final inspection. Is this possible? No, because everyone makes errors. Ever hear of the term "zero defects," which was a program originally started as a quality control program by the Martin Marietta Corporation back in the 1960s for the Titan Missile program that carried the Gemini astronauts into space? What a great goal!

Because all non-value-added steps add cost to your product, it makes your product less attractive to your customers. You need to transform your company into a Lean organization. This will take time. Taiichi Ohno started his Lean journey in 1949 and was still continuing the journey when he wrote his book in 1975. The transformation of your company may not take thirty-four years but it will take years—not weeks or months. This is truly a business transformation, not just a project. It reshapes the way your company acts and thinks and, no matter what level you achieve in your journey, be it one of the 75% who use the tools or one of the 3 to 5% who achieve total transformation, you have taken positive steps to improve your company.

Why Do We Need Lean Manufacturing and Business Systems?

The answer to this question is simple: We cannot do without it. As our businesses grow, they become riddled with hidden waste that, over time, raises the cost of doing business and slows down the product time-to-market for our customers. This is not only a production problem, but also a development issue because approximately 80% of a product's cost is designed in by the product engineers. There are ways to mediate and reduce this 80% number, and I discuss these later in the book.

Many people and companies believe that Lean manufacturing, the Toyota Production System (TPS), was designed for large companies with mass-produced products and is not applicable to the small business. Actually, the opposite is true. The system was originally designed to produce small quantities of numerous types and configurations of products, similar to a job shop. The system is very elastic and can flex to continuing product and market conditions, far better than old-fashioned ideas of a manufacturing company. If you are to be competitive and successful today, you must be able to produce product on demand and with high quality at a cost that is equal to or close to an emerging country's cost; otherwise, your customers will take their business to those emerging countries.

One company I was talking with believed they were a job shop, doing short runs and, as a result, they did not feel they could restructure into a value stream production floor layout, which is better for higher volume and dedicated management control. The more we discussed their customer production volumes, the more they became aware that 80% of their volume came from one customer and that it was usually the same parts. All of a sudden, we were able to implement a production flow value stream that could be used to redesign the production floor and implement kanbans.

Chapter 2

Fundamentals of Lean Production and Business Systems

Nine Critical Wastes in Business

Toyota identified seven major types of waste (non-value-added costs). I like to call these "the magnificent seven" because they identify a significant portion of the waste found in all business operations. Some may be more obvious as manufacturing waste but you can also identify the same types of waste in your office, sales, and development organizations.

Jeffery Liker, author of *The Toyota Way*, added the eighth to the list and a company I was working with added the ninth—all of which capture, I believe, the most complete list of waste (non-value-added cost) to our products today.

Let's learn about each one (the first seven items are the original Toyota seven wastes):

1. *Overproduction*: This is the most damaging of all the wastes because it produces more product than you have orders for, which means you over-staff, which creates excess inventory, adds carrying costs, and wastes valuable building floor space.
2. *Inventory*: Excess inventory (as my associate said, "Inventory is evil"). Excessive amounts of raw material and finished goods cause longer

lead times. Goods stored for a long time can become obsolete, corroded, or otherwise damaged and should be scrapped. Not to mention the labor cost associated with scrapping the part plus the cost of the part adds up to a lot of wasted cash. Excess inventory hides delivery or quality problems with suppliers or products, equipment downtime, excessive set-up times, and improperly balanced production lines and production bottlenecks.

3. *Waiting (idle time)*: Idle time or waiting time means that the machine operator is idle (not doing anything of value added to the product) while they wait for the next part to arrive or a machine to complete running a part. It can also mean the office worker who is standing in line for the copier. Some of the causes may be a production bottleneck, late arrival of parts from the supplier or warehouse, a machine or tool has broken down, etc.

4. *Unnecessary movement of material*: Moving material (WIP or finished goods) into or out of storage when not necessary; moving material long distances to get to the next processing step. An example would be moving finished goods from the finished goods warehouse back to production for rework or moving material from one department or building to another for the next processing step.

5. *Overprocessing or incorrect processing*: This is one of my favorite wastes, especially in regulated industries—when unneeded steps are needed to process a part or document. An example of a document being overprocessed was an Engineering Change Order I did for a small label used by our field service staff. Because it was a medical instrument, it took thirty-two signatures of approval before the new label could be released to production. Incorrect processing is when a defect is created as a result of a process that is not needed to satisfy the requirements of the part specifications. Overprocessing can also mean producing a part with higher quality than is needed. This may be a result of poor part design.

6. *Motion*: Any movement by an employee that does not add value to the product is wasted motion. This can mean reaching, walking, looking for tools, reading unnecessary paperwork, ergonomically incorrect movements, etc.

7. *Defects:* Incorrect processing of a part or product that results in reworking, repairing, scrapping, or needing a production deviation for use. Any steps taken, including inspection, which did not create a part or

product at an acceptable quality and specification the first time, would be considered waste.

8. *Unused creativity*: Not listening to or engaging an employee with knowledge that can be used to improve products and processes within your organization is truly a lost learning opportunity for all. The ideas your employees have can result in reducing lost time, improved employee skills, improved quality levels, and improved customer satisfaction. Management and engineers are not the only ones with ideas.

9. *Environmental*: Although relatively new to the list, it fits nicely with the new push for "Green Lean." Consider the non-value-added costs associated with this area, such as disposing of corrugated boxes, plastic bags, bubble wrap, and the like. There are huge opportunities here for a reduction in utility costs, trash disposal, and pollution control.

Now you have an understanding of what deadly wastes are. Can you see any opportunities for elimination of waste (non-value-added tasks or processes) within your organization? Later in this book I will help you identify your non-value-added tasks and processes.

Concerning Elimination of Waste

Whenever you are considering eliminating waste, you must also consider improving efficiency:

1. Improving efficiency makes sense only when it is tied to cost reduction.
2. Look at the efficiency of each operator and each line. Then look at the operators as a group, and then at the efficiency of the entire plant (all lines) (Ohno, 1988).

When you look at your plant as an entire system, it is very easy to find cost reductions and improve efficiencies.

Fundamentals of Lean Manufacturing

The fundamental principles of Lean were developed as a way for Toyota to catch up with American automobile manufacturers after World War II. These fundamentals have proven to be a sound business model, one that is unsurpassed at this time. The fundamentals are very simple and should be easy to follow:

- *Production leveling*: Level load the production line so that everyone is equally busy from workstation to workstation, from the beginning of the production line to the end, with all supporting lines equally balanced to support the main line.
- *Production flow*: Rearrange your factory into work cells and then production lines based on value streams.
- *Cost reduction*: Continuous improvement, rapid continuous improvement, and numerous other terms all relate to the same thing: the continuous elimination of waste in a company's systems.
- *Just-in-time*: Build what you need when you need it. Do not build to store in WIP (work in process) or finished goods inventory. If a company can achieve this ideal level of production, the end result will be zero inventory levels. Although few, if any, companies ever achieve this level, it is the ultimate goal. Think what your company might be like if you achieved this ideal state. You would save significant factory square footage, excellent inventory turns, and, as a result of the inventory turns, reduced inventory carrying costs. That means less borrowed money and thus less interest cost. All these cost savings drop directly to the bottom line for improved profit. Another advantage is that in most cases your cash-to-cash cycle will be reduced.
- *Common-sense ideas*: These are ideas that are simple and make a lot of sense. The ideas are not complicated or even difficult to implement, yet they provide excellent return for the time, effort, and cost expended. (For example, simply changing the way one company handled rejected material and processing of the paperwork reduced the time to close one scrap ticket from weeks to days.)
- *Automated machine intelligence*: When automating a machine, be it an assembly-line machine, a CNC (computer numerical control) machine tool, a paint line, etc., you will produce scrap faster than you can believe unless you have an automatic stop on the machine. This is a stop that will automatically detect the first defect and shut down the automated system immediately upon recognizing the first defect. Can you do this with no automated lines and equipment? The answer is "yes."

▪ *Power of teams and individuals:* Optimizing and utilizing the skills of individual team members, while creating specialized skills as needed, strengthens your company's team members. When you combine all these skills and then begin orchestrating their usage is when you begin to truly see the power of teams and individuals. Like a football coach who lets the quarterback call his own plays, you as a manager must be secure and confident enough to let your staff and production workers call their own plays. This is your ultimate goal.

The Five Whys

You may have already heard of the five **whys**. This form of problem solving helps search out the root cause of a problem. The idea is to ask **why** questions five times, each time taking another step deeper into a problem. Although this sounds simple, I assure you it is not. It takes practice and patience to achieve success. The method of five whys is officially called the "Socratic method," for the originator of the teaching method, the Greek teacher Socrates, and is designed to teach your employees to think about each question asked before they answer. Part of being a good manager and Lean leader is being a good teacher. For example, suppose two parts would not assemble correctly:

1. Why did the two parts not go together?
   The attachment holes between part "A" and part "B" did not align.
2. Why was there a misalignment?
   The hole in part "B" was out of position.
3. Why was the hole in part "B" out of position?
   The fabrication department made it wrong. They followed the print.
4. Why was the piece part printed wrong?
   The drawing had an engineering error.
5. Why was there an engineering error?
   The engineer made a math calculation error.

We now have an answer to the root cause of our problem, and we can fix it with the proper corrective action:

Instruct engineers to be more careful in their calculations and then correct the engineering piece part print. This specific problem should not recur because it was properly corrected.

One of the problems when asking the five whys is that people resist you asking the questions when they know they are not following the proper procedures for their own work. If you build your system on the scientific practice of asking the five whys, you can get to the root cause of your problems, which are often hidden by other symptoms.

Critical Importance of Management Commitment

I *cannot emphasize enough* the critical importance of you and your management team from the top all the way to the leader on the production floor or in the office knowing, understanding, accepting, and personally practicing and driving the change to a Lean culture. You as the leaders of the company set the tone and create the culture of the organization. It is critical to the success of this implementation and ongoing sustainability that you and all your staff commit to making these changes because if this is not a team effort and a team sustainability goal as well, you will not fully reap the benefits of Lean.

I have seen companies start out with lots of enthusiasm and energy around Lean manufacturing, only to watch the focus of Lean fade as a new crisis for the company enters the picture. Sometimes it is a new manager who enters the picture and does not fully understand what Lean is. If Lean is to be successful, you must teach and train that person in the Lean culture.

Now let us discuss one factory I worked with. This factory made complex electromechanical instrumentation for medical customers. When Lean was introduced to the factory, it was viewed as just another fad, the "flavor-of-the-month," just another management initiative. Extensive training was given to the Lean leadership team, which then trained the factory floor personnel. It took a year of regular meetings with non-management staff to convince the factory personnel that Lean principles would not be used as a tool to eliminate their jobs. When they finally became comfortable with this, they embraced the Lean concepts. Consequently, some of the middle management staff, although saying they supported Lean, never really supported the changes that would affect their departments. This happened for two reasons: (1) they did not want to lose their power in the organization although some of the power was only perceived power, and (2) their goals and objectives were not directly tied to the overall success of Lean and its implementation in the factory. That is, they were not 100% committed to Lean and its principles. The next situation this company experienced was a very significant quality issue with some of its products; this resulted in a refocusing of resources away from Lean to fix these problems. When this happened, the management staff reverted to its old ways, and Lean tools were forgotten and the company lost a significant amount of the improvements they had achieved.

All of this is a perfect example of lack of management commitment to sustain Lean production.

Guidance: Upper-Level and Middle Managers Must Be Committed to Sustainability

 Our basic instinct in a crucial situation, be it personal or business, is to revert back to our basic skills and training, better known as our comfort zone because it has worked for us in the past. You must stay committed to your new direction to achieve your long-term goals, no matter how easy it is to revert back. If you revert back, you will have to do the work all over to regain ground, and that rework is nothing but waste.

Establish Your Lean Team and Lean Leader

This is an area that does not get enough attention and one that has the potential to have a significant impact on the organization. ***The team is the leader of the culture change***. As a small business, the team may be as small as one person, yourself, but no larger than one person from each department. It could be yourself and the person you leave in charge when you are gone, or it could be all of your employees. In a very small shop, everyone might get together and learn the basics and make the changes together. If you are a slightly larger company and can afford a dedicated person half-time or full-time, this would be an excellent idea.

This is not a place to put someone whom you do not want to progress in the organization. This team is an excellent place to position people for advancement. Used correctly, the team can showcase a person's leadership skills—or lack thereof—before placing him or her into a significant role of responsibility.

The Lean Coach

In a small company it is always difficult to find enough time and people to accomplish what needs to be done; if you are in growth mode, whether a small or larger company, it is even more difficult. But to be successful with Lean, you will need to identify someone as the "Lean coach." Because this position would be a staff-level position reporting to the company owner, Vice President of Operations, or the plant manager, you want to use one of your "rising stars." This is an excellent way for them to see and learn all aspects of the business; this person will become your in-house expert on Lean production. For that reason, you want someone from your organization who is a leader in change management. Someone who gets excited about making things better and at the same time someone who people will listen to and support. This person needs the respect and support of the top management staff in your organization. The person may well be someone whom you are grooming for a higher position.

I have found that once this person learns the Lean principles and concepts and has successfully implemented some of them, he or she becomes very passionate about Lean and wants to work even harder to transform the company. Just think what all of that passion and energy can do for your company when you give this person the support and backing that he or she needs to succeed.

The job of the Lean coach will include

1. Leading creation of value stream maps
2. Facilitating and coaching kaizen events
3. Teaching Lean tools, concepts, and philosophy
4. Educating themselves on Lean and bringing back new ideas to the company
5. Directing the development and deployment of the Lean operating systems (metrics, principles, audits, glass walls, standardized work, supermarkets, work cells, etc.)

The more difficult jobs they have include

6. Coaching and teaching all levels of company leadership about Lean
7. Internally promoting Lean transformation

8. Transforming the company to a value stream management structure if the company desires

9. Successfully engaging other departments, outside of production, in using Lean

Why do I say these last four jobs are more difficult? Because the Lean coach must be more politically savvy to accomplish these jobs successfully.

The Lean coaching position is not a trivial position; it is one that needs both legitimate and perceived power, one that requires a person who

- Is smart (quick study)
- Loves learning new things
- Likes to read books
- Is passionate about improving processes
- Is hands-on (get your hands dirty)
- Has leadership skills (good listener, do-the-right-thing, etc.)
- Has strong interpersonal skills
- Is an excellent communicator (written and spoken)
- Is a systems thinker
- Is skilled and knowledgeable in the use of spreadsheets, graphs, data, presentations, etc.
- Has excellent problem-solving skills
- Is not afraid of confrontation
- Is open to new ideas
- Is a well-organized individual

Guidance: Rubber-Stamped Lean Coach

Lean leader wanted, must have Lean Six Sigma black belt! How many times do you see this in a job ad? A lot of companies believe they need someone who is *certified* in Lean; after all, if they have a "black belt," they must know their subject and must be successful at applying the tools. Many universities and professional organizations offer certifications in Lean manufacturing and Six Sigma. These programs certainly have merit, in that they provide some basic training in the philosophy and tools needed to understand Lean, and in today's job market such credentials help you get a job. But do you really need them? My experience and others in the field can tell you that there is *absolutely no substitute for hands-on experience* when it comes to implementing Lean. Formal education cannot substitute for years of experience in manufacturing; only with experience and hands-on trial-and-error has one learned what works best for a work cell shape or if a process is stable enough for one-piece flow. A coach with five to ten years of serious Lean experience is worth far more than someone with a black belt and little experience on the production floor. Also remember the distinct difference between Lean and Six Sigma: Which one do you really need?

Lean Coach and Consultants

The Lean coach, whom you should have picked from among some of your most talented employees, has been named; he or she has begun reading books on Lean and has now begun the new position but has never before transitioned a company. How do you get him or her a mentor (teacher)? None of you in the company knows anything about Lean? Although this book is designed for your Lean coach and you to use as a workbook to build your Lean operations system without the aid of a full-time consultant, I understand that there are times when a little help is needed. I would suggest that when this happens, the use of a consultant as a coach for a week or two, or even a month, is completely acceptable. The consultant should be just that: a coach. The consultant should not be doing the work, but rather coaching and training your in-house Lean coach. You may want to consider this unless the person you pick for the in-house Lean coach has someone who he or she can contact for help. You may also want to consider the use of a consultant to audit your progress and help answer any questions that might arise. This auditing is helpful to establish where you are in the process of Lean implementation so you can plan your next steps.

Lean Team

When creating the team, think about all the functions within your company and have each area represented. This you want to do for continuity and organizational support.

This team will meet twice a month for the foreseeable future; I would recommend two uninterrupted days at a time, to help learn Lean concepts and principles as well as guide the company and the staff through the culture changes ahead.

This team will need to learn and understand how to use the tools provided to them. These tools and concepts will be used to teach Lean principles to other levels of staff and managers.

At this time, we should have two levels of training either in-process or complete:

1. *Senior management staff:* Read this book together and understand what is needed to implement Lean manufacturing and how to change the company culture.
2. *Lean team:* The Lean team should be trained by the Lean coach (leader) and members of senior staff who understand and can teach Lean concepts to the Lean team.

Going forward, it will be the responsibility of the Lean team leader to teach the remainder of the company staff Lean principles and concepts.

Why do I approach the teaching of Lean in this way? I do this because Lean manufacturing is something that is best learned as a team. You are transforming your company to a learning and doing organization, one where everyone is free to express their thoughts and ideas and to use these opportunities to improve processes and eliminate waste.

Let us talk about another way to form this team. If your company is fortunate enough to have an Industrial Engineering department, this is an excellent department in which to find your change agent. Industrial Engineers are trained in systems thinking and in operations improvements. It is possible to use your Industrial Engineers as Toyota does, as a true profit center, where they will continually look at your processes and eliminate waste within them. Industrial Engineering in many ways is a forgotten field, yet its goal is to improve business processes. I would suggest that all companies can benefit by having an Industrial Engineer on staff.

You may still find some lack of understanding regarding Lean principles and concepts and how to apply them; if this happens, I recommend the use of an outside consultant to help clarify such concepts and facilitate their application within your organization.

Lean Production and Your Employees

The introduction of Lean manufacturing methodology to your employees can be a difficult task. Employees look at it as just another management idea that they must contend with. Some think of it as the flavor-of-the-month and it will eventually go away, and there is no need to get too excited about it; others look at it as a way to get rid of people. You will hear, "They are going to make changes to our processes and then they can get rid of some of us." It is very important to communicate early on to your employees that *no one will lose their jobs because of Lean manufacturing, that actually the opposite is true.* As you improve your processes, product flow, on-time delivery, cost, and quality, you will most likely be asked to deliver more products by your customers. As a result, you may have to increase production but because of improved productivity, you may not have to add staff; thus, your employees' jobs become more stable. On the other hand, business situations may require you to adjust staffing levels but it will not be due to Lean manufacturing.

How do you convince your employees that Lean is good for them? From my experience, it will take about a year of seeing some changes happen without people losing their jobs before your employees will accept the idea that Lean is not a tool to be used to eliminate staff.

Schedule weekly meetings with a cross-functional group of employees—no more than ten employees at a time. Create a group with a mix similar to that below:

1. Assembly
2. Fabrication
3. Quality
4. Manufacturing Engineering
5. Warehouse
6. Procurement
7. Planning
8. Senior-level manager

Make the meeting approximately one to one-and-a-half hours long. Schedule the meetings during the lunch hour and provide lunch. Everyone likes a free lunch, not to mention some time off work.

Your Lean leader should lead the meeting because he or she is the true change agent. In the initial meetings, the Lean leader and senior-level manager teach the employees Lean concepts and principles; allow only about thirty to forty-five minutes for teaching, and allow the other fifteen to thirty minutes for a question-and-answer period. You will find the questions are slow in coming, but once the ice is broken, you will get lots of questions and most likely run over your time allotment for the meeting. Continue these instructional training meetings until everyone—including managers—have been through the "lunches" at least once.

Once you have completed the full cycle of training, you should schedule a second round of meetings to review the training and answer additional questions. By this time, most people should have been exposed to a continuous improvement event and participated in several Lean activities that will allow them to ask better, more focused and meaningful questions. Continued reinforcement of Lean principles and how to use Lean tools is critical to the success of your Lean transformation. When trying to change the culture of an organization, you must continuously reinforce why the change is needed and what the new culture will be.

Some Will Leave Us (Making the Really Tough Decision, Removing Human Roadblocks)

You cannot sustain change, if it is not enforced, until it becomes a part of your culture. Your higher-level management team needs to take the necessary steps to ensure the momentum is sustained even if it means removing uncommitted managers from their positions. You as managers must have honest, forthright discussions about such situations. I know that such discussions are not easy, but they must be held. If you do not address these issues, this journey will end with only partial success and it will then regress backward until most, if not all, of the hard-fought-for ground and savings are lost.

Because this is a change in the way you do business, a culture change, not everyone can or will make the changes with you. If you are committed to such change, you must remove the roadblocks. Most mangers do not have a problem removing machines that cannot do the work or are worn out from years on the job. Also, if a production worker is not performing to expected levels, you do not find it difficult to remove them, although it may take a lot of paperwork to back up their dismissal. Why then do managers have difficulty removing other managers who do not meet expectations? This element of success for Lean is too easy to let slide. After all, "Ted has worked for the company longer than I have"; or "Ted and I have been best friends for years, I just can't let him go." If you have found Ted to be an obstruction to the implementation and success of Lean, then you must remove him from his current position. Remember that it is management that sets the tone for success. Ted has not necessarily lost his value to the company and he can be moved to another position that does not directly influence the implementation of Lean. Nonetheless, if he resists or does not want to make the move, then you have no other choice but to terminate his employment. You must have employees and managers open to and embracing change.

Lean Systems versus Six Sigma

Many times in discussion I am told that Lean and Six Sigma are the same thing. Some companies tell me that they have hired a Black Belt and they do not need help with Lean. Unfortunately, these people are somewhat misinformed. There is a distinct difference between Lean systems and Six Sigma. Many companies will try to simultaneously implement both systems to achieve what they believe to be maximum results in a very short time. Although some of the goals are the same and some of the tools from one system can be used in the other system, they are somewhat different and, without proper definition, can be confusing.

Let us look at the definition of each one:

Lean manufacturing: A methodology, based on the end-user customer's perspective, that is *used to reduce and eliminate wasteful non-value-added cost resulting in unnecessary steps in a manufacturing or business process* which will, in turn, increase the velocity of the product through the system, improve quality, improve efficiency, and reduce cost. I like to call this a macro system. It looks at the "big picture."

Six Sigma: A structured business strategy used as a problem-solving method that seeks to improve the quality of a manufacturing or business process or product by identifying and *removing the cause of defects or errors related to the variability in process, product design, and component parts*. It uses mathematical data and statistical analysis to create a product or process that can produce highly repeatable defect-free products. A process operating at six sigma is one in which 99.99966% of the products produced are expected to be defect-free. This is the equivalent of 3.4 defects per million opportunities for errors. An example is a printed circuit board. One board has many opportunities for errors—each solder joint where a component is attached to the board itself is a possible error. Another way to say this is that an opportunity for error is a point where a customer requirement is either met or not met.

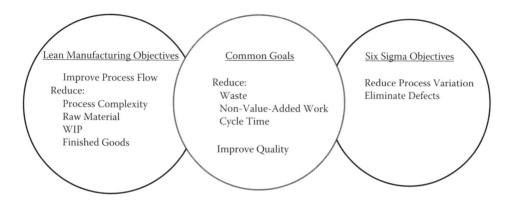

Figure 2.1   Lean versus Six Sigma goals and objectives.

Example: One circuit board = (225 components × 2 solder joints per component) = 450 chances for errors. A customer expects all solder joints to be good. Therefore, you could only have 4.5 errors out of 2500 circuit boards produced.

I like to call Six Sigma a micro system because it looks in more finite detail at the problem than the larger scope of Lean manufacturing.

Figure 2.1 shows you the difference between Lean and Six Sigma as well as their common goals.

The metrics used to track the performance of the factory are somewhat similar for both Lean and Six Sigma. In this book I focus on Lean production for the small company; therefore, with the exception of this explanation of Six Sigma and a discussion later on metrics, I have concluded our look at Six Sigma.

Chapter 3

Tools for Continuous Improvement

Step 1: Hands-On

Now that you have a basic understanding of Lean manufacturing and why it is good for your company, you can begin to apply this learning to real-life situations. One of the biggest values of Lean manufacturing is that it makes problems visible and thus easier to find while at the same time creating "order out of chaos."

Example: Order out of Chaos:

Suppose you are in a large shopping mall parking lot and there are no parking lines marked on the pavement; cars have parked wherever they want: forward, backward, sideways, crooked, even boxing in one car. Why? Because there is no order to the parking lot, no system. Now we paint lines on the parking lot pavement, showing the proper parking position for cars and trucks. With the addition of parking lot lines, people will park correctly as the visual signals indicate—thus creating order out of chaos.

Nevertheless, the first thing to do is a little housecleaning. We call this 5S.

Housekeeping: 5S

When I started in manufacturing some thirty years ago, the only factories that were really clean and orderly were electronic and medical device manufacturing companies, and that was partly because of the cleanliness that was needed to ensure quality products. Although other manufacturing companies were clean and neat, more factories than not had metal chips and oil on the floor. In plastic molding operations, it was not uncommon to find hydraulic fluid leaking from machines. One molding shop I was in placed wooden pallets on the floor to walk on due to large quantities of leaked oil. Although much of this has changed today, there is always room for improvement in all companies.

We will be using 5S to support the smooth flow of product through the factory. This will allow us to maintain proper *takt time*, which lets us meet our delivery demands from the customer. What is takt time? Takt time is calculated as the frequency at which you deliver product to your customer; based on this, you determine the frequency at which a product must be delivered from the assembly line to finished goods to replace the product that was shipped.

Back to 5S, this requires that you spend some time cleaning up and organizing your work area so you can work smoothly and efficiently. This holds true for the office as well as the production floor.

As we move forward in this book, do not forget that everything I teach is also applicable to the office. Pride in your work area will transfer to pride in your factory and ultimately pride in your company. By implementing a 5S program, you are creating a series of activities that eliminates wastes that contribute to errors, defects, and possible injury in the workplace. Here are the five steps in 5S (Figure 3.1):

1. *Sort:* Sort items and keep only what is needed to do the job. Get rid of extra tools and supplies not needed.
2. *Straighten (organization):* A place for everything, and everything in its place.
3. *Shine (cleanliness):* Clean your tools and work area—and also the machines you use.
4. *Standardize:* Create a procedure and system that will allow you to maintain and monitor the success of the first 3 Ss.
5. *Sustain (self-discipline):* Maintaining a standardized work area is an ongoing process, one that uses continuous improvement to eliminate waste.

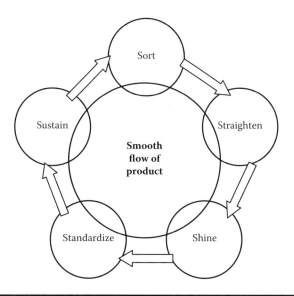

Figure 3.1   5S.

What you are creating is a set of visual controls for each work area. By doing this you can quickly see if you have the correct parts, tools, supplies, and instructions to correctly assemble your products.

Sort the material in the work area. Once completed in an area, mark items that are rarely used with a red tag. Preprinted red tags (Figure 3.2) can be found at office supply stores or on the Internet; just search for "5S red tags." This tag will show the proper disposition for the material or tool. Remove the surplus material and tools from the area and place in a centralized separate collection area. This could be a conference room, isolated corner of production, etc.; you want some place where people will not go and reclaim this material for use. Next, decide how to dispose of the surplus material. You may decide to keep some tools as backups, give some away, sell them, or just throw them away. For the backup tools, store them in a secure place with limited access so they do not find their way back to the production floor unless they are needed.

Does all this really work? One medical device company with about forty assembly workers removed over $20,000 worth of surplus tools from the production area in less than a year. They did not have to buy a replacement tool for three years. Part of this savings derived from eliminating the need for individual toolboxes for each employee, thereby eliminating many duplicate tools. Instead, each workstation was set up with its own tools.

Next, you need to "straighten" the work area (see Figures 3.3 through 3.6). Create specific locations for each item used in the work area; here you may

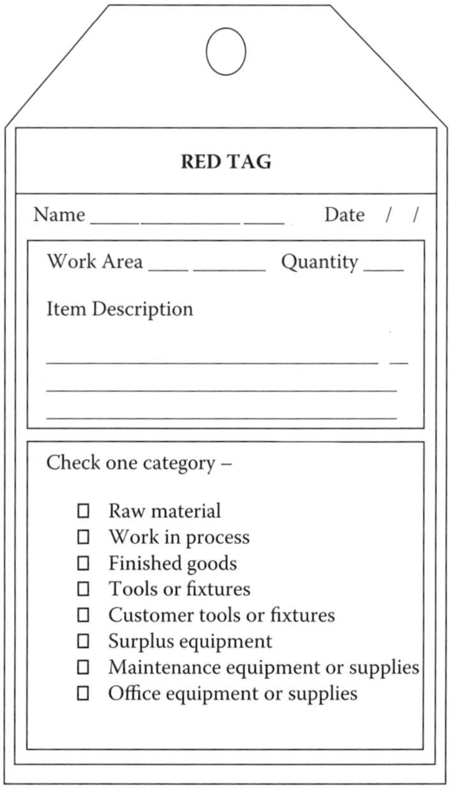

```
                         RED TAG

Name _____        Date  /  /

  Work Area ____ _____    Quantity ____

  Item Description

  _____ __
  _____
  _____

  Check one category –

       □  Raw material
       □  Work in process
       □  Finished goods
       □  Tools or fixtures
       □  Customer tools or fixtures
       □  Surplus equipment
       □  Maintenance equipment or supplies
       □  Office equipment or supplies
```

Figure 3.2   Red tag.

want to use shadowboards, foam cutouts, or other means to place tools only in a specific location (Figures 3.7, 3.8, and 3.9). You may also wish to label locations if tools have similar shapes. Placing these tools in specific locations also makes it very easy to see if a tool is missing. If it is, then rather than searching for it, it may be more time effective to get a new one from a supervisor or tool crib.

The operator should be able to easily reach the commonly used tools and parts in the work area without moving. These tools and parts should be placed in front of the operator or on tool balancers over the actual work area. The operator should have these tools within a normal arm's reach; for the female worker, this is fourteen to twenty-four inches, while for the male worker it is fifteen to twenty-seven inches. In the standing position, the recommended work area is thirty-four to forty-eight inches above the floor.

Shine at the end of each shift allows sufficient time for clean-up; start with ten to fifteen minutes and adjust as needed. This is not time for idle socializing. The operators should clean their tools, machines, and work

Figure 3.3   Work area before 5S.

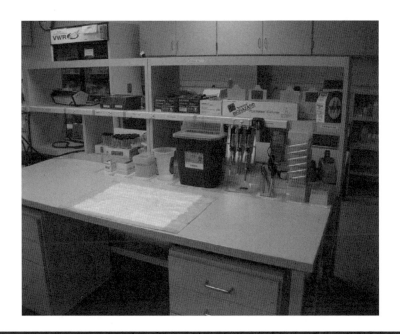

Figure 3.4   Work area after 5S.

Figure 3.5   Storage room before 5S.

Figure 3.6   Storage after 5S.

surfaces; sweep the floor in their area; and otherwise make the area neat and clean. Some companies require their operators to place all trash along a main aisle for pickup by the janitorial staff.

Standardize creates the rules to sustain the first 3 elements of 5S. It is management's responsibility to ensure that the 5S program is sustained within the organization, and the best way to do this is by creating a daily,

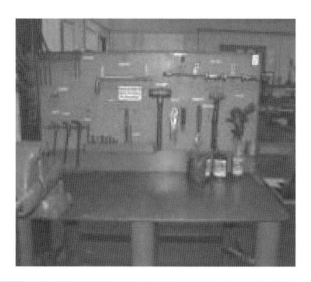

Figure 3.7   Workbench after 5S.

Figure 3.8   Tool drawer after 5S.

weekly, and monthly audit system. There will be more on standardized work in Chapter 8.

Sustain is where accountability comes into play with the operator, lead, and supervisor responsible for the daily and weekly audits, while management holds those three accountable with the monthly audit. But how is management held accountable? I discuss an audit system for the factory later in Chapter 6.

Figure 3.9   Toolbox after 5S.

Chapter 4

Beginning Your Journey

Waste Walk

Now that you have a basic understanding of the nine wastes, it is time to get out of the conference room and go on a gemba walk. *Gemba* is a Japanese term that means "go to the place" or "go see." To perform our waste walk, we will go to the place and see for ourselves.

Our walk begins at the end of the production cycle—that is, the finished goods warehouse—and proceeds backward through product packaging, final inspection, product test, assembly, raw material production floor delivery, raw material warehouse, receiving inspection, and finally ending on the raw material receiving dock. Why do we go backward through our factory? The answer is very simple; remember that we are always looking at our processes and products from the perspective of our end user, our customer. Also, working backward through the processes and departments actually provides a new perspective on your factory and processes.

Here is how the walk works: Your Lean leadership team (let us assume that your team has nine members) will do the walk. Do not delegate this task; remember that one of the fundamentals of Lean manufacturing is accountability and it lies with you. Your leadership team needs to know what the estimated waste is in your company. Each person on the team is given a task based on the nine Lean wastes. During the walk, you will keep track of your findings on paper and report back to the team after the walk is complete. This will be a snapshot in time. Your findings will be used to calculate the cost of waste in your production system.

As a small shop, you may not be able to break up the waste walk into separate categories as shown in Table 4.1, so just break up these tasks in an appropriate manner among the people on the waste walk.

You may have noticed that we did not assign the waste called "underutilized people." This is difficult to analyze at this time; thus we will do this after we have changed the culture a little.

Now let us take the information from each of the team leaders and see how to use the data. We call this "going to the whiteboard"; we do this periodically in this book for detailed examples.

To the white board:

Plant Manager: Waiting (Idle Time)

20 people × 5 minutes each = 100 minutes (assume typical/worker)
100 minutes × 7.5 hours/day = 750 minutes/day
750 minutes/day ÷ 60 minutes/hour = 12.5 hours/day
12.5 hours/day × $20/hour labor = $250/day
12.5 hours/day × 256 days/year = 3200 hours/year
$250/day × 256 days/year = $64,000/year

Materials Manager: Excess Inventory

Inventory report shows $3,000,000 average monthly inventory
Lean required 2 weeks of inventory: $1,500,000
Excess raw material inventory = $1,500,000

Finished Goods: Overproduction

78 pallets of finished goods
78 pallets × $15,000/pallet = $1,170,000
20 pallets shipped/day
20 pallets × $15,000/pallet = $300,000
Overproduction = $870,000

Table 4.1 Waste Walk Tasks

		Waste to be Identified
Plant manager	Watch and count how many people are idle (appear to be doing nothing).	Waiting
Raw material manager	Estimate the number of available weeks of production stored in the raw material warehouse.	Excess inventory
Finished goods manager	Count the number of finished goods pallets in the finished goods warehouse.	Overproduction
Quality manager	Not doing things right the first time, which causes rework or scrap. Does the product meet customer expectations? Include the cost of inspecting for defects.	Defects
Production manager	Estimate amount of work-in-process material (WIP) found sitting between all processes.	Overproduction
Purchasing manager	Look for areas where you can eliminate such things as bubble wrap, cardboard, hazardous chemicals, etc.	Environmental
Planning manager	Look for the movement of material around the factory. Estimate the average distance moved. Determine the number of times something is moved.	Transportation
Manufacturing engineering manager	Watch people and equipment for signs of excessive motions (i.e., walking to get parts or tools, long reaches for tools, etc.). Estimate time lost: 1 walking step = 1 second	Excessive motion
Lean leader	Watch for and estimate the number of occurrences and cost.	Operations or processing that may not be needed

Production Manager: Overproduction

1.5 pallets of WIP between each process
1.5 pallets × 15 process steps = 22.5 pallets of WIP
22 pallets × 200 parts/pallet @ $5/part = $22,000 of WIP

Quality Manager: Defects

15 defects/day × 1 hour average fix time = 15 hours/day
15 hours/day × 3 people idled/fix = 45 hours/day
45 labor hours lost/day × $20/hour = $900/day
$900/day lost × 256 days/year = $230,400/year
12 scrapped parts/day × $55 each = $660/day
$660 scrap/day × 256 days/year = $168,960/year
  $230,400/year lost time
  $168,960/year scrap cost
  $399,360/year defect rate = $1560/day defect cost

Purchasing Manager: Environmental

Bubble wrap: use 10 rolls/month at $40/roll = $400
Cardboard boxes: use 1000/month at $2.00/box = $2000
Raw material from suppliers:
  Shipments/month: 3000 boxes at $2.00/box = $6000
  Total environmental cost/month = $8400 or $100,800/year = $394/day

Planning Manager: Transportation

Moved 24 pallets to raw material warehouse
24 pallets × 500 feet/move = 12,000 feet to warehouse
24 pallets × 500 feet/move = 12,000 feet to production = 24,000 ft
24,000 feet × average transit time of 3 minutes = 72,000 minutes
72,000 minutes/60 minutes/hour = 1200 hours × $15/hour = $18,000
$18,000/day × 256 days/year = $4,608,000/year

Manufacturing Engineering Manager: Excessive Motion

Observed 20 operators in 60 minutes
20 operators walked 8 feet to get parts

20 operators × 8 feet = 160 ft × 1 second/foot = 160 seconds
160 seconds × 7.5 hours/day = 1200 seconds/day
1200 seconds/day/3600 second/hour = 0.33 hours/day lost production, or
$7/day
0.33 hours/day × 256 days/year = 85 man-hours lost/year
$7/day × 256 days/year = $1792/year

Lean Leader: Overprocessing

Found two operators who were processing two different parts. Neither operator could tell me why they had to do the process; they felt it was not needed.

Combined processing time for the two processes = 0.007 hours/part
0.007 hours/part × 500 parts/day = 3.5 wasted hours/day
3.5 hours/day × $20/hour labor = $70/day
$70/day × 256 days/year = $17,920/year, or 3.5 hours/day × 256 days/year =
896 hours/year

Cost of Waste

Waste	Cost/Day
Waiting	$250
Excess inventory	$1,500,000
Overproduction	
Finished goods	$870,000
WIP	$22,000
Defects	$1,560
Environmental	$394
Transportation	$18,000
Excessive motion	$1,792
Overprocessing	$70
	$2,414,066 in excess waste

Current Lean Status

The first step in preparing for your Lean journey is knowing your current
status of Lean production. You may already have some elements of Lean
production and not even know it. After all, how can you know if you have
improved if you do not know what the starting point is?

Lean Assessment Form					
Area to be assessed _____					
Who requested asssessment _____					
Assessor _____					
				Assessment Scores	
		Date	Initial	1 year	2 year
People Flow					
Is there a recognition to become lean		6/11/2011	0.5		
Is there a serious commitment by senior company management to implement lean		6/11/2011	0.5		
Is there evidence of employee participation at all levels		6/11/2011	0.5		
Is there a training program for employees at all levels		6/11/2011	0.5		
Is there a visible continuous improvement program. Has it been sustained for a period of time (the seven wastes)		6/11/2011	0.5		
Has error proofing been implmented in product design		6/11/2011	0.5		
Has error proofing been implemented in process design		6/11/2011	0.5		
	People Flow Total		3.5	0	0
Information Flow					
Are there documented current and future state maps		6/11/2011	0.5		
Is there an understanding of the three flows		6/11/2011	0.5		
Have visual controls been established		6/11/2011	0.5		
Is there evidence of standardized work at all levels		6/11/2011	0.5		
	Information Flow Total		2	0	0
Material Flow					
Has 5s been implemented and sustained		6/11/2011	0.5		
Is there a focused layout on flow manufacturing		6/11/2011	0.5		
Has a pull system been implemented within the factory and sustained		6/11/2011	0.5		
Has a pull system been implemented with raw material suppliers and sustained		6/11/2011	0.5		
Are lead times understood and mapped		6/11/2011	0.5		
Has quick changeover of tools been implemented and sustained		6/11/2011	0.5		
Has total preventive maintenance been implemented and sustained		6/11/2011	0.5		
Has material flow been optimized to reduce waste		6/11/2011	0.5		
	Material Flow Total		4	0	0
	Overall Score		9.5	0	0

Assessment Scoring	Status of lean Implementation	
.5 = Aware of lean principles - no implementation	Beginning	0 - 39
0.75 = Initial training begun - no implementation	Improving	40 - 79
1 = Knowledge of principles - some implementation	Succeeding	80 - 91
2 = Knowledge of principles - aggressively pursuing implementation	Leading	92-100
3 = High level of knowledge - partial implementation		
4 = High level of knowledge - high degree of implementation		
5 = Full integration of lean between manufacturing, finance, sales & marketing, development and administration. Maybe within plant, division or company based on implementation strategy.		

Figure 4.1 Lean Assessment Form

For this purpose, we have compiled a Lean survey form (Figure 4.1). You can find a blank form on the included CD.

To begin the survey, you will need yourself and your Lean leader as a minimum team. Do not take more than three persons, including yourself, on this survey trip; any more people will only add confusion to this process. Make sure that these people are very objective and open with their comments and have a basic understanding of Lean production from either practical experience or studying this book.

Chapter 5

Value Stream Maps: The Amazing Tool (Critical to Your Success)

What a Value Stream Map Is and Why You Need It

The value stream map (VSM) is critical to your success at driving waste out of your company. Please take the time to read and truly understand this chapter; it will be of great benefit later in your Lean journey.

Like all journeys, we start at the beginning and end at our destination. Similar to driving from Minneapolis to Dallas, we would use a map to find the appropriate roads to travel and which direction to go; we might even look at the map to determine the shortest or quickest route to get there. But what is a value stream map? A value stream map creates a visual display, or road map, of your manufacturing process, showing each value-added and non-value-added step that adds cost, process time, and other significant time to your product's delivery to the customer. This ultimately leads to what we know as *lead time*. It is the link between material, information, and process flow. Because a complete value stream map for your product covers all the actions from the time a customer places an order to the time it is accepted for use by the customer and you receive final payment, the map can become very lengthy and complex. Therefore, I focus here only on how the value stream map is used on the Lean production floor.

Specifically, we will be creating a large visual picture of your production floor, and will focus on one area of the floor for ease of understanding the mapping process. When completed, we will analyze the data on the map and use that information to plan our continuous improvement goals and which projects to work on. Once you have mastered and understand how to make and read the map, you can branch out and expand the map to include other elements that support the production line. These maps can be combined with maps from your suppliers or sister plants to truly see the entire "big picture" value stream.

Why a Value Stream Map Is Critical to Your Success

- It lets you see the entire flow of product through the factory, not in just one process.
- It provides a common language from which everyone can understand the goal and use the same terms to describe the manufacturing processes and flow.
- It makes all the steps in the process visible so they can be easily understood and analyzed. Otherwise, issues and problems remain hidden.
- It creates a baseline from which you can formulate and implement a continuous improvement plan.
- It allows you to clearly visualize how your factory should flow.
- A good value stream map is a blueprint for Lean implementation, as well as factory and process redesign.
- It helps you see the source of waste in your operations.
- It shows the linkage between material, information, and people flow.
- Combined with numerical information used to run your production floor, the value stream map becomes an excellent quantitative tool for short- and long-term strategic planning.

Guidance: High-Level Manager Must Lead Value Stream Improvement

Your value stream map team must be led by a high-level manager. Why do you need this? The value stream mapping tool is often thought of as a technical tool that lower-level individuals can create. However, the true value lies in the right people seeing the waste and becoming excited about eliminating it. By having a high-level manager leading the creation of the value stream map, they can direct a shared realistic vision for the future that can then be transformed into actionable plans that they are excited about and can hold people accountable to. A value stream workshop can take from two to five days and should have a dedicated team and place to meet. Do the value stream development in continuous sessions; do not break it up or you will lose momentum. A well-planned and facilitated workshop can have unbelievable results. The workshop should have the key functional specialists who touch the process in it. The high-level manager should be someone who has responsibility for all of the main processes. In some cases, this is not possible due to corporate department reporting structures. If this is the case, the high-level manager must have the support and backing of other senior managers in the company so that he can exercise ultimate authority over the resulting outcomes of the workshop. An example of a high-level manager may be the plant manager, director of operations, or owner of the company.

How to Create a Value Stream Map

Current State Map

The first map you create is called the current state map; it identifies and shows all the processes, inventory, personnel, setups, and information needed to make your product. Remember that as you create this map, you are not looking to fix problems at this time, but rather just identify the current requirements and conditions on the production floor. Another advantage is showing the links between processes, material, information, and people, which reveal hidden waste that you do not easily see. This reveals numerous wasteful situations that will be addressed.

Creating the Map

You can create this map on a whiteboard, a wall with sticky note paper, on a large piece of paper (11 × 17 inches), or using one of the available software packages designed for this purpose. You will make changes and corrections to your map before you are finished, so I suggest waiting to use any software packages because they are slower to work with.

Gather Your Data

First, gather your data for the map; this is done by a gemba walk (remember: gemba means "go to the place"), so start in the shipping department. Why the shipping department and not the receiving department? Because, we always start with the process closest to the customer. Walk through the plant with your team and gather all the needed information. You may elect to send team members to specific areas to gather information but I have found that when the entire team follows the process, it makes them more aware and knowledgeable of the entire value stream.

Be sure to show the completion date on your map. You will use this as a reference point. Now place the map in a prominent location; I like to place a copy on the production floor for everyone to see and the original in the conference room that has been identified as the "Lean manufacturing conference room," a room that is available for Lean meetings at all times.

Guidance: The Fix-It Trap: "I Know How To Fix That Right Now"

 Do not get caught in the "I know how to fix that right now" trap. Be patient and methodical, and you will truly reap significant rewards in waste reduction and production flow improvement if you do. It is only after you create the future state map that identifies flow and the overall system that you can move forward.

Follow the steps in Table 5.1 to create your current state value stream map. Steps 1 through 10 and 16 represent material flow; Steps 11 through 15 are information flow; and Steps 17 and 18 are your timeline.

The timeline is the time it takes for one part to move from receiving through to shipping; subsequently we will look at only one part as it moves through the system as opposed to looking at many parts.

After Step 15, stop and look at your map and think about how each process knows what to make for its customer, following the producer process and when to make it. Ask yourself if each of the producer processes pushes material to the next operation, or if the customer pulls the material from the producer. A push system means the process produces regardless of what is needed by the next process downstream and literally pushes the

Table 5.1 Current State Map

Step	Data Needed	Data	Image
1	**Customer data:** Quantity of pieces/month Shipping container size Number of production shifts at supplier Shipping frequency	 475 Box = 25 parts 1 Daily	Place this factory image in upper-right corner of page and fill in customer name and data. Bob's Boat Trailers — 475 pcs/month; Box = 25 parts; 1 shift; Daily shipments
2	**Production process:** Place your first box at the bottom-left corner of the page about two inches up from the bottom and one inch in from the left paper edge; work from left to right. Leave approximately 1–1½ inches between process icons. C/T = Cycle time, in seconds C/O = Changeover time, in seconds, minutes, or hours Uptime = Available machine time with efficiency factored in (i.e., 80% uptime = 2280 seconds/hour)	Place the name of the process in the top rectangle box. 14.4 1.5 hrs 80%	Machining — C/T = 14.4 sec/pce; C/O = 1.5 hrs; Uptime = 80%; EPE = 4 weeks; Work time = 2 shifts

continued

Table 5.1 (continued)   Current State Map

Step	Data Needed	Data	Image
	Available work time	2 shifts	
	○ = Number of operators required to operate process (One operator equals 3060 seconds/hour)	1	
	EPE = Production batch size. EPE = stands for every part every interval.	4 weeks	
3	**Inventory:** Inventory = Work-in-process (WIP) inventory located between each process step		Insert this symbol between each production process that has WIP between them.
	Days of production available = days inventory will last without replenishment		I
			1800 pieces
			20 days
	If similar inventory is located in another location, use two triangles with data to indicate two separate locations and added days of inventory.		
4	**Inventory:** To the left of your first process icon, place one icon for the material located in the raw material warehouse.		I
	Days of production available = days inventory will last without replenishment		100 bars
			60 days

5	**Inventory:** To the right of your last process icon, place one icon for the material located in the finished goods warehouse.		△ I 40 boxes 42 days
6	**Shipping:** Place one process icon to the right of the last icon to represent shipping.	Place the name "shipping" in the top rectangle box.	Shipping
7	Now compare your value stream map to the one in Figure 5.1. They should be similar except for the data and number of processes identified.		
8	**Shipping and delivery:** Draw a double-line arrow between "shipping" and the "customer." Next, add a "truck" or other similar (plane, boat, etc.) icon in the middle of the arrow representing the method of transport. In the truck, identify the frequency of delivery.		

continued

Table 5.1 (continued)   Current State Map

Step	Data Needed	Data	Image
9	**Raw material delivery:** Place the "factory" icon in the upper-left corner of the page. Then draw a double-line arrow between the "factory" and the "inventory" icon on the left side of the page. Next, add a "truck" icon in the middle of the arrow. In the "truck," identify the frequency of delivery.		Dumbell Steel Co.
10	Now compare your value stream map to the one in Figure 5.2. They should be similar except for the data and number of processes identified.		
11	Place a process box at the center top of the page. Label MRP	Production Control Computerized MRP or manual system	Production Control

12	Draw a single-line arrow from the "customer" to "production control," indicating transfer of information. Insert data in data box.		
	Forecasts	30, 60, 90 days, etc.	→ Manual information
	Orders	Daily, weekly, monthly	⚡ Electronic information (does not include fax)
13	Draw a single-line arrow from "production control" to the "supplier," indicating transfer of information. Insert data in data box.		
	Forecasts	Daily, weekly, monthly, etc.	→ Manual information
	Shipping instructions	Daily, weekly, etc.	⚡ Electronic information (does not include fax)
14	Draw a single-line arrow from "production control" to each of the process steps to which you supply a build schedule. Insert schedule timing in data box.		
	Schedule	Daily, weekly, monthly	→ Manual information ⚡ Electronic information (does not include fax)

continued

Table 5.1 (continued)   Current State Map

Step	Data Needed	Data	Image
15	Compare your value stream map to the one in Figure 5.3. They should be similar except for the data and number of processes identified.		
16	**Show material push:** Insert "inventory push" icons where needed between the process blocks. This shows inventory is pushed rather than pulled to the next operation.		
17	**Timeline:** Draw the timeline under the process boxes. Place the hours, days, or weeks of inventory as shown. Place the cycle time for one part as shown.	Data for the timeline is taken from the data boxes and inventory triangles directly above the line.	
18	Add data box to the right-hand end of timeline. Production lead time (non-value-added time) Processing time (value-added time) Waste in system (this is what the customer will not pay for)	Add days of inventory. Add processing time. Subtract processing time from production time. Convert time to hours or days (your choice).	
19	See finished value stream map in Figure 5.4		

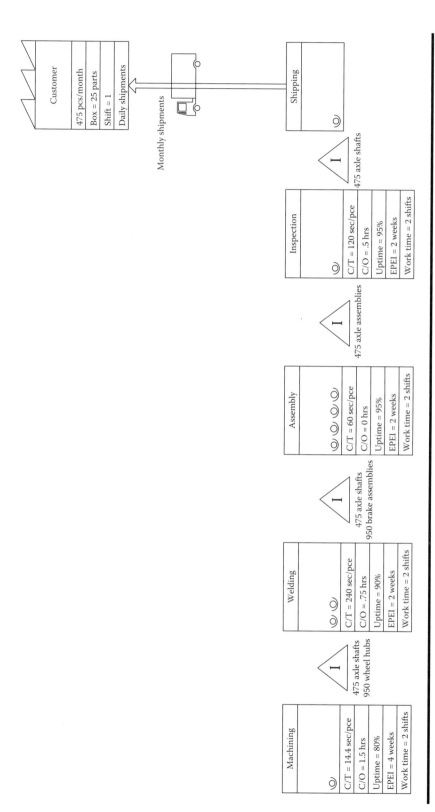

Figure 5.1   Current state value stream map, phase 1.

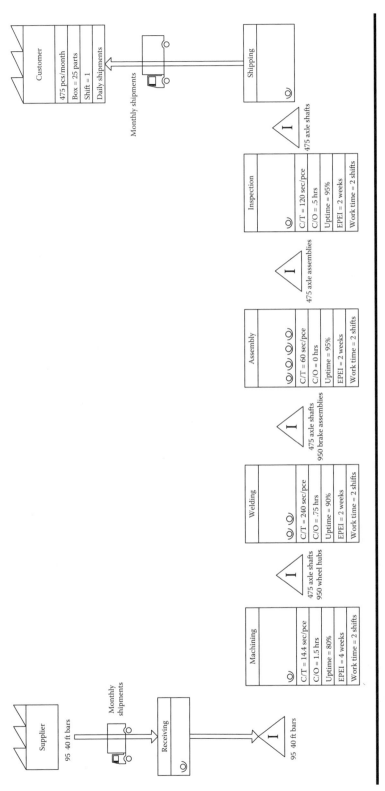

Figure 5.2 Current state value stream map, phase 2.

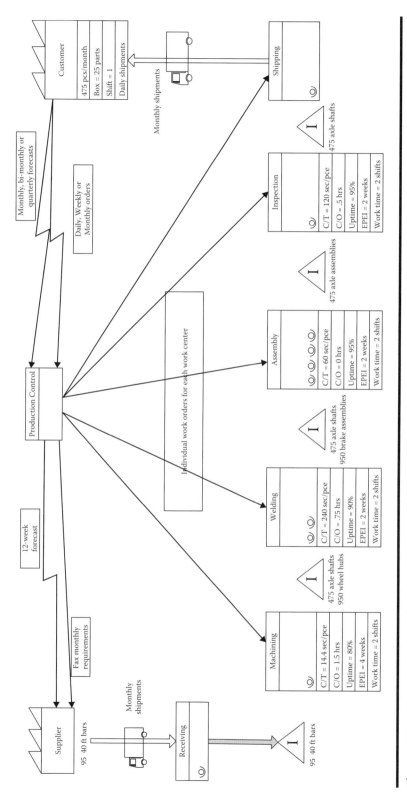

Figure 5.3   Current state value stream map, phase 3.

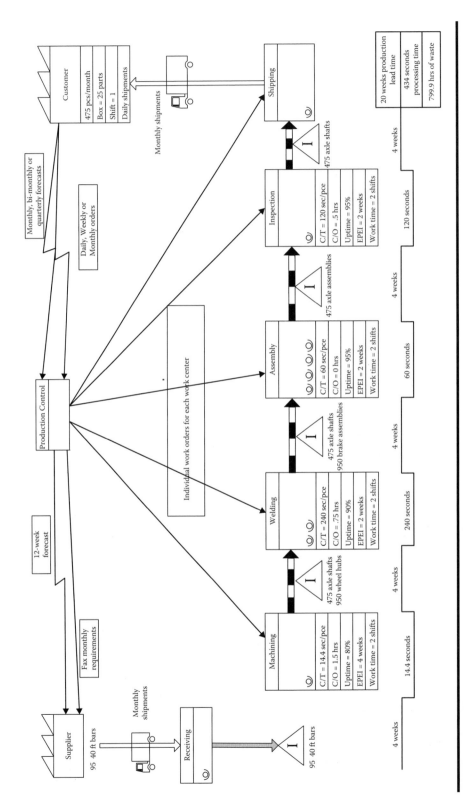

Figure 5.4 Current state value stream map, complete.

material to the next process. A push system typically results from producing to a schedule that comes from a centralized scheduling system that tries to predict what the next downstream process needs; these processes are typically computer-run MRP (material requirements planning) systems. Because production does not always run smoothly, the accuracy of these predictions is never correct. This type of manufacturing is referred to as "batch" manufacturing. Now you can indicate these material movements on your value stream map.

By looking at the map, you can see the actual flow of material through the processes and out the shipping door to the customer. It also shows you how information flows through the process; but if this is a value stream map, where does it show "value added time" that the customer will pay for versus the waste we want to eliminate? The final step is to add the timeline to the bottom of the map (Figure 5.4); go to Step 17 in Table 5.1.

Now you have completed your current state value stream map; as you become more familiar with creating these maps, you can expand them into many other processes. You may want to look deeper into one of the process blocks on this map by creating a separate map for that process or create another map of a part or assembly that feeds into a process block on the map. As you create the maps, you become more aware of the waste in your processes and the opportunities for continuous improvement that exist.

The final item that you add to the map is the data box showing your days of inventory and processing time (see Table 5.1, Step 18). You can see the difference in the two times but to make it more apparent or striking, subtract the processing time from the material time. This makes the amount of waste in the system jump off the page at you, and this is the time you want to eliminate. I like to convert the total waste to hours or weeks for the real impact.

The total days of inventory is your current lead time to the customer; reducing this time not only reduces your lead time to the customer, but also the cost to your company. Make sure you have placed the date you completed your current state map on the map in the area of the data box for your timeline.

In Figure 5.4 you can see that we have completed our current value stream map.

Now that you know how to make and read a value stream map, when you visit another factory or supplier and see a map there, you will be able to quickly identify how much waste they have in their system.

| 20 weeks production lead time |
| 434 seconds processing time |
| 799.9 hours of waste |

Figure 5.5 Current state process times.

How to Read a Value Stream Map

Now that you have completed both the current and future state value stream maps, you have some understanding of how to read them. We need a better understanding so we can determine which projects we might want to attack. First, look at your current state map in the lower-right corner; you should find a box like the one in Figure 5.5. In this example, the bottom row shows 799.9 hours of waste, which is the difference between your production lead time and the actual hands-on processing time: in this case, 20 weeks minus 434 seconds of processing time. You can easily see the waste that you need to eliminate (Figure 5.5).

Here is a key to the value stream map. Any company creating, using, and displaying the map correctly is showing you how much waste they have in the process they have mapped. There is nothing wrong with this, as a company displaying this information is also, most likely, trying to reduce the amount of waste. You want to work with companies that are actively pursuing continuous improvement because they are usually the more progressive companies.

Future State Map

The second map is the future state map, which shows the final design of the factory or process after a specific period of time. This map shows the new flow of product, material, people, and information through the factory. Typically, you begin with a future state map that has a completion date of six to twelve months in the future when compared to the current state map's completion date, although your map may have a longer or shorter time period. Keep in mind that this must be somewhat of a stretch goal. As an outside facilitator, I would meet with you and your team and establish goals to be accomplished before my next visit, and these would be challenge goals to help you move quickly and maintain momentum while still getting your daily work done. You may find that creating the future state map is somewhat difficult to do. Do not worry; the maps become easier the more you do them. This is why I think someone who has done a number of value stream maps would be a good facilitator for your first maps. This is where a consultant or teacher with this type of experience is valuable. Still, you can create these maps yourself by following the steps in this book.

Use the same team that did the current state map to do the future state map. Why? These people now know your process and should be able to identify the areas of waste to attack in order to "Lean out" the factory. Begin by asking, "What do we want the flow to look like after six or twelve months?" and then draw that flow. This is the point where your vision of the future factory is put down on paper. What will your process or factory look like with waste removed?

What you are trying to do here is create a production pull system that delivers one part to the next process when it is needed, while not overproducing product. Remember that overproduction is the worst waste of all and produces additional hidden waste. Hidden waste exists in the form of excess inventory, increased carrying costs, and extra facility space required, which then requires more material handlers and handling, additional equipment such as forklifts, pallet trucks, racking, etc., all requiring extra personnel to shuffle material around. Overproduction results in focusing on making more than is needed and not always the correct parts, which can lead to shortages of parts due to a lack of machine time to produce the needed parts when required.

Automated processes are great when needed for high-volume production but for a small shop, they may not be the most effective use of capital. You can create a lot of problems for yourself with automation. Automation is just a great way to produce lots of scrap more quickly and efficiently than manually producing it. I am not saying do not automate, but automate only when it is necessary, cost efficient, and strategically important. I have worked for companies that effectively maintain used surplus World War II equipment to this day because it is the most efficient and cost-effective method of production. Hence, as you prepare your future state map, think about keeping your production systems simple and efficient. Keep in mind that you always want straight, continuous flow. Always look at the map and think left to right, or customer backward to the previous process. You are trying to connect the customer to the raw material in the shortest possible time while ensuring the highest quality and lowest cost. Remember what we said about 5S: it is to make product flow easily through the factory. This is exactly what you are trying to do with the future state map. Make the product flow easily through the factory to the customer.

The Toyota Production System has outlined six steps for us to follow:

1. *Continuous flow:* Continuous flow has the goal of producing one part at a time and only when it is needed. This is the most efficient way to produce any product and should be the ultimate goal of any manufacturing business. You may need to begin by using a combination of continuous flow and pull manufacturing since it would be extremely difficult to implement continuous flow over the entire production floor at one time. As you become more familiar with the continuous flow processes and continuous improvement you can advance to a higher level of continuous flow.

2. *Takt time:* Takt time is how often you should produce a product to match the demand of your customer. What does the word "takt" mean? It is a German word meaning "beat." Example: Your customer pulls from your inventory a specific product at the rate of 200 parts per day.

   To the white board

$$\text{Takt time} = \frac{\text{Average working time/day}}{\text{Customer demand/day}}.$$

$$\text{Takt time} = \frac{27{,}000 \text{ seconds/day}}{200 \text{ parts/day}} = 135 \text{ seconds or 2.25 minutes.}$$

   The *beat* of your factory is one part moving from production to the shipping warehouse every 135 seconds to replace the part that just shipped to your customer. Where did the 27,000 seconds come from? We used a 7.5-hour workday times 3600 seconds per hour. You can adjust the number of work-hours per day for your factory. If you have two shifts, use 15 hours. We will use takt time at the pacemaker cell when we establish the pull rate on the production floor. Takt times are noted in the data boxes on future state maps.

3. *Schedule using a pacemaker cell:* When using a supermarket to replenish the production line, you can use a pacemaker cell to control all the processes preceding the pacemaker cell. This cell is set up to produce product at a rate equal to customer demand and therefore schedules the remaining upstream work cells without using a paper schedule. You always place the pacemaker cell as close as possible to the end of your manufacturing process. In our example, that would be one part every 135 seconds. This then would create a pull system from all upstream processes at a rate of

one part every 135 seconds. All other downstream processes from the pacemaker cell are based on first-in-first-out (FIFO) demand.

- Just for clarification, think of the production line as a stream. Visualize the flow of water moving from left to right as you stand in front of the pacemaker cell, so processes done to the left of where you are standing would be called upstream processes and those to your right would be downstream processes.

In job shops and custom product manufacturing, the pacemaker cell may need to be further upstream from the customer.

4. *Create pull at the pacemaker cell:* Many companies, even today, release large batches of work to multiple work cells on their production floor. As a result, they create many problems for themselves.

- Each work cell on the production floor can begin to shuffle work orders to meet their own needs, not the needs of the customer. As a result, this increases the lead time and in many cases someone has to expedite the order. This would be a good time to ask the question, "Why do you need an expediter?" If you are in control of the shop floor and meeting customer demand, the expediter position is not needed and can be removed from the process. The person performing the expediter job is not laid off; instead, he or she is reassigned to another position in the company; in that way you keep their knowledge and skills within the company.

- Work typically occurs in peaks and valleys, which can cause production delays. When coupled with the first problem listed above, this can many times result in the use of overtime to meet the expedited demand of the customer. Rescheduling the work cell then causes a continuous cycle of expediting orders to meet customer demand.

- It becomes very difficult to determine if you are on schedule or not. Will we meet customer demand on time?

- There is no visibility to the actual schedule demand of the customer; therefore customer shipping requirements are not known on the production floor. Is your shipping department the only one that knows your customer demand?

- Responding to changing customer demand for the product becomes extremely difficult and often creates an overproduction situation.

- Quality problems become less visible because errors are not caught quickly, again causing longer lead times and poor customer satisfaction.

5. *Load leveling the production mix:* Since the advent of modern production and the creation of the Economic Order Quantity (EOQ) equations,

manufacturers have used batch production to try and maximize machine utilizations and reduce setup times. This may have worked well during the 1940s to 1980s. Today you cannot afford to carry large quantities of inventory. For this reason, you need to "level load" the factory. You need to make product more often in smaller quantities and with more setups to satisfy your customers; because of this, you need to schedule a mix of small-quantity, quick-changeover parts with large-quantity, longer-changeover parts each day. By alternating between the two product types at the pacemaker cell, you can respond more quickly to changes in your customer's demand. This does mean more change-overs and keeping a greater variety of parts at the line to reduce setups. This is why setup time reduction is important to a Lean factory. It is a difficult balance for sure but one that can provide significant improvements to the management of the production floor.

6. *Supermarkets:* Before delving into supermarkets and their advantages, I need to explain what a supermarket is. The term "supermarket" was created by Taiichi Ohno in Japan to describe the new warehousing method that was being used at Toyota. Ohno, while on a trip to the United States, was so impressed by the modern supermarket and its method of stock rotation and placing similar items in one location that he set up a similar system for his warehouses at Toyota. From that time on, they were known as supermarkets. Example: You are building an electromechanical device that includes a robotic arm assembly. The robotic arm assembly is a subassembly of the main electromechanical device, and all the parts for the robotic arm would be placed in the same location in the supermarket (warehouse). When parts are picked up for the robotic arm subassembly, the material picker would not have to walk all over the warehouse to find parts for that assembly. There will be more discussion about the supermarket in Chapter 13.

■ *Supermarkets (mini-marts) on the production floor:* Because there are areas on the production floor where it is not practical to use continuous flow, you must revert to batch handling of parts. Examples would be processes with unreliable lead times, long lead times from suppliers, or processes that absolutely require batching such as injection molding, production heat treating, stamping, etc.

Your production planning department will want to schedule these areas independently from the rest of the value stream for two reasons: (a) "That's the way we have always done it" and (b) "You

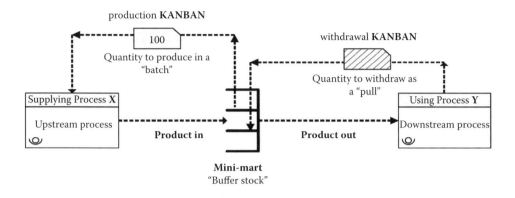

Figure 5.6   Mini-mart.

cannot physically link two different scheduling systems and have it work." Resist the idea that you have to schedule those areas separately. Control the production from these work cells by linking them to their downstream customers using a "mini-mart." A mini-mart is a "small" quantity of inventory used to buffer between two processes that either have a significant difference in process times or have different production methods, such as batch-versus-pull systems. What would this look like? See Figure 5.6.

Note the difference between the two kanban cards. The withdrawal kanban shows diagonal lines in it while the production kanban card does not. Also, you put the quantity to be produced inside the production kanban card.

The "mini-mart" located in the center of Figure 5.6 belongs to process "X" because the open side of the mini-mart icon faces process X. This also indicates that this mini-mart is used to schedule process "X."

1. Process "X" produces product in a batch to be used by process "Y."
2. Material from process "X" is placed into the "mini-mart."
3. Process "Y" withdraws or "pulls" material from the "mini-mart" as needed.
4. When the "mini-mart" reaches a predetermined level of inventory, a signal is sent back to process "X" to produce more product to replace the product used by process "Y."

As you can see from Figure 5.6, we use both the batch and pull production methods without separate scheduling between the two processes. Process "Y" schedules process "X" using kanban withdrawals. Then process "X" uses a production kanban card to produce the replacement quantity for the mini-mart.

What makes this different from the old min-max inventory level system? In a min-max inventory situation, you can hold old inventory without knowing it; with the mini-mart (supermarket), you rotate your stock using up kanban signals in sequence.

The use of kanban signals between the two processes will then provide an accurate scheduling demand to the upstream process, while not needing to accurately guess the product demand further downstream. We will talk more about the kanban signal in Chapter 12. We have now effectively eliminated the need for one production work order for the upstream process. On the production floor, a mini-mart is typically placed next to the supplying process so they can see how much the next downstream process is using and when. This allows process "X" the opportunity to plan its production schedule without help from the production scheduler in the office. Another waste saved!

Guidance: MRP – Material Requirements Planning and Forecast

The use of MRP scheduling for the production floor is unnecessary because all scheduling is done on the production floor using kanbans and pull. This is not to say that MRP is not needed. We must use sales forecasts to determine our budgets and get an idea of production demand for the year. These forecasts, although not very accurate for the most part, are what they are. Enter the forecasts into your MRP and use the resulting material requirements for negotiating material purchases and prices for the year. However, in a Lean factory, MRP is not used to schedule the production floor and work orders, which for the most part are a thing of the past.

Before you set up a mini-mart, make sure you really need it. Look again at the upstream and downstream processes; are you certain there is no way to create continuous flow between them? Remember that each mini-mart created increases WIP inventory, adds to the cost of inventory, takes up floor space, adds more material handling, and is more material to rework if a quality problem is found.

Creating the Future State Map

On the future state map you will use many of the same icons as you did for the current state map, but a few new ones will be added to show new methods of material and information flow. Let us begin to create our future state map. First, visually look at the process and gather your data. Ask yourself the following questions and discuss with your team. To be successful, you must be honest about your answers. Let me take one question as an example.

1. What is the takt time for the product or process?
2. Do you build product for direct customer shipment, or to place in a finished goods warehouse?
   If you build for direct customer shipment, you are most likely making custom products for each customer. This might be a one-of-a-kind automated machine. If your product goes to a finished goods warehouse before being shipped to your customer, then even if it is custom made for one customer, you select "to place in finished goods."
3. What is the point in production that will become the pacemaker cell?
   You will have a lot of discussion on this subject. Your basic instinct is to place it at the beginning of the production line, but remember to place it as close as possible to the customer.
4. What is the best product mix for the pacemaker cell?
5. What will load leveling look like at the pacemaker cell?
6. What improvements must be made to the production process to allow for continuous flow?
   ■ Look at reducing the changeover time.
   ■ Look at the process times. Can they be reduced by eliminating waste inside the process?
   ■ Look at changing the assembly process to reduce the number of people required.

This process will be repeated many times over as you continue to improve each of the operations and processes within your organization. Let's now begin to create our future state map by following the steps in Table 5.2.

One thing to note on the future state map is that directly above the welding process, you will find multiple kanban cards coming from the mini-mart. This indicates that the production signal being sent to the welding process is to be produced in "batches" to refill the mini-mart.

When you have reached your goals on this map, it becomes your current state map and you must create a new future state map. This process will be

Table 5.2 Future State Map

Step	Data Needed	Data	Image
1	**Use an 11 × 17 sheet of paper** **Customer data:** Place this factory image in upper-right corner of page and fill in customer name and data.		Bob's Boat Trailers 475 pcs/month Box = 25 parts 1 shift Daily shipments
2	**Production process:** Place your first box at the bottom-left corner of the page, similar to your current state map. (Note: We have added takt time to the data box.) Now update the data box with your goals (i.e., C/O from 1.5 to 0.5 hours) Takt Time = customer pull rate C/T = Cycle time in seconds C/O = Changeover time in seconds Uptime = Available machine time with efficiency factored in (i.e., 80% uptime = 2280 seconds/hour)		Machining Takt Time = 324 sec C/T = 14.4 sec/pce C/O = .5 hrs Uptime = 80% EPE = 1 weeks
3	**Inventory:** Inventory = work-in-process Be sure to add your supplier, receiving and raw material inventory to your value stream map.		Insert this symbol between each production process that has WIP between them. I

4	**Inventory:** To the left of your first process icon, place one icon for the material located in the raw material warehouse.		△ I 10 bars 6 days
5	**Inventory:** To the right of your last process icon, place one icon for the material located in the finished goods warehouse.		△ I 20 boxes 21 days
6	**Shipping:** Place one process icon to the right of the last icon to represent shipping.	Place the name "shipping" in the top rectangle box.	Shipping
7	Compare your value stream map to the one in Figure 5.7. They should be similar except for the data and number of processes identified and the left-hand column with supplier at the top.		

continued

Table 5.2 (continued)   Future State Map

Step	Data Needed	Data	Image
8	**Shipping and Delivery:** Draw a double-line arrow between "shipping" and the "customer" and icon for "mode of transportation." Add text showing frequency of delivery.		
9	**Raw Material Delivery:** Place the "factory" icon in the upper-left corner of the page; then draw a double-line arrow between the "factory" icon and the "inventory" icon on the left side of the page. Next, add a "truck" icon in the middle of the arrow. In the truck icon, identify the frequency of delivery.		
10	Compare your value stream map to the one in Figure 5.8. They should be similar except for the data and number of processes identified.		

11	Place a process box at the center top of the page and label "production control."	Production Control
12	Draw a single-line arrow from the customer to production control, indicating transfer of information. Insert data in data box. Forecasts Orders	30, 60, 90 day, etc. Daily, weekly, monthly	Manual information Electronic information (does not include fax)
13	Draw a single-line arrow from "production control" to the "supplier," indicating transfer of information. Insert data in the data box. Forecasts Shipping instructions	Daily, weekly, monthly, etc. Daily, weekly, etc.	Manual information Electronic information (does not include fax)
14	Compare your value stream map to the one in Figure 5.9. They should be similar except for the data and number of processes identified.		

continued

Table 5.2 (continued) Future State Map

Step	Data Needed	Data	Image
15	**Show material pull:** Insert "inventory pull" icons, where needed, between the process blocks.		 Max X pcs Indicates First-in-First-out flow (show max. pieces to move at one time) Supermarket (open side is the fill side) Pull Signal (pull from the previous process or supermarket)

16	**Timeline:** Draw the timeline under the process boxes.		
17	Add data box to the right-hand end of timeline.	Data for the timeline is	Inventory · Process Time
	Production lead time (non-value-added time)	Add days of inventory.	
	Processing time (value-added time)	Add processing time.	
	Waste in system (this is what the customer will not pay for)	Subtract processing time from production time.	
		Convert time to hours or days, your choice.	
18	See finished value stream map, Figure 5.10.		

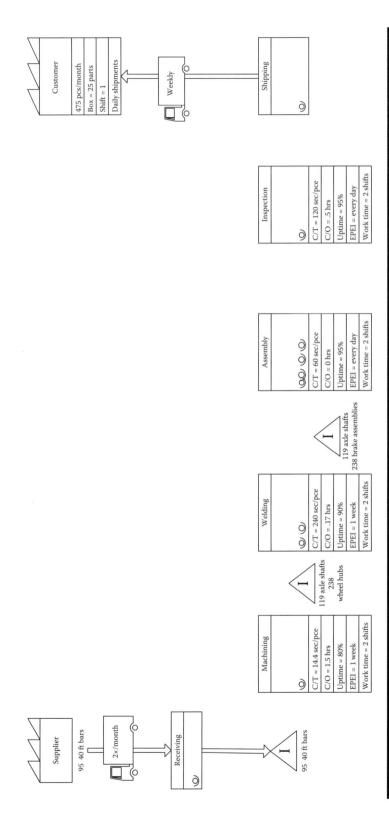

Figure 5.7   Future state value stream map.

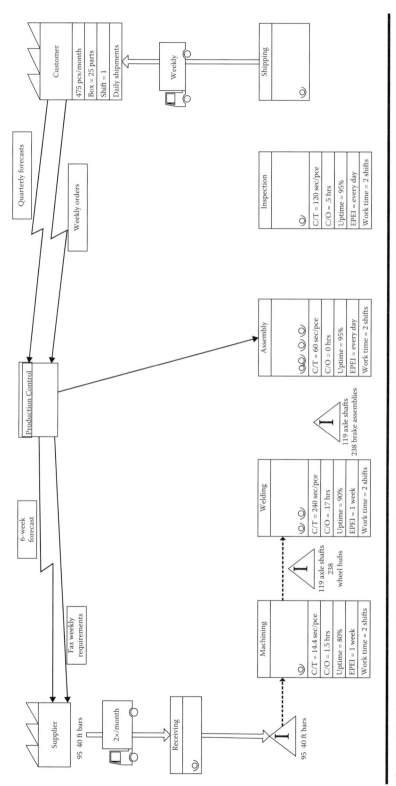

Figure 5.8 Future state value stream map in process.

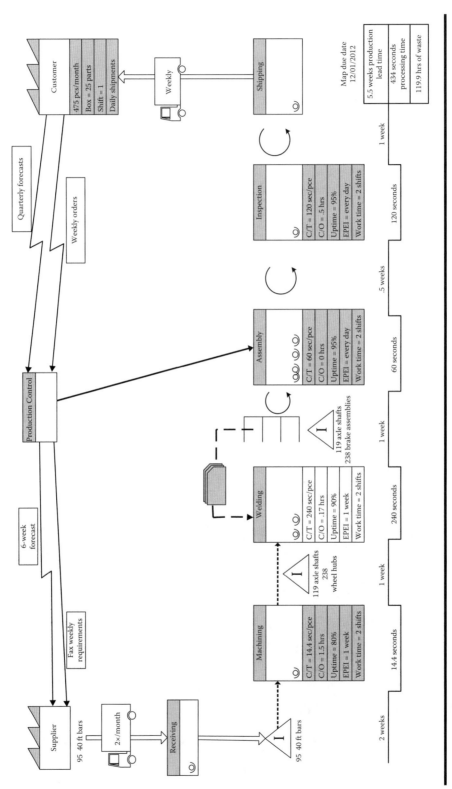

Figure 5.9 Future state value stream map.

Figure 5.10   Value stream timeline.

repeated many times over as you continue to improve each of the operations and processes within your organization.

Now let's look at the timeline in Figure 5.10. In our example there is four weeks of inventory between each of the processes shown. The processes are on the lower step of the line, while the inventory is on the upper step. It is easy to see that we need to reduce our inventory levels between processes, that four weeks is just too much unless we are trying to buffer for an extra lead time in processing.

Also, in the example you will notice that there is one process that takes 240 seconds. Can you reduce this time? Can you combine multiple processes, and eliminate inventory and process time all at the same time?

Now look at the individual processes in Figure 5.11. You have one person welding parts with a cycle time (C/T) of 240 seconds. Changeover time (C/O) is 0.75 hours (or 45 minutes). You have an uptime for the employees and their equipment of 90% of the time they are at work (or 6.75 hrs). This means the work cell is available for production 6.75 hours out of each shift. The EPEI (every part every interval) is two weeks. This means that based on your set-up time and number of parts produced you need to set up and run the part once every two week; thus, you have one changeover to a new part number every two weeks. This also means that you will have to produce enough parts for inventory and production to last at least two weeks; you will most likely produce a few more just to be safe. Sound familiar? Finally, you have work time; this indicates that you are producing on two shifts (Figure 5.11).

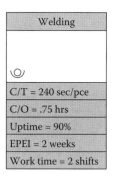

Figure 5.11   Welding process times.

Now look at your current state map and notice all the direct lines running from production planning to each of the process blocks; these represent work orders that control each of the processes. Ideally you need to reduce this number to 1 and have it control the pacesetter cell or even zero if you get to a high-level pull system.

Next, Compare the Current State Map to the Future State Map

Now you need to determine what improvements must be done to achieve the final results for the future state map. First, compare your totals located in the time line total box; see Figure 5.12.

If you look at the future state map example, you will find that there is also a plan for reducing some setup time. If you want to add setup time to these blocks of information, go right ahead; just make sure what you place in these blocks is the total of all setup on your map for the current and future states so that you can show the difference in the improvement target block.

Ok, this looks a little daunting to complete in the allotted time frame but you need to set challenging goals.

Current State	Future State	Improvement Targets Needed
20 weeks production lead time	5.5 weeks production lead time	Lead time reduction = 14.5 weeks
434 seconds processing time	434 seconds processing time	Processing time = 0
799.9 hours of waste	119.9 hours of waste	Waste reduction = 680 hours

Figure 5.12   Comparison of current state map to the future state map.

Guidance: "To Achieve Your Goal, Sometimes You Have to Run on the Edge of Out of Control"

 This was a teaching point from my sensei: it simply stated that if you wait to make a change until it is perfect, you will never complete your goal. Instead, make your changes even if you do not have a perfect plan or all the details for the change. There is nothing wrong with making another change later to improve the process again.

Now you can break down how you are going to achieve the goal you set for yourself. Look at Figure 5.13. I have added seven "kaizen bursts" to the current state map. Each of these bursts represents a continuous improvement project that you must complete to achieve your final goal.

1. Reduce changeover time in welding by 79%.
2. Remove three weeks of inventory from between welding and assembly processes.
3. Eliminate four weeks of inventory between assembly, inspection, and shipping processes.
4. Remove three weeks of inventory from between machining and welding processes.
5. Eliminate all work orders except for the pacesetter cell.
6. Reduce raw material inventory stocks by increasing the delivery of smaller orders of raw material.

You will find that your biggest improvements in lead time reduction will most likely come from reductions in WIP, raw material, and finished goods inventory.

Now take your current state map and future state maps, compare them, and identify where your continuous improvement activities will need to take place to achieve the future state goal for the process you have mapped out. Remember that this is a journey, not a race, and that you will have time to complete all the tasks you identify over time.

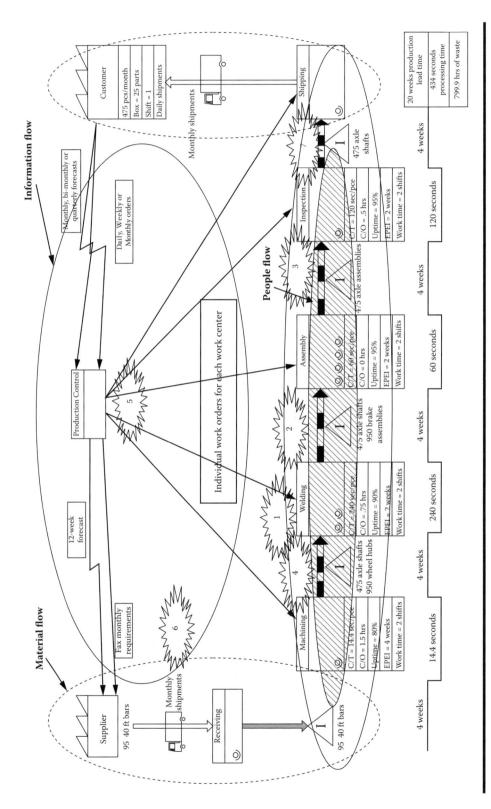

Figure 5.13 Kaizen burst.

In Figure 5.13 you can see that we have completed our future stream shapes that represent the three major flow systems in production: Information, Material and People. You can tell by the map that all three of these ellipses intersect, which shows how important each area is to the other. If you make a change to one it will affect the others.

Chapter 6

Identify Your Projects

Continuous Improvement Projects

Because you know where your kaizen events are needed, you can break them down into projects that you can tackle individually. First let me remind you that kaizen events should be used when it is necessary to work cross-functionally on a major project that will create a breakthrough or paradigm shift in the way you do business. Other, smaller continuous improvement projects can easily be done within the departments they are affecting without the use of a kaizen event.

Note that all but one of the "kaizen bursts" shown on the example current state map are cross-functional in nature.

Continuous improvements include

1. *Reduce changeover time in welding by 79%.* This is the only non-cross-functional project on our list. This is because we can make the improvements we need to reduce changeover time almost entirely within the welding process cell itself. Let us call this our "single minute tooling change project." In Lean manufacturing terms, this would be called SMED (single minute exchange of dies). Because all changeovers are not limited to metal stamping dies, I prefer the term "quick change-over tooling," as the whole idea is to reduce tooling and setup time to zero.

2. *Remove 3 weeks of inventory from between welding and assembly processes.* This would be accomplished by setting up a mini-mart

(supermarket), thus minimizing buffer inventory, eliminating push inventory, and allowing us to pull inventory into assembly.

3. *Eliminate 4 weeks of inventory between assembly, inspection, and shipping processes.* Our idea for these three work cells is to eliminate all inventories with the exception of WIP (work-in-process). We will create separate work cells or combine these processes into one work cell, and set up kanban signals that will allow us to pull rather than push inventory into each work cell and between operators in the work cell.

4. *Remove three weeks of inventory from between machining and welding processes.* To do this, we need to create a work cell for both the machining and welding processes and control the production demand from the welding process back to the machining process, with the welding process pulling inventory as needed from kanbans between machining and welding.

5. *Eliminate all work orders except for the pacesetter cell.* We can eliminate work orders for each process we have, as we now control the production build for each work cell by the demands of the following cell using visual controls. But if we have multiple products produced on the same assembly line, we need to identify what product is being built. We may be able to do this at the beginning of the line with production signal cards (which we explain later) or at the pacesetter cell, which should be placed as close as possible to the customer.

6. *Reduce raw material inventory stocks by increasing the delivery of smaller orders of raw material.* This is a larger undertaking and requires cross-functional support from materials, purchasing, planning, and the production floor. This is where we start predetermined material delivery routes to the production floor.

Identifying Your Projects from Your Maps

During all your kaizen events and projects, it is important to remember to gemba. Take a walk with your team to the area you want to change so that all of you see what needs to be done.

When you are asking people to try new things, it is important for you, the person giving the instructions, to verify for yourself the results of your request. Therefore, it is important for you to visit the actual location of the change, be it on the production floor, in the office, or at another factory. Why is this important? Because it is extremely important that you gain the trust and respect of the people you are asking to change the way they do things; and without that trust, people will not follow through with the change.

When you visit the site of the change, you may find that the change was not successful or it was incorrect. When this happens, you must immediately admit, with sincerity, that the change was wrong and admit the mistake. This will go a long way toward securing the trust and respect of the people affected by the change. Then the next time you ask someone to change a process or method they are doing, they will be more willing to cooperate.

You must teach your staff to utilize the same method in order to teach this skill to others and for you to see that your business can accomplish remarkable improvements. When you are on a gemba walk, take the opportunity to teach about continuous improvement and identify new areas for improvement. One of the most important aspects of any such walk is to identify areas for improvement and discuss them with the people on the walk. It is also important to include the people who will be affected by the change.

Explain the change to them and get their input; they do not always have to agree with your ideas, but ask them to "Just Try It" for a day. If you are not careful, you will end up in an endless debate as to whether or not a change will work. If you cannot get the support of your staff, just get them to "Try It" for a day or two; then be sure and check back to see how things went. Most people want to help and improve things, so keep their spirits and enthusiasm raised by following up with them—and remember that you are trying to transform your company into a learning company to help sustain company growth.

Which Project to Do First?

It is always difficult to decide which improvement project to tackle first. You always want to do one that will have the biggest impact to show yourself and others that this is a wonderful way to do business and how much money and time you can save the company. But you must be careful and take on a medium-sized project in which you can use many of the concepts and tools you will learn in this book. When using the example project list created from our current and future state value stream maps, pick one area to work in. If you have an assembly line on the production floor, this is an excellent place to start. However, if you are a component manufacturer, such as machining, injection molding, metal forming, etc., then I would pick a medium-volume component with which to work and determine which kind of work cell you can create to improve the flow of this product through your factory. I should note here that a discussion of scheduling individual work cells appears in Chapter 11. Also, these work cells, although similar to focused factories, are not the same thing. A focused factory is much more similar to what I call value stream management, which is a totally separate topic.

From our example in the book, let us pick the project to eliminate inventory between assembly, inspection, and shipping:

1. Eliminate four weeks of inventory between assembly, inspection, and shipping processes. Our idea for these three work cells is to eliminate all inventories with the exception of WIP (work-in-process). We will create separate work cells or combine these processes into one work cell, and set up kanban signals that will allow us to pull rather than push inventory into each work cell and between operators in the work cell.

This is still a rather large project to tackle all at once, so let us break it down into smaller elements:

1. Eliminate four weeks of inventory between assembly, inspection, and shipping.
2. Redefine assembly and inspection work cells to meet Lean principles.
3. Set up kanban signals between assembly, inspection, and shipping.

Now we have three more defined projects that still need further definition to make them easier to work with. Let us pick Project 2 as the one we want to do.

Redefine assembly and inspection work cells to meet Lean principles. This gives us a good project definition and allows us to begin working on the project. Because this book is designed for small companies, I will use some abbreviated steps to help achieve the desired change. However, for a high degree of waste removal from your processes, I would suggest more analysis in some areas. It is not necessary to follow the kaizen processes outlined in this book, but some of the elements are helpful in identifying and documenting the success of your project and reporting on the progress of the project. The steps to take in working with this project are as follows:

Team gemba: Take your team and "go see" the area you want to improve; while at the site, take pictures of the area to help identify the changes required.

Discuss, in general, the changes that need to be done and make a sketch of the current layout of the area.

In the conference room, begin by breaking down the elements of the assembly process. These elements do not need to be super-fine in detail but should be clear enough to define the steps of the process. Also, do the same in the inspection area. You may already have manufacturing process sheets with timed elements identified. If you do, it makes this step easier. Now lay your assembly steps out in sequence with their allocated process times (Figure 6.1).

If you do not have any process cycle times identified, you will need to do so.

If you have never done time studies before, you will need a stopwatch and the work element form available on the included CD. Breaking down a process into individual work elements and doing time studies is a little art and a little science; industrial engineers and technicians are trained in

Part/Model Name:		Process:		Operator:		Prepared By:	
Part/Model Number:		Department:		TAKT Time:		Date: / /	

Process Cycle

No.	Process Step Description	Break Point	1	2	3	4	5	6	7	8	9	10	Lowest Repeatable Time	Adjustment	Adjusted Elemental Time
1	Get light assembly from bin	Begin reach to bin	15	17	23	14	18	17	16	15	14	20	14	3	17
2	Return to trailer removing part	Begin turn after getting part	10	12	13	9	10	13	12	12	10	8	10	4	14
3	Slide light assembly onto bracket	Part touches bracket	20	22	23	24	20	22	23	24	20	22	20	0	20
4															
5															
6															
7															
8															
9															
10															
11															
12															
13															
	Sum of process steps (Overall Cycle Time)		45	51	59	47	48	52	51	51	44	50	44 / 51	7	51

1) Observe the operation & fill in the "Process Step Description" column as well as the associated break points
2) Using a stopwatch, time each event and enter the data into the columns, do this for 10 process cycles
3) Sum each *column* and enter the value at the bottom "Sum of process steps"
4) For each process step, review the data for each *row* and enter the lowest repeatable time in the column (NOT THE AVERAGE TIME!)
5) If the numbers on either side of the diagonal line do not match, use the "Adjustment" column to correct until they do
6) Use this data to complete the "Standard Work Combination Sheet"

Figure 6.1   Time Study Observation Form.

detail to define the process and work elements, and do the time studies, all of which can take multiple days and hours for a truly exact result. However, because most small companies have limited resources, we will limit the amount of detail and time we spend on creating timed elements.

Go to the work area and write down each of the work elements you see that are required to make your component or assembly. There is no need at this time to break them down into really fine detail because you are only looking for the major elements within the process. It is important to note cycle times where the operator is waiting (idle) for a machine, oven, test fixture, etc., to complete a cycle. Once you have completed the list, take each element and, using a stopwatch, time the elements one by one. Be careful when timing and always pick the same start and stop points (also known as the breakpoints), usually when a person picks up or puts down a part or tool, within the element to check the time. Gather a minimum of ten cycle times for each element. Total each *column* (see Figure 6.1); now take the lowest repeatable time for each *row* and place it in the column labeled "Lowest Repeatable Time"; this includes the "Sum of Process Steps" row. Place the answer from the "Sum the Lowest Repeatable Time" column in the box with the diagonal line. If the two numbers in the diagonal box are not the same, subtract the two to arrive at the adjustment number. Next, add the adjustment factor to each row as needed to make the two numbers equal. This will give you a satisfactory time for the remaining work you need to do. Complete this task for each of the elements; you will need these numbers to help balance the work within the process (completed form shown in Figure 6.2).

STANDARD WORK FLOW - Office/Production Assembly				
Area	Trailer wiring	**Date:** 10/11/08		**Work Instruction Sheet**
Operation	Install tail lights	**Process:**	Attach left-hand light to trailer	**Sheet 1 of 1**
No.	**Major Steps**	**Time (seconds)**	**NOTES**	
1	Get light assembly from bin	15		
2	Return to trailer while removing nuts	15		
3	Slide light assy on to left hand mtg bkt	3		
4	Screw on two nuts	10	Hand tight only	
5	Tighten nuts with wrench	12	Use torque wrench tighten to 20 inch lbs	
6	Attach wiring harness plug to light	10		
7				
8				
9				
10				
	Total Time:	65		

Figure 6.2

Guidance: Time Study Basics

When taking a time study, if someone is interrupted during your timing you will need to stop and redo the time. Sometimes an operator will get ahead of you while you are taking the time study. If this happens and you have not had time to reset your stopwatch and get ready for the next element, you will need to stop and redo the time.

There are two methods people use when using a stopwatch.

1. Time one element over and over.
2. Time one element and move to the next one when all elements in the process are complete.

I have found over many years that timing one element over and over until I have the number of readings I want and then moving to the next element worked best.

Other things to remember:

1. Separate operator and machine time.
2. Identify times when the operator is idle.
3. Identify times when the operator is loading or unloading a machine or fixture.
4. Study only trained operators for the process.
5. Position yourself so you can see the operator's hand, body, and foot movements.
6. Always be respectful and courteous to the operator.

Now you can eliminate waste within the process. Look at your work element breakdown; find any time where the operator is idle or waiting on a machine to complete a process and determine if you can have the operator doing something else. Can one operator run more than one machine? Can an inspection step be included? Look for any time where the clamping or unclamping of parts could be automated or parts automatically ejected from a machine or fixture. Keep in mind as you review your process that automation costs money. What can you do to eliminate or improve the process without large capital outlays? Look at the operator's time; is it really fully utilized? When creating the work balance chart for the work cell, each operator's time is placed on a bar chart and some Lean practitioners will add details within each work element to show individual tasks. Again, because you are a small company, a simple bar chart will do. Next, add the takt time line indicating how often one product needs to be completed and leave the work cell. Now look at the bars on the chart. Do any of these extend above the takt time line? How many are below the takt time line? Now you need to redistribute the work between the operators in the cell. Let us assume that you have five operators in the cell. Now distribute the work by filling the first operator's time to within 10% of takt time; next, do the same for operator number two, three, and so on until you have as many operators at 90% of capacity. Any remaining time is left with the remaining people in the cell. You may find that you have too many workers in the cell; if this is true, redistribute them to other tasks in your company. Once the balancing is complete, the work elements for each person should be less than the takt line, thus allowing for the comfortable completion of work in time to meet the customer demand. Now you have a dynamic scheduling tool to help determine the number of people you need in each cell. If the customer demand goes up, the takt time line will come down closer to the top of the work elements. As long as the takt line is above the work elements, you are fine; on the other hand, should the takt time line go below the top of one work element, you will need to rebalance the work cell. The rule of thumb is that if the amount of time that must be redistributed is less than half a person, then look for more ways to eliminate waste in the work cell. If it is more than half a person, you will need to add another person to the work cell (Figure 6.3).

Next create a process balance chart for the assembly and inspection areas combined. This gives us a very good visual from which to balance the entire line (Figure 6.4).

In our example, assume that for each workstation there is one person. The assembly process consists of five work elements and inspection is one work element. Also add the customer demand takt time to the chart.

Now that the work cell balance chart is complete, begin looking at how you can balance the work within the entire line.

You are trying to create continuous flow to balance the line between all work cells, just like you would within a work cell. For the time scale on both charts, minutes have been used in place of seconds; this was done for ease of calculations. It is recommended that you use the lowest measurement increment possible. On your charts I would use seconds for the

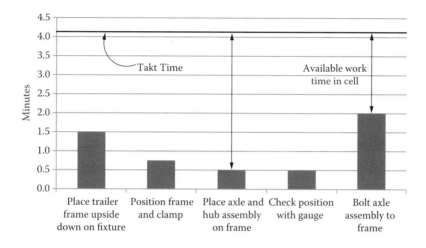

Figure 6.3   Work balance chart for frame and axle assembly.

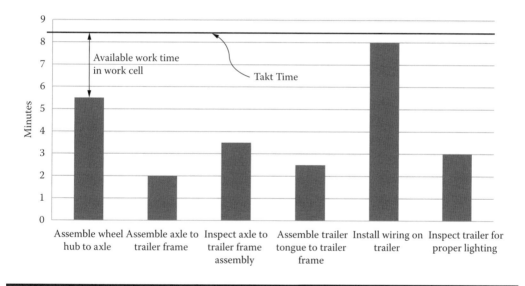

Figure 6.4   Work cell balance chart for trailer assembly line.

time scale. Now you have balanced the assembly line and combined some of the inspection steps into other workstations. You can see that you have now reduced the number of operators to four from the original total of six. Notice that the last workstation is less than 50% of the takt time, and you should look at the other three workstations to see if there is any waste to be removed so you can eliminate the fourth station. As a small company, you may not have the time to perfectly balance a work cell or production line, but taking the time to make some improvement to the balance of the line improves throughput and frees up personnel for other tasks.

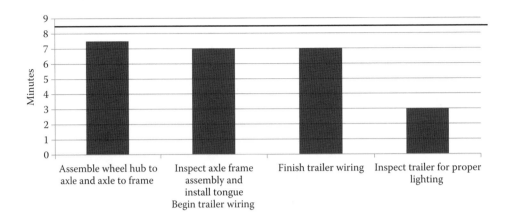

Figure 6.5   Assembly line balance chart.

There are five different ways to set up work cells to redistribute the work-load. Because you are trying to keep things simple, I have shown you the most typical way to do this by splitting the work between operators in the work cell (Figure 6.5).

Machine Tools and Takt Time

To determine if your machine tools can meet takt time, you only need a simple calculation.

To the white board:

Machine cycle time	= 32 seconds
Load time	= 5 seconds
Machine start time	= 2 seconds
Unload time	= 5 seconds
Changeover time per part	= 1 second (see below)
Total machine time	= 45 seconds

120-second changeover time divided by 150 pieces/batch = 0.8 seconds

Ideally, you would allow yourself approximately 10% available time in each of the work cells and on the assembly line to allow for fluctuations in takt time and minor delays in production.

If your machine's total cycle time is still above the takt time, you can use other methods to bring the cycle time to within proper limits—things such as using more than one machine or running the machine off-line from the regular production line.

We have been taught over the years that the most efficient way to run a machine tool is at or near capacity; and while this is great for the individual machine tool, it is not necessarily good for the entire production line. In the case of Lean manufacturing, we are optimizing the efficiency of the entire production line, not just one machine; and as a result, we have a highly efficient factory.

Smoothing the Flow of Production

One of the main problems companies face is erratic customer demand, and this causes all sorts of problems for you, the small business owner. You find yourself constantly adjusting the number of people you need on the production line or working overtime to meet demand. Large numbers of companies experience what is known as the "hockey stick effect." This is where you find yourself rushing to get more product out the door at the end of the month and at the end of the business quarter. If you happen to be a smaller, publicly owned company, this is done to help bolster sales numbers for the end of the month or sales quarter.

Figure 6.6 shows what the "hockey stick effect" would look like graphically. Does it look familiar? Because with Lean production you want a stable, balanced production floor that you can easily manage and that allows for continued balance flow to your customers, you can use what is known as a *pacesetter cell*, supermarkets (finished goods warehouse), and mini-marts (buffer stock between work cells) to smooth out the production line while ensuring that you meet your customers' demands.

Customer demand is not the only thing that affects production; there are also supplier delivery problems, product quality and design issues, machine breakdowns, as well as staffing level fluctuations resulting in a need for a way to smooth out production. To compensate for these variations, over the years companies have added inventory to allow them a consistent level of product to ship to their customers. It is better to address these types of variations as quickly as possible. Waiting for daily production review and then assessing which problems are found allows an entire day of product to be produced with errors or worse, not produced at all.

What you need to do is monitor production and its problems at the lowest possible level. Depending on your type of product and customer takt time, this could be daily or even hourly. From my experience, I find that hourly monitoring is a nice balance because it is long enough to show if we are meeting our demand and short enough to respond to problems quickly.

In some companies you may want even shorter times to respond to problems. How do you determine what is a good interval in which to check the assembly line? One method is to check the line based on takt time. How many parts do you pack per box? Then multiply it by the takt rate, as in the following example:

Calculate the pitch:

$$45 \text{ pieces} \times 8 \text{ minute takt time} = 360 \text{ minutes} = \text{every 6 hours}$$

This gives us a "pitch" of six hours, so management would check for problems every six hours. In this example, the six hours seems a little too long to me; I would adjust this to every four hours.

Now we have two new terms: both *pitch* and *paced withdrawal* are used at the pacemaker cell to detect problems. They are not to make operators work harder or faster.

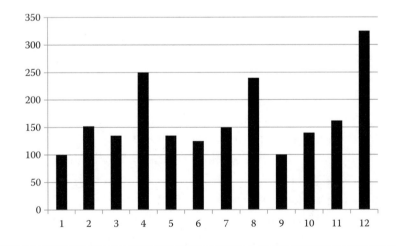

Figure 6.6   The "hockey stick" effect.

Balancing Product Mix in the Work Cell

Many small companies have multiple customers requiring the use of the same machine tools or even sharing of assembly production lines. The question is: How do I balance and schedule this work within my work cell? Many people are skeptical of how to schedule multiple parts in a work cell with Lean manufacturing but it is relatively easy. You may hear or see the term "every-part-every-interval" (EPEI). EPEI indicates how often a process can produce its high-running parts. An example would be if a process can produce its high-running parts every four hours, then the EPEI would be every-part-every-four hours. What would this look like? Use the simple plan below to schedule a one-shift operation with deliveries every four hours.

There are numerous ways to build a scheduling and work cell balance board, but for the small company I prefer the design in Figure 6.7. The idea is that your production planning department places work orders or, in the case shown, schedules kanban tags showing what needs to be produced and when. I like the kanban tag method because it gives the work cell some flexibility in how they schedule their work. Each tag has the same information:

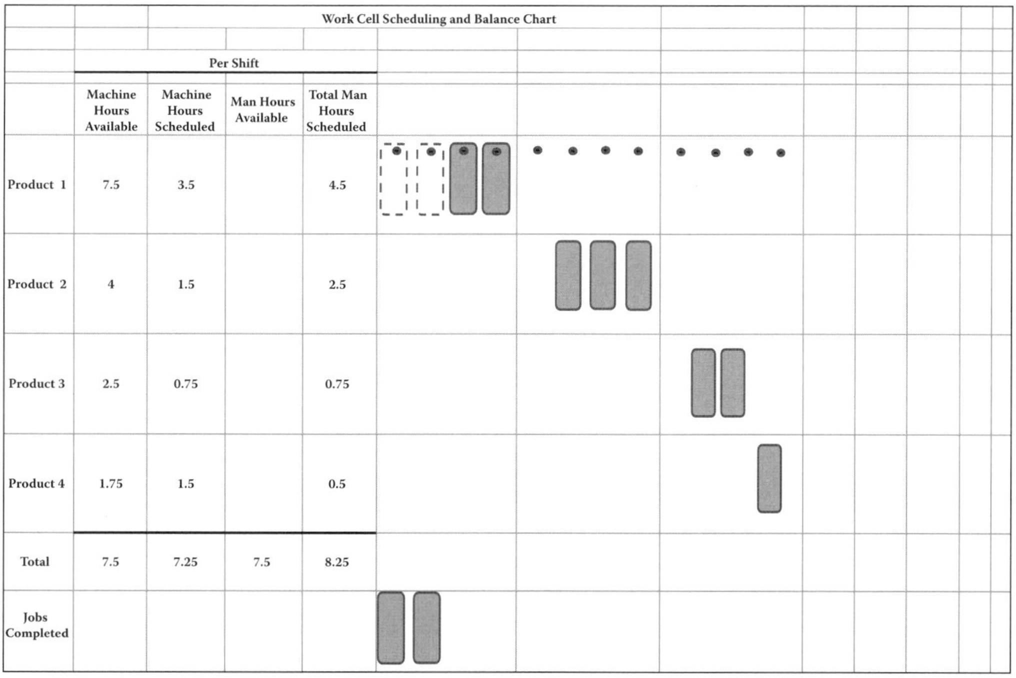

			Work Cell Scheduling and Balance Chart							
		Per Shift								
	Machine Hours Available	Machine Hours Scheduled	Man Hours Available	Total Man Hours Scheduled						
Product 1	7.5	3.5		4.5						
Product 2	4	1.5		2.5						
Product 3	2.5	0.75		0.75						
Product 4	1.75	1.5		0.5						
Total	7.5	7.25	7.5	8.25						
Jobs Completed										

Figure 6.7   Work cell scheduling and balance chart.

- Part description
- Part number
- Quantity to be produced
- Man-hours required
- Machine-hours required
- Setup time required

The cards are laminated and the quantity is written on the card so the card can be reused. If the card needs additional information updated, it needs a new card created. I have used this example to show how to create a visual scheduling system that easily shows the status of production for a machine tool, molding machine, packaging department, or any other place you would like. All you have to do is adjust the columns to fit your need. Each cell holding cards is divided into four sections using four hooks. In this example, if you needed a setup time, we have skipped one hook to show a fifteen-minute setup time. If you needed a thirty-minute setup, we would skip two hooks. You can see by the total row that our machine still has fifteen minutes of production time available and our manpower is overcommitted by forty-five minutes. Management can easily see that overtime may be an option or adding another person to the work cell to ensure production is completed in the time available may be the best idea. As each kanban demand card is completed, it is placed at the bottom of the chart showing the progress for the day. It is easy to see if the daily production will be met.

This is just one method of scheduling and balancing a work cell although there are other designs and methods. When your small company grows, you may need to consider more advanced Lean scheduling and balancing systems but this method works well for almost all businesses. In an assembly process, placing this scheduling system at the pacesetter cell will automatically schedule the remaining upstream processes for each product.

Implementation

When implementing your first work cell, you must be very careful to make it a success. All of the production staff will be watching and all of the skeptics will be waiting to say, "I told you it would not work." The following items will help you make this a success:

- Create an implementation plan using the A3 format.
- Using the A3, show the goals you wish to attain.
- Show the planned schedule.

It is imperative that management is in full support of the project and reviews the project on a regular basis. I discuss more about implementation, A3 reports, and project planning in the kaizen section in Chapter 7.

For the work cell to run properly, you need Standard Work Charts for each of the workstations in the cell. If you are fortunate enough to have these in real-time on the computer, it is great; but most companies still rely on paper standardized work charts. Many companies call these production process sheets but the key here is to have a "standardized process sheet" that is actively maintained so anyone can use it and build a quality product. In the Lean environment, we expect and demand that these sheets include the detailed process used at each workstation, including all of the little adjustments needed for a quality product. Operators cannot keep these little unwritten processes to themselves. A more detailed discussion about standardized work is in Chapter 8.

Once the work cell is in place, it will usually take two to three weeks for the operators to feel comfortable in the cell. The operators will experience a learning curve in the cell. You will find that between 70% and 80% of your target goals will be met in the first week the cell is operational. The remainder of the goal will most likely be met in the following two weeks. The work cell's success is everyone's responsibility, and management needs to give their full support. By the end of the third week, the work cell team and its supervisor should be updating the operator's balance chart and standardized work chart. Keep in mind that maintenance of the work cell is not the responsibility of management or engineering—it is the responsibility of the team leader and supervisor.

Audits

The best way to maintain sustainability and to keep continuous improvement moving is through the use of an audit. The audit should be constructed to hold each level of management accountable to the next level of management. Audits should be done daily, weekly, and monthly. The following is a good example of an audit system.

◼ Daily: Team leader reviews checklist for work cells under their responsibility.

◼ Weekly: Production supervisor for the area reviews the work cell checklist as a check against the team leader to make sure they are doing things correctly.

◼ Monthly: Plant management reviews all work cells and holds the production supervisor responsible for accuracy and errors.

These audits are designed so that team leaders and supervisors spend approximately twenty to thirty minutes doing the audits while the managers' audits take between forty-five and sixty minutes. A plant manager may spend as much as a day doing an audit, but in most cases it is closer to two to three hours.

Table 6.1 shows a list of potential assessment items. These happen to be for a medical device company. Once you have determined your areas of assessment create a laminated card with the information you want to audit listed on them. Place the cards in the work cell where they are visible and readily available. Be sure and use the cards during each audit.

Detailed items to audit are unique to each work cell and are identified on laminated 3 × 5-inch cards. Each "aspect" is a separate card, with all the cards held together with a metal ring (Figure 6.8).

Although this is a fairly elaborate audit system, it gives you an idea of what one might look like. This company found a dramatic change on their produciton floor within two months of implementing this system. Prior to that time, they had standard worksheets called SOPs (Standard Operating Procedures) that were not up to date, they had chemicals that had expired on the production floor, and their kanban bin quantities were not accurate.

Who Should be Audited?

All departments are included in the monthly audit; this means production, inspection and test, raw material warehouse, receiving, and receiving inspection. You may have other departments that you would want to include.

The audit form in Figure 6.9 is for use by the supervisor and managers. Each week it is the responsibility of the supervisor of each work cell to complete an audit of the cell based on the audit cards created. As the supervisor audits each section required, i.e., safety, tool calibration, maintenance, etc., he initials the proper box on the assessment form. If he finds a problem he

Table 6.1 Standard Work Flow: Office/Production Assembly Trailer

Aspect	Potential Area of Assessment
Work cell cleanliness	• Workbench surfaces clean • Floors swept clean • Sinks clean • No improper storage • Supplies put away • No benchtop / workstation paper clutter • No clutter underneath benches • Tools and fixtures in proper location
Command center utilization	• Monthly productivity sheet is up-to-date • Daily production form is up-to-date • 5S sheet is up-to-date • Cell assessment form is up-to-date • Assessment building block card (ABC) cards are present
Use of LEAN flow	• Follow standard work instruction • Follow work cell flow diagram
Proper bin use	• Adequate supply of equilibrated/thawed reagents available • Proper kanban levels for consumables maintained • Kanban cards in good repair • Bin label present and in good repair • Bins in proper locations • Parts match bin description • No bin dumping • Part quantity must match bin quantity

must fill out the form in Figure 6.10, which requires assigning responsibility to someone to correct the issue found, and then have the responsible supervisor or manager sign off that the corrective action was completed. When the supervisor audits the work cell, he is holding the work cell leader responsible for properly maintaining his areas of responsibility. When the plant manager audits the work cell, he is holding the supervisor responsible. As the plant manager audits each work cell he scores the area, i.e., for safety, maintenance, etc., with a "1" or a "0." A "1" if the area is satisfactory and a "0" if it is not. The column is then totaled with a maximum perfect score in

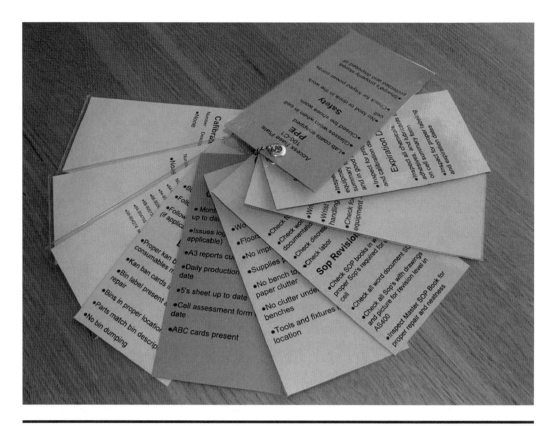

Figure 6.8 Audit system.

this example of "10." If the plant manager finds a problem and scores a "0," he must fill out the form in Figure 6.10 and provide a reassessment date on the work cell assessment form.

Stabilizing Your Processes

After you have created your work cells and have an audit process in place, begin to think about how stable your processes have become. If the individual work cells and machines do not have an uptime and reliable delivery of between 75% and 85%, it will be difficult to smooth out production using the pull method of production control. This is a good point to spend more time working on improving the stability and dependability of each work cell. Once you have achieved the desired uptime, you can move ahead with production pull. If you do not wait to improve your processes at this point, you will find it more difficult to implement your pull system later.

Cell	Lead Initials Assessment Complete					Supervisor / Manager Assessment Score	
Month/Year	WK 1	WK 2	WK 3	WK 4	WK 5	Monthly	Re-Assess
1) Safety Procedures Followed							
2) Tools Calibrated							
3) Expiration Dates							
4) Maintenance Done							
5) Work Order/Deviation Control							
6) Standard Work Revision Control							
7) Work Cell Cleanliness							
8) Command Center Utilization							
9) Use of LEAN Flow							
10) Proper POU Bin Use							

Assessment Scoring: The highest score achievable is 10. 1 point will be given for each of the 10 aspects of compliance if all requirements are achieved. No points will be awarded for a given category if any non-compliance is identified. Total scores of 6 or lower will require re-assessment.

Totals

Initial / Date

Findings:

Comments:

Reviewed By Reporting Manager: _____

Sign/Date

Figure 6.9   Work Cell Assessment Form.

Cell	Assessor	Assessment Date
	Assigned to	Date

Correction Action Instructions:	1) One correction action form will be completed for each non-compliance.
	2) Provide details on what and how you corrected the non-compliance.
	3) Sign and date after completing the correction action and return to Lead.
	4) Return completed forms to your reporting Manager for review and sign off.

Non-compliance description: Circle which aspect of compliance was affected.   PPE/Safety   Calibration   Expiration Dates   Maintenance

Work Order/MD Control   SOP/Rev Control   Work Cell Cleanliness   Command Center Utilization   Lean Flow   Bin Use

Correction action:

Completed by	Date

Reviewed By Reporting Manager:

Sign/Date

Figure 6.10   Correction Action Form.

Chapter 7

Your First Kaizen Project Team

What Is a Kaizen Event (Continuous Improvement Event)?

The word *kaizen* is a Japanese word meaning continuous improvement. A kaizen event is a team activity that is intended to create a "significant improvement" in the process being investigated. These events should be used when you need significant cross-functional help to affect the improvement desired or one that will be difficult to accomplish due to complexity or politics. There are two types of kaizen events:

1. *System (flow) kaizen:* Focuses on the overall value stream and is typically performed by management.
2. *Process kaizen:* Focuses on an individual process. This is for work cell teams and team leaders.

In the small company, you will most likely experience kaizens that are a combination of the two (system and process), where managers and supervisors are sometimes members of the kaizen team.

Many people mistakenly believe they need kaizen events to change a process, because kaizen is part of the larger goal of continuous improvement. I want to make sure that everyone understands that continuous improvement is one of the desired outcomes from the culture change you are undertaking, and that a kaizen event is one of the tools in your Lean toolbox. Do not expect to use kaizen events for every change you want to make; change should be a continuous process where little changes that are processed and implemented at the work-cell level make a difference and do not require a kaizen event to achieve. Kaizen events are intended to make a "significant" change in the way we do something.

Team Makeup

Your team should be made up of people knowledgeable about the process you are trying to change. The team leader is anyone you believe will show leadership and provide guidance and direction to the team. In a very small company, the team leader is an active member of the team while in a large company the team leader functions more as a facilitator. The team should consist of no more than seven people, and preferably five. In a smaller company, the team may be less than five; however, I prefer to have teams made up with an odd number of people—three, five, or seven. Why? The odd number allows one person to be the tie-breaker when voting on decisions made by the team. You want team members who actually use the process that is to be changed because the users almost always know how to shorten and improve the process. Also, if they are involved in the decision of how to change the process, they will more readily embrace the change and help make it a success.

Kaizen Event Process

Once you have selected the team, you can begin planning your event. Shown below is a typical kaizen event covering a one-week time period. Some events run shorter and some longer, but for the example here we use a week time frame. Please note that the schedule uses Six Sigma identifiers for each significant step in the process. These are Define, Measure, Analyze, Improve, and Control (DMAIC); these steps were used on this chart because the company I was working with was more familiar with these terms than with the Plan–Do–Check–Act (PDCA) process. These two processes—DMAIC and PDCA—in effect cover the same information, and I tend to use them interchangeably in this book because the two systems have a common origin. There are two large differences, however. One is that DMAIC used with Six Sigma must stop after each step and be reviewed and approved by a committee before moving to the next step, and it uses statistical data to help in analyzing a problem. The PDCA method is much more informal and does not need any formal approval before moving to the next step and for the most part uses basic mathematics, although statistical data is always helpful. As a result of less organizational steps to overcome, PDCA tends to be a simpler and quicker method to use when looking at processes. In fact, you may do multiple repetitions of PDCA as you work through your problem very quickly. Whether you use the DMAIC or PDCA is somewhat irrelevant; the main outcome or result of either system should be in the retained learning you as an individual and the corporation achieve when you have finished the project and explain to others in the company what you have learned.

Table 7.1 provides an example of a weekly kaizen schedule and gives you a very good idea of what a very formal kaizen event entails. As a small company, you may not want such a formal system; however, it is a very good learning tool from which to decide what your kaizens might look like.

Looking at the schedule in Table 7.1, you will find Lean training every morning. Instead of one day of intensive training, I have divided it into several shorter sessions. The first day is basic Lean training, an overview, while each of the following days focuses on the tools to be used that day to help in problem analysis and resolution. These tools are typically

- Spaghetti diagrams
- Value stream maps
- Pareto charts
- Time study forms
- Financial data
- Fishbone diagrams
- Cause-and-effect diagrams

By the time the kaizen is complete, you may not have learned all of the tools but you will have a very good start on your Lean knowledge. In the next kaizen, you will learn more tools.

These are not the only tools you might use but they are the most common ones used in a kaizen event. Here you have some time for "theme," which is where you discuss what the problem is and why you are working on it. You also refine the problem statement to be very definitive about what you are trying to change. At this point, it would be helpful to go see, with the team, what the problem is. Walk the problem backward from the final

Table 7.1   Proposed Kaizen Schedule

Times Are Flexible	Monday	Tuesday	Wednesday	Thursday	Friday
8 a.m.	Kickoff meeting	Training on Lean principles	Training on Lean principles	Training on Lean principles	Follow-up items
9 a.m.	Training on Lean principles	Begin populating the A3 template	IMPROVE	Collect all "after" data for metrics	Finalize A3
10 a.m.	DEFINE	Finish data collection, charts, & diagrams	Develop improvement plan based on analysis	Update A3 report	Presentation preparation
11 a.m.	Theme	Brainstorm visual for data collection	Try storming and implement	CONTROL	Final presentation
12 p.m.	SMART targets	ANALYZE	Try storming, implement, and measure improvements	Sustainment of changes made during kaizen burst	Celebration
1 p.m.	MEASURE	Determine root cause of defects/problems	Try storming and implement	Develop documentation and control plans	If needed, team continues
2 p.m.	Develop data collection plan	Identify sources of variation	Try storming and implement	Prepare newspaper	Maybe we can go home
3 p.m.	Observations of waste	Prioritize improvement opportunities	Brainstorm visual for process improvement	Communication plan	
4 p.m.	Leaders' alignment meeting	Leaders' alignment meeting	Leaders' alignment meeting		

step to the very beginning step of the process to get a different perspective on the issue. Take notes along the away. Once that is completed, you can move on to create your SMART goals.

SMART Goals

Part of the planning process for any continuous improvement project is to set some goals to know if you have truly improved your process. There are guidelines for setting good SMART goals and they are as follows:

Specific: Set goals that are specific in nature. Do not say, "reduce process time"; this is too vague. Say, "Reduce process time by 5%."

Measurable: The goal to "reduce process time by 5%" is both specific and readily measurable.

Achievable: Do not set goals that are out of reach, such as losing twenty pounds in two weeks. Know what is achievable and go for it. Example: lose two pounds per week for ten weeks. Plan for success.

Realistic: Goals should be realistic with a little challenge to them but not too easy. To "reduce process time by 1% is too easy, and to reduce process time by 10% may be unobtainable, but to reduce process time by 5% is realistic." You must be honest with yourself when you do this.

Time frame: You need an end date for which you can measure your success in achieving your goal. Allow enough time for the change to become established after it is made, but not so long that you forget why the change was made. One to four weeks after a change is implemented is a reasonable time frame.

A simple goal target sheet is shown in Table 7.2; you can also use SMART goals on an A3 report.

Listed in Table 7.3 are a number items and their method of measure that we have used on our target sheets and A3 reports. You are free to use any measure you would like but be sure and keep them simple and easy to understand. You will find in the list provided that there is a line for business process members included. This is done because many of the measures you see here can also be used when you do kaizens in the office.

Now the fun really begins. Begin gathering information and data that will be used to change your process. This data can take the form of value stream maps, spaghetti diagrams, financial data, etc. Break up the team and send

Table 7.2 Target Sheet

Location: _____
Department: _____
Project Description: _____ Date _____

Target	Measurement	Before	After	% Difference

Table 7.3 Target Sheet Measurements

Items	Measurement	Items	Measurement
Setup time	Minutes	WIP dollars	$
Crew size for setup	Number	Operator travel distance	Feet
Units per operator hour	Units/operator	Sum of process cycle steps	Seconds
Daily clock man-hours	Man-hours	Non-value added	Seconds or minutes
Crew size standard work	Number	Annual scrap savings	$
Daily output	Units	Search time	Seconds
Floor space	Sq. ft.	Walking distance	Feet
WIP units	Units	Personnel redeployed	Number
Parts travel distance	Feet	Business process members involved	Number
Throughput	Minutes	Process steps	Number
Walking distance	Steps		

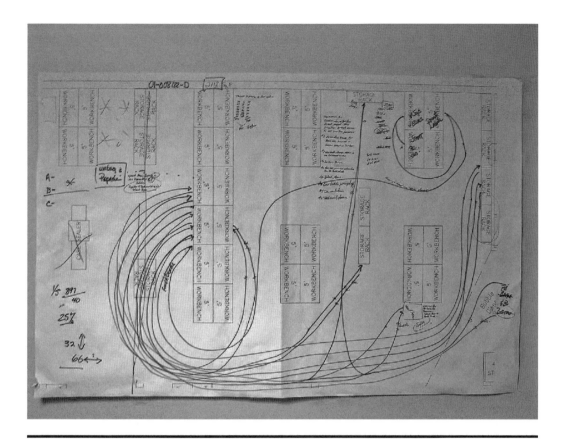

Figure 7.1   Spaghetti diagram.

them out to gather the data. A spaghetti diagram is fun. Start with a copy of the plant, office, or a work cell floor layout; it must be large enough to work with, a preferable size is 11 × 17 inches or larger, but not too large because you are going to carry it with you. Start at the beginning of the process; now trace on the layout the stops you make to complete the entire process that you are interested in changing. Think of this as a picture where you connect the dots by numbers to show the hidden picture. Figure 7.1 provides a very good example of a spaghetti diagram. What you see here is a current state diagram of a manufacturing floor; I suggest you do another diagram after you have changed your process and then compare the two to see how successful your changes have been at eliminating the number of lines. As a measure of success, on your target sheet you could even include the reduction in lines on the spaghetti diagram or the number of times the lines cross each other.

At the end of the day you fill out the daily activity report showing what you have accomplished during the day and what you plan to accomplish the

	Date:	**Week of 2/15/2011**
	Kaizen Burst Name:	**Assembly Angels**

	Monday's Objectives	Member(s) Assigned
1	Team introductions	Nancy L.
2	Kickoff meeting	Major M.
3	Lean training	Mike E.
4	Establish SMART goals	Team
5	GEMBA (go to the place go see) walk	Team
6	Create data collection plan	Team
7		
8		

	Tuesday's Objectives	Member(s) Assigned
1	Begin collecting data	Bob, Carol, Ted, Alice
2	Begin working on A3	Major M
3	Brainstorm data	Team
4	Determine root cause	Team
5		
6		
7		
8		

	Wednesday's Objectives	Member(s) Assigned
1		
2		
3		
4		
5		
6		
7		
8		

	Thursday's Objectives	Member(s) Assigned
1		
2		
3		
4		
5		
6		

Figure 7.2   Kaizen burst team daily activities.

next day. The example in Figure 7.2 shows one day of work complete and what the team expects to complete the next day. Do not fill out this form more than one day in advance as activities can change from day to day. Why does the form stop on Thursday? The form is designed for a week-long kaizen event, with Friday only being a kaizen review meeting and with the results outcome being information for management and a celebration of success.

Now you have a quick daily management update; keep this to about fifteen minutes and do not let it go beyond twenty minutes. These short update meetings allow for management to be updated on the progress of the kaizen and provide input by providing suggestions such as, "Have you thought about …?" or "Think about …." Management is not there to direct the project as the team is self-directed.

The next day you compile and review your data and begin to brainstorm possible solutions after you have identified the root cause of the problem you are fixing. You then begin to prioritize possible fixes to the problem. Next, develop your implementation plan, which is based on your analysis of the data, root cause determination, and the selection of what the team believes is the best solution to the problem. Now this is really exciting because you get to try out your solution, and hence the term on the calendar, "try storming" (see Table 7.1). Try storming is not unlike brainstorming but you actually get your hands dirty and try the solution in real life. If you find significant issues with the solution, you can easily go back to the team and reevaluate the solution. Once you have a solution that works, it does not have to be perfect; you collect your after-implementation data and update the A3 report. Keep in mind that you are doing continuous improvement in the form of the kazien and you can always go back and readjust your solution at a later date. But the most important thing at this point is that you have come up with a solution using the data, not your instincts, and applied it to help correct the problem. It may not be perfect but you have taken another step toward improving your processes.

Sustainment of the change can be difficult, so the team will often make a change and at the end of the kaizen event they walk away from the change, leaving someone else to ensure that the change stays in place. Before you go to the final report-out meeting with management, you need to formulate a sustainment plan that identifies who is responsible for the change after the kaizen is finished. This is simple to say and difficult to do. Because management is ultimately responsible for ensuring that the implementation of Lean is successful, do not be afraid to identify a first-line supervisor and his or her boss as the responsible parties. All the people in the factory and the office need to learn that it is not the team's responsibility or even the team leader's responsibility to ensure that the change sticks; rather it is their own responsibility.

Wrap up the kaizen with a final presentation of the target report using the after-implementation data and showing the difference between "before" and "after" results. Compile a list of action items that need to be completed before the kaizen event can be called complete. See Figure 7.3 for an example of a kaizen event form that we discuss further in this chapter.

Team Name: _____

Project Leader: _____

Directions:
1) Fill each row with implemented Kaizen improvement items that your team completed during the Kaizen event.
2) At the end of the Kaizen event add items to the list that must be completed (maximum 30 working days allowed).
3) After the Kaizen event is over fill in the audit dates for the next 30 working days.
4) Perform cell audits every week for 30 working days.
5) Project leader will give a status report at every lean team leaders' meeting until all task numbers are complete.

Follow-up Audit Schedule
6) Audit dates should be every week, separated by approximately 5 working days
7) Indicate if items are complete and being sustained by scoring a 1 or 0
8) Score a 1 for every week they are sustained, a 0 on the weeks they are not

Task #	Problem to be addressed	Kaizen (improvement) Action	Responsible Person	Expected audit date / Actual Date / Due Date	End of Kaizen event (action complete)	1 week (Yes = 1, No = 0) 1/12/12 — 1/20/12	2 weeks (Yes = 1, No = 0) 1/19/12 — 1/19/12	3 weeks (Yes = 1, No = 0) 1/26/12 — 1/27/12	4 weeks (Yes = 1, No = 0) 2/3/12 — 2/7/12
					1/6/12				
1	Gather data on issue to be resolved	Collect data for analysis	Team	1/2/12	1/2/12	1	1	1	1
2	Ensure data is compiled and usable by team	Compile data	Strand	1/3/12	1/3/12	1	1	1	1
3	Decide how to resolve issue	Prepare change plan	Team	1/4/12	1/4/12	1	1	1	1
4	Physically try proposed process	Try storm change plan	Team	1/5/12	1/5/12	1	1	1	1
5	Final report out of Kaizen team to management	Final report to management	Team	1/6/12	1/6/12	1	1	1	1
6	Complete final changes needed in work cell	Finish changes to work cell	MElbert	1/7/12	1/22/12	0	1	1	1
7	Update all standard work affected	Update process standard work	Nlatzke	1/10/12	1/9/12	1	1	1	1

Total value of events to be complete (Number of events × number of weeks in audit) — 42

Total events to complete — 7

Total events complete (input total manually) — 4 — 42 / 41

Percent achieved — 57% — 98%

Week sustainment scores: 6 7 7 7

Maximum sustainment score achievable — 7

Achieved sustainment score

Note:
1) Add new rows in middle of spreadsheet if needed so totals will not be affected
2) Shaded totals will calculate automatically

Figure 7.3   Kaizen Event Form.

Plan–Do–Check–Act

Whether you are a small or large company, everyone must plan their projects, and the wonderful thing about a kaizen event is that it creates shared goals and activities for a dedicated team to focus on. Although we call kaizens an event, they are actually quick, highly focused mini-projects that require a certain amount of preparation. To accomplish a successful kaizen event, follow the "Plan–Do–Check–Act" (PDCA) method of project management (Figure 7.4). PDCA is a repetitive process that uses the results from one step to build on the following steps. This method is commonly used for the control and continuous improvement of processes and products. It is also known as the Deming cycle or Deming wheel. Plan–Do–Study–Act is another name for the same process. This method is most commonly used for process improvements, and the method will be used over and over again as you improve your process.

With any event or project, it is important to follow the PDCA method. Some people believe that Six Sigma is a better method and it may be for some companies; however, many small companies do not always have the luxury of extended time to solve their problems. It is more important for the small company, or any company for that matter, to have a disciplined method of problem solving. Toyota does not use Six Sigma as we know it; instead, they have a very well-developed problem-solving process of their own that they follow. They also do not have certified people in Lean Six Sigma; rather, they have trained their employees in their method of problem solving, thus making them all problem solvers.

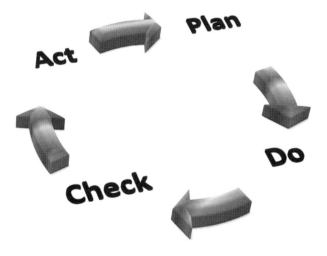

Figure 7.4   Plan–Do–Check–Act.

Using Plan–Do–Check–Act and A3

Any initiative you start can be difficult to maintain; thus, you want a system, particularly for problem solving, that is relatively simple to use yet has the necessary structure to ensure that it is easy to understand and provides all the necessary information for yourself and other people in the company to use and make decisions from. When performing kaizen events, there is a need to clearly define and resolve a problem. Using the PDCA method, you have this tool; when combined with the A3 reporting format, it becomes an excellent project tracking and reporting tool. What is nice is that the tool works! It gives you a step-by-step process through which you can investigate and solve a problem while providing excellent visibility through which to communicate the status of a project.

Some small companies may feel that PDCA does not fit their organization, or that it is too complicated and that the form is too busy to really be used effectively. They eventually find that the A3 report compiles lots of information into a small space and has an intuitive flow; a story about the project can be told in five or ten minutes. When discussing kaizen events, we talk about the need for a newspaper or action item follow-up plan. This plan is included on an A3 report, showing even the steps remaining after the kaizen team has officially finished its tasks.

I should state here that the use of an A3 report is not required with a kaizen event but it is an excellent tool with which to report the progress of the kaizen team. The A3 is not really a report but rather a storyboard that easily and concisely shows the progress and results of a project. What does A3 mean? A3 is the largest piece of paper (11 × 17 inches) that could fit in a fax machine when Toyota developed the form. People tend to use A3s to present problem-solving stories or a status story, although they are also used for project proposals and to convey information. Our focus in a kaizen event is to use them as a problem-solving story.

The A3 report follows a standard format (Figure 7.5) that is best printed out on A3 paper in landscape form to maximize the amount of information you can show and make it easy to read. You want to keep all A3 formats the same so all reports look the same, and the information presented is always in the same place making the reports easier to read for everyone, although the content and size of each section will vary as the project and reports progress.

The elements of PDCA do not overlay exactly with the original A3 format. I like the combination of the two when creating a storyboard for kaizen events. Larger companies are more apt to use this type of report than

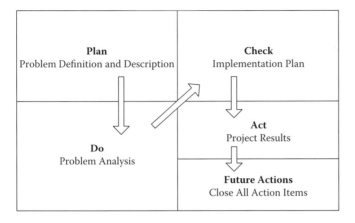

Figure 7.5   Plan–Do–Check–Act–Future Actions.

smaller companies, primarily because of the time it takes to create the form. I have also worked with companies that have incorporated the Six Sigma DMAIC (define, measure, analyze, control) process into an A3. This shows that the A3 is a tool that can be adjusted to meet the needs of every organization. If you find that you do not like the tool, go back to the original Lean reporting tools. When an A3 is created in daily steps while performing a kaizen event, they can expect to spend a half hour to an hour at the end of each day preparing this form. You may also find that you only need to do an A3 every other day during a five-day event. Again, flexibility is the key. When creating the A3 report, try to remember the following:

■ Avoid excessive wording.
■ Use arrows or lines to help show the flow of information within the blocks of information and on the page.
■ Use bullet statements whenever possible. Use three to four such statements in a section—no more.
■ Whenever possible, present data in graph form that is quickly and easily understood.
■ Be very careful with the scale on your graphs. Different graphs with similar data can be confusing.
■ Size your fonts and graphs accordingly so they can be easily read.
■ Do not try and cover too much information. Stick to three or four main points.
■ Stick to black and white; no color graphs or charts. Keep it simple.
■ Make the report visually balanced on the page. This will make it easier to read.

To complete an A3 report, take the following steps (Table 7.4):

1. *Heading section:* Complete this section and add any additional information you feel would be important, such as facility name, work area name, etc.

   Plan—Define the problem: Make sure your problem statement is specific in nature. Do not make the statement too broad because it will be difficult to tell exactly what you are trying to change. Example: "Reduce process variation in molding process on machine #14." This statement is too broad. A better statement would be, "Reduce process variations while molding part number 70-1958." Show the problem graphically if you can, using charts, graphs, pictures, etc. If possible, identify the impact on the business in dollars, late shipment, lost productivity, etc. and provide a compelling reason to resolve the problem. Add your SMART goals in this section.

   Do (problem analysis): Pictures are worth a thousand words; use charts, graphs, diagrams, etc. to show how you narrowed down the problem to the root cause. Do not list possible causes, just the root cause. *Check:* Show how you verified and how you found the root cause of the problem.

   Act: Provide short- and long-term corrective action plans and identify who is responsible for ensuring that the action plan is completed by the specified due dates. Show whether or not the actions have been completed.

   Results: Here you want to show the results of the changes you made. Using graphs or charts is an excellent way to compare the original state to the now-current state. Show how this change has impacted the business. Show how the change has been sustained. As mentioned earlier, use only four or five bullet items to show your results.

   Future steps: List any future steps needed to complete or sustain the changes. Be sure to identify the necessary resources needed to complete these steps (i.e., money, manpower, etc.). The last thing to note is "who is now responsible to ensure the change is maintained."

Identifying who is responsible for the changes after the team has completed its tasks is important because everyone has a tendency to revert back to their old ways of doing things unless they are held to a new standard. When anyone unfamiliar with the project looks at the A3 report, they

Table 7.4 A3 Report

[Project Title]	

Team:
Leader: 1
Co-Leader: 2
Team Members: 3
                       4
                       5
Facilitator   If used
	Improve (Do):
	Show your action plan to correct the problem. Be sure to include the person responsible for each action to be taken and the completion date.

Define Problem (Plan):
Problem Statement:
 	
S.M.A.R.T. Targets:
  1.
  2.
  3.
  4.
  5.
  6.	

Measure: Summarize and list the data you have gathered to be used in the next phase, which is analysis.	**Control (Check):** Summarize the results of the improvement project or problem correction.
Analyze: Show a summary of the analysis of the data and what the root cause of the problem is.	**Future Steps (Act):** If you find additional steps needed to improve the project or further correct the problem, list them here. Be sure to include the person responsible for each action to be taken and the completion date.

should be able to create their own story of the problem that matches the team's story.

Upon completion of the A3 report, hold reviews with the team and interested managers, and solicit feedback, paying close attention to any questions regarding clarification of information that the reviewers may have. These comments are not meant to criticize but are an attempt by the reviewer to fill in voids in your presentation; thereby better understanding what you are trying to say. View this as an excellent learning experience and a way to improve your next A3.

Some people have tried to condense this report into an 8½ × 11-inch sheet of paper or even into a PowerPoint slide. Whenever I have done this, some information has been physically distorted or even lost. Although 11 × 17-inch paper is an inconvenient size for us here in the United States, I would suggest you try and stay with this format. Your biggest outcome of the A3 report is in the process of creating consensus within your team and thus a satisfactory outcome to the plan. By the time the final report is shared with your upper levels of management, everyone should have seen the report and nothing should be a surprise to anyone. It is not uncommon for some companies using this format to come to a final decision in less than ten minutes. When used in a kaizen event, there is no need for a final decision to be made from the report on the last report-out meeting as management has already had a chance during the previous days to give input to the team.

Some companies have found that teaching their managers how to create an A3 report can be problematic if the managers do not already have good problem-solving skills and tools. You may find it effective to have someone come and teach good problem-solving methods and then use the A3. Any company with good problem-solving skills will go a long way toward improving product quality and improving processes. The appeal of an A3 being a simple, one-page report can create problems, especially when people try to outdo each other and generate fancy graphics to cram more and more information onto the page. The key point of an A3 is a clean, simple, no-nonsense tool with which to gain consensus, solve problems, and get results. Most of all, it is a communication tool.

If you find the A3 method cumbersome or complex, or if you would like to keep things even simpler, use the kaizen event forms shown in Figure 7.6. These are designed to be simple and easy to use.

Kaizen Toolbox

To make your kaizen events more efficient, a toolbox filled with all the needed supplies (Figure 7.7) is an excellent idea. I have created a proven toolbox supply list, as shown in Table 7.5.

Kaizen Event Form

Team Name: _____

Project Leader: _____

Directions:
1) Fill each row with implemented Kaizen improvement items that your team completed during the Kaizen event.
2) At the end of the Kaizen event add items to the list that must be completed (maximum 30 working day time allowance)
3) After the Kaizen event is over fill in the audit dates for the next 30 working days
4) Perform cell audits every week for 30 working days
5) Project leader will give a status report at every lean team leaders meeting until all task numbers are complete.

Follow-up Audit Schedule

6) Audit dates should be every week separated by approximately 5 working days
7) Indicate if items are complete and being sustained by scoring a 1 or 0
8) Score a 1 for every week they are sustained a 0 on the weeks they are not

Task #	Problem to be addressed	Kaizen (improvement) Action	Responsible Person	Expected audit date / Actual Date / Due Date	End of Kaizen event	1 week Yes=1 No=0	2 weeks Yes=1 No=0	3 weeks Yes=1 No=0	4 weeks Yes=1 No=0	5 weeks Yes=1 No=0	6 weeks Yes=1 No=0
					8/3/2010	8/10/2010	8/17/2010	8/24/2010	8/31/2010	9/7/2010	9/14/2010
					8/3/2010	8/10/2010	8/17/2010	8/20/2010	8/30/2010	9/6/2010	9/12/2010
1	Need a method to signal where parts are located for CC	Put signs on shelves	Dennis/Kurt	8/3/2010	6	1	1	1	1	1	1
2	Need a method to signal that parts are in downstairs Market	Color and write location on bins	Dennis/Kurt	8/3/2010	6	1	1	1	0	1	1
3	How to indicate red bin	Devise notification system	Dennis/Kurt	8/3/2010	6	1	1	1	1	1	1
4	Need two carts for bulky items	Create second cart	Artie	8/17/2010	6	0	0	1	1	1	1
5	Phantom assemblies are in area	Determine cut in date of carts	Dave	8/17/2010	6	0	1	1	0	1	1
6	How do we prioritize carts	Create FIFO area for carts. Mfg will have to help prioritize if there's an	Dennis/Kurt	8/20/2010	6	0	0	0	1	1	1
7	Old inventory in area	Transfer back to market	All	8/20/2010	6	0	0	1	1	1	1
8	Top covers not on BOM	Write ECO to move covers to Chassis line	Tony	9/6/2010	6	0	0	0	1	1	1
					48						

Total value of events to be complete (Number of events x number of weeks in audit) | 8 | 48 | 3 | 4 | 6 | 6 | 8 | 8

Total events to complete | 8 | 48

Total events complete (input total manually) | 8 | 48   Maximum sustainment score achievable

Percent achieved | 100% | 35   Achieved sustainment score

73%

Note:
1) Add new rows in middle of spreadsheet so totals will not be affected
2) Totals will calculate automatically

Figure 7.6 A3 report format.

Figure 7.7   Kaizen toolbox.

Table 7.5   Toolbox Inventory List

	Qty		Qty
Calculator	1	Ruler	1
Packet of dry erase markers	1	Stopwatch	1
Red permanent marker	1	Staple puller	1
Green permanent marker	1	Standard desk tape—roll	1
Black permanent marker	1	Masking tape—roll	1
Eraser—whiteboard	1	Package of black pens	1
Scissors	1	Push-pins—box 2	
Post-It notes:		Stapler	1
Large	4	Memory jogger	1
Medium	4	Lean enterprise jogger	1
Small	4	Bag of checkers	1

Now the obvious question! Why a bag of checkers in the toolbox (see Table 7.5)? Before physically making changes on the production floor, you may find it helpful to lay out a production line on the table using sticky notes. Next, use the checkers to indicate kanban locations and quantities. This allows you to run a manual simulation of the production line in the conference room. No fancy software packages needed here.

Guidance: Kaizen Events

When selecting your kaizen team, attempt to pick a team of people who are open minded. I like to have one person on the team who has nothing to do with the process because that person will ask questions no one else would even think of. That person's questions will be open and unbiased. Also, all team members have to understand that no one person controls this process; there are to be no hidden agendas to move the decisions of the team one way or another. YOU MUST LET THE DATA DRIVE YOUR DECISION, nothing else. No preconceived ideas. If you as a team leader believe someone is trying to move the team in one direction, for their own reasons, without looking at the data that person should be spoken to or removed from the team. THIS IS A TEAM PROJECT WITH DECISIONS MADE BY THE TEAM FROM THE DATA PROVIDED.

Chapter 8

Continuous Flow

Introduction

Now we need to create continuous flow on the production floor. Many people believe they already have continuous flow but is it continuous without stopping or is there stored inventory between processes? We will create flow based on Lean principles in this chapter.

Many companies have what is known as *process village layouts*; a different way to say this is similar machines and processes are grouped together, such as all machining centers together, all lathes together, all sheet metal brakes together, etc. This method of factory layout is very common. In this type of layout, the product does not really "continuously flow"; it starts and stops as it moves through the different processes, being held up many times, as we found out in our value stream map. As a result, it is difficult to respond quickly to ever-changing customer demands even if you maintain large amounts of WIP (work-in-process) inventory.

Step 1: Determine Family Mix

Determine what your product family mix is. This you do by creating a matrix of products and processes; Figure 8.1 shows you how to construct the matrix. I like to add a column for percentage of company sales. This allows you to decide which area you would like to focus on first. By looking at the matrix, you also get an idea of where you may want to place the pacemaker

		Process Steps								% of Annual sales
		Machining	Forming	Welding	Deburr	Sub-assembly	Paint	Final assembly	Test	
Products	Medical	X	X		X	X		X	X	35%
	Aerospace	X	X		X	X			X	20%
	Automotive	X	X	X	X	X	X	X	X	15%
	Heavy Equipment	X	X	X		X	X	X	X	10%
	Boats		X	X		X	X	X		10%
	Toys		X	X	X	X	X			10%

Figure 8.1   Product Family Matrix.

cell for those products. In this case, some products could have a pacemaker at test, while others have it at subassembly.

Before you begin to rebuild your product line for continuous flow, make sure you have enough capacity to sustain production for your other customers.

Step 2: Build First Production Cell

Start by building your first production work cell. You want to keep the cell simple; this will support another principle of Lean manufacturing, which is to minimize capital expenditure. Pick an area of the product that will

■ Be relatively easy to do
■ Show success early on
■ Be one in which the employees embrace change
■ Be one where with success work cell employees will champion more change

Step 3: Create Goals and Results Chart

Before you begin rearranging the production area, create an objectives sheet for the area you have selected. This will allow you to quantify your improvements. Be sure to take before-and-after pictures because this is a wonderful way to look back on your accomplishments.

As you can see in Figure 8.2, we have five columns that contain specific information showing our goals for the work cell or process improvement

Process Name ____________________

Team Members ____________________

Date ____________________

	Current State	Targeted Improvement: Future State	Targeted Improvement: Percentage Change	Actual Improvement: Future State	Actual Improvement: Percentage Change
Does process have continuous flow?	No	Yes	100%	No	0%
Floor space reduction (sq ft)	1,626	1,275	22%	1,128	31%
Lead time reduction (work days)	15	9	40%	13	13%
Production per shift (actual/target)	256 / 175	325 / 325	21% / 46%	300 / 325	15% / 46%
Productivity (pieces/employee/hr)	6.8	14.4	53%	13.3	49%
Number of employees	5	3	40%	3	40%
Does process have continuous flow?	No	Yes	100%	No	0%
Is process stable or unstable?	Unstable	Stable	100%	Unstable	0%
Is work cell the pacemaker? Is work cell effective?	No / Yes	Yes / Yes	100% / 0%	No / Yes	0% / 100%
Streamlined/simplified process (eliminate unnecessary process steps)	75	50	33%	60	20%
Reduce number of physical employee steps taken to do process	150	25	83%	30	80%
Inventory reduction (Raw material, WIP, Finished goods)	$10,000	$5,000	50%	$4,800	52%
Number of errors/employee/day	3	0	100%	1	67%

Figure 8.2 Goals and results chart. Shaded columns calculate automatically.

and the actual results. This goals and results chart should be posted on the work cell or department's glass wall. This way, everyone can see how much the work cell or department has accomplished in eliminating waste.

Stabilizing Your Process

Everyone wants to move quickly in creating new Lean processes but one of the first things you need to do is stabilize your current process. If you have not done any work in this area, you most likely will find plenty of work to do because most processes at any manufacturer are somewhat unstable. Instability is in every process—from its inception through to its current state—even processes that are in Lean factories can be somewhat unstable, which is one of the reasons for continuous improvement programs.

What is stability in a process? We achieve stability in a process when we can consistently and repeatedly deliver the same amount of product at the same quality level when requested. We certainly do not expect to achieve an instantly stable process because stability comes in steps as we improve the process. The first step would be to deliver product that meets customer requirements at least 85% of the time or greater. This means you have to know your customers' requirements and having them well documented is critical. As you stabilize your process, the percentage of on-time delivery and quality of the parts increases to 100%.

"But I do have consistent processes. I am already delivering on time to my customers." I hear this often but when one begins to discuss how to tell if a process is stable, much of the time the customer's process is not stable. How can you tell if a process is stable? Ask the following questions:

- Is there a high degree of variability, either in pieces per hour or pieces per labor-hour?
- Is there a visibly consistent pattern of work at the workstation?
- Do WIP (work-in-process) quantities vary significantly from batch to batch?
- Are there random piles of WIP on the production floor?
- When describing or discussing an operation, do you hear words like "usually," "normally," "most of the time, " followed by "except when"?
- Has an abnormal process become the norm?
- Ever hear, "We trust the operator to decide on the process"?

These are all warning signs that you do not have a stable or even a standardized process on which to build your Lean process. To build a process of continuous flow on the production floor, you must have stable processes.

As you use the processes on the production floor over and over again and teach other employees how to use the processes, over time every person will add their own steps to the process, steps that they believe makes the process easier for them. But, over time, we begin to think of these modified processes as the normal way of doing things. All of the variation that each individual added to the process in good faith has now created a process that is unstable because each person now does the process differently. Consistency is what is needed in a process; and with consistency of a process procedure you can identify what is not needed.

Standing in the Circle

Here is something I never heard of and thought was a little ridiculous to begin with. My trainer described an exercise his Japanese trainer at Toyota had him do. I thought it was a joke until I heard another well-known Lean expert, Jeffrey Liker, talk about it. It is called the circle exercise and is used to train you to see more than you think you do. If you take this process seriously, the amount of information you can gather about your production floor, office, or warehouse is unbelievable.

The exercise works like this. You stand in a make-believe circle and observe a process, manufacturing area, or even the entire production floor if it is small. This is not a sprint; it is a marathon. Stand in the circle for three to four hours and then continue to stand, up to eight hours. You will find that for the first three to four hours you tend to see the same thing over and over and become bored; but for the next three to four hours your mind begins to identify small differences in the processes and before long you have a list of things to change. When you are in the circle, take notes to identify what things need to be changed. My trainer told me that the first time he did this, he did not see very much. When his teacher asked what he had learned, he said, "I don't see any problems." His teacher said, "No problem is big problem" and sent him back to the circle. The second time he came back with pages of things to change, he gave them to his teacher, and said, "Here are the things that need to be changed," and his teacher immediately gave them back to him and told him, "Go fix these problems." Jeffery Liker, in his book *The Toyota Way Fieldbook*, compares the circle exercise to a marathon and how runners say they "hit the wall" around mile 20 of a 26.5-mile race and from hitting the wall they mean they transcend to another level. Standing in the circle is said to be similar in nature: When you have stood there long enough, you begin to notice things that need to be changed because you have transcended to another level of awareness. Now I thought this was ridiculous until I tried it, and I will tell you that I am a skeptic by nature. Well, it works! I have now used this method many times in different companies to get an awareness of how the production area is run and what some of the problems are. Fortunately, some days you do not have to wait four hours. The more I practiced this, the better I became at seeing problems. I do not want to say that this was a revelation to me because I have spent my entire adult life working in manufacturing, but I am amazed at how quickly I was able to see problems. At one company I worked for, the production people would see me standing on the floor or sitting on my stool observing the production floor and they would come up to me and ask what I was watching. I would tell them and they would actually tell me, "Watch this step closely" or "Have you already noticed...?" I am now a firm believer in the circle exercise.

Standardized Work

Before beginning a discussion of standardized work, there are two things we need to clarify. First, many companies have become ISO certified and as such have procedures that have been created for different activities in production, the office, and other areas of the company, and one of the questions I often hear is, "Is standardized work a controlled document per ISO requirements?" I am not an expert on ISO but have participated in many ISO audits over the years in companies using Lean tools and not using Lean tools. My experience has been that when you explain to an auditor what the standardized work document is and how it is used, they typically do not have any issues with it. *Remember that standardized work is a tool used to analyze a process for waste. It is not a work instruction, which is an ISO-controlled document, used to direct the operators and assemblers in how to produce a product and is also used as a training tool.* I have also found that if your company is a "regulated company," which typically applies to FDA

(Federal Drug Administration) or DoD (Department of Defense) regulations, the auditors like Lean tools because they enhance and complement the regulations already in place.

Lean tools relate to all areas of ISO 9001 but the best example is the kaizen event, which directly links to the ISO requirement for continuous improvement. My experience has been that when you apply Lean manufacturing tools, ISO auditors have been very happy with the results.

Using Standardized Work

Standardized work is a very powerful tool when it comes to analyzing the waste in a process. Step-by-step work instructions provide a road map from which you can determine the overall waste in a process. Because the first thing you look for are large amounts of waste rather than the fine waste found deep in a process, you start by analyzing three basic steps:

1. Identify the basic work steps (not elements – elements are finer detail).
2. Record the time for each step (record work time and wasted time).
3. Make a sketch of the work area, showing the operator work flow.

Any time you start an analysis of a process, look at the biggest wastes first; they are typically "excess motion" and "waiting time." Always work from the highest level of waste down to the smallest so that your sequence of analysis would be

1. Walking out of the area: count the steps.
2. Walking within the area: look at the walking pattern, count the steps.
3. Operator is stationary (sitting or standing in one position): watch hand motions.

Use a stopwatch to record the time that each step or hand movement takes. Once you have your times, enter them into a simple chart like the one shown in Table 8.1.

From Table 8.1 you can see that there are eighty (80) seconds of walking time, which is 31% of the total time for the process. The first thing to look at is to reduce waste from walking. Next, look at the breakdown of walking time. You can see that 50% of the time is going to the warehouse to get parts, while the other 50% of the time is walking to and from the

Table 8.1 Standard Work Breakdown

Step	Description	Process Time	Walk Time
1	Get parts from warehouse	5	40
2	Place 6 parts in assembly fixture	12	0
3	Glue parts	18	0
4	Take parts to oven	0	20
5	Bake parts 2 minutes	120	0
6	Get parts from oven	10	0
7	Take parts back to bench	0	20
8	Unload fixture	12	0
9	(Start process over)		
	Total Time (seconds)	177	80

oven. What can you do to reduce the amount of time it takes to get parts from the warehouse? Can you have a material handler deliver the parts? Can you include getting the parts from the warehouse when you take parts to the oven? Think of all the possible ways to reduce the walk time. There are many. Think about how you can make the process flow better by looking at the sketch you made of the area. How many times do the walking lines cross each other? Do you have to backtrack to do any of the other processes? Keep the process flowing in one direction.

Reducing Variability

To achieve stability, you need to reduce variation in your process. Variability comes in two forms—external and internal—and each is a serious problem when trying to stabilize processes for Lean manufacturing.

■ *Internal variability:* Is self-inflicted and this is the variability you have control of in your process. One of the most common forms of internal variability is found when applying human and machine resources. Planned and unplanned employee absences can account for as much as 10% to 20% of annual workdays. When a machine or work cell is unmanned, new work is not started and WIP is not completed. The rest of the staff is reassigned to other hot jobs and more jobs at other machines are not started; the resulting domino effect creates a backlog of pending hot jobs. Once this domino effect starts, it is very difficult to stop without working overtime, hiring temporary workers, or maintaining the extra staff needed to cover for the shortages when they occur.

■ *External variability:* Is primarily related to customers, but can also come from suppliers and the design of the product itself. Design variability comes in the form of different sizes and shapes of components as well as the overall complexity of the product. If you cannot correct these variables, and in all likelihood that would be difficult, the best you can hope for is to design the process to compensate for them. Product demand and model mix are two common customer variables that make balancing your internal human and machine resources even more difficult. The best that most companies can hope for is to minimize the variability. You most likely will not eliminate all the variation but you can isolate it by creating continuous flow and pull manufacturing while using standardization of the processes.

After eliminating as much internal and external variation as possible you will find your product lead time will have decreased.

Leaders' Standard Work versus Work Instructions

We hear the terms "standard work" and "work instructions" used all the time when talking about Lean, and many times they are confused and used incorrectly. It is important that you know and remember the difference. As mentioned before,

> *Remember that standardized work is a tool used to analyze a process for waste and as an audit tool for management. It is not a standardized work instruction, which is used to direct the operators and assemblers in how to produce a product and is also used as a training tool.*

We have stated this again because we feel that so many people are confused by the terms. The difference between the two is explained next.

Team Leader's Standard Work

This is a list of daily, weekly, monthly, or even quarterly activities that need to be done on a regular basis. Shown in Figures 8.3 and 8.4 are two examples for team leaders who are the first level of supervision on the production floor. Do not confuse this with the production supervisor who is one step up from the team leader. Team leaders typically have four to six people or work cells that they oversee. This position is best described as a working foreman for some companies. The activities of these people are fairly detailed, yet not as detailed as an actual work instruction that the people they lead use. In the example in Figures 8.3 and 8.4, you can see the team leaders have hourly, daily, and weekly tasks, while the people using the standardized work instructions need only focus on the work they are doing and the instructions they read on the work instructions to assemble and produce individual components and assemblies. This particular example comes from a booklet with the hourly work on the left page and the daily and weekly page on the right. The back of each page is left blank for notes and comments. The size of this booklet was designed to fit in the pocket of a shop coat.

Team Leader Standard Work							The roll of the team leader is to manage and insure that all safety, quality, productivity, government and ISO regulations are maintained as required by the company. The leader is also responsible for responding quickly to a sudden and unexpected changes or deviations including but not limited to standard work, flow of material, personnel issues, etc. The leader is a strong advocate for continued improvement and uses the lean tools to be an effective manager of people, process and flow.
Week Of :							
7/10/2010							
							Hourly
M	T	W	TH	F	SA	6:00–7:00	Review e-mail.
M	T	W	TH	F	SA	7:00–8:00	Meet with team members, assign job duties and discuss related issues. Send absence report to supervisor.
M	T	W	TH	F	SA	8:00–9:00	Set line flow rate to takt rate. Create and post daily production demand sheet. Record hourly production.
M	T	W	TH	F	SA	9:00–10:00	Record hourly production. Meet with supervisor to review staffing, parts and technical issues.
M	T	W	TH	F	SA	10:00–11:00	Record hourly production. If needed adjust hourly production demand.
M	T	W	TH	F	SA	11:00–12:00	Record hourly production. If needed adjust hourly production demand.
M	T	W	TH	F	SA	12:00–1:00	Lunch
M	T	W	TH	F	SA	1:00–2:00	Record hourly production. If needed adjust hourly production demand.
M	T	W	TH	F	SA	2:00–3:00	Record hourly production. If needed adjust hourly production demand.
M	T	W	TH	F	SA	3:00–4:00	Record hourly production. Meet with team to discuss daily issues, 5S area.

Figure 8.3 Team leader hourly.

Team Leader Standard Work								
Week Of :								
7/10/2010								

							Daily	Weekly
M	T	W	TH	F	SA	6:00–7:00	Process production scrap	
M	T	W	TH	F	SA	7:00–8:00	Notify supervisor of issues that could affect meeting daily demand	
M	T	W	TH	F	SA	8:00–9:00		
M	T	W	TH	F	SA	9:00–10:00		Conduct lean audit of work cells using audit cards
M	T	W	TH	F	SA	10:00–11:00		
M	T	W	TH	F	SA	11:00–12:00	Review and process scrap and discrepant material reports	
M	T	W	TH	F	SA	12:00–1:00	Discuss shift throughput and related issues. Plan overtime if needed	
M	T	W	TH	F	SA	1:00–2:00		Review staff training records Create weekly training plan
M	T	W	TH	F	SA	2:00–3:00		Team members 5S entire production line
M	T	W	TH	F	SA	3:00–4:00		

Figure 8.4 Team leader daily and weekly.

Manager's Standard Work

As you move up the company organizational chart, the hourly, daily, weekly, etc. work activities are less structured due to the nature of each individual's work. Because of this, we have created a different form for manager's standard work, as shown in Figure 8.5. Again, this is an example and you can structure your form any way you like, but we like this format and I actually use it myself. This form includes daily, weekly, and monthly activities. Because of work and the manager's unexpected meetings and demands on their time, they can only schedule their day based on the whole day, as opposed to an hourly schedule. If you are at the vice president or president level, you may only be able to schedule on a weekly or monthly basis.

We have incorporated a number of items into this form (Figure 8.5). It is designed to be a trifold form so it will fit easily into a pocket or day planner. At the top of the form there are six small blocks for the days of the week. This is your attendance record; you draw a line through each day that you are present. For each day that you complete the tasks you have listed,

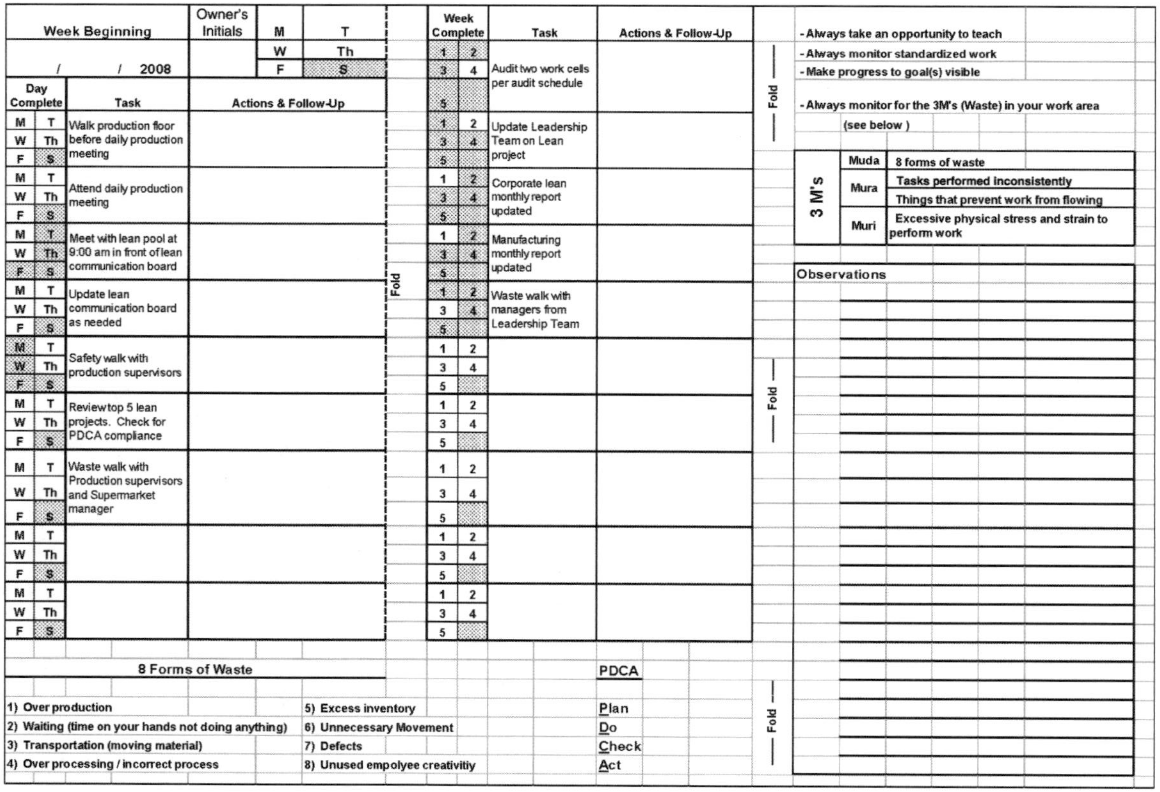

Week Beginning	Owner's Initials	M	T	Th
___/___/2008		W	F	S

Day Complete (M W F / T Th S) | **Task** | **Week Complete** (1 2 3 4 5) | **Actions & Follow-Up**

Day Complete	Task	Week Complete	Actions & Follow-Up
M T / W Th / F S	Walk production floor before daily production meeting	1 2 / 3 4 / 5	
M T / W Th / F S	Attend daily production meeting	1 2 / 3 4 / 5	
M T / W Th / F S	Meet with lean pool at 9:00 am in front of lean communication board	1 2 / 3 4 / 5	
M T / W Th / F S	Update lean communication board as needed	1 2 / 3 4 / 5	
M T / W Th / F S	Safety walk with production supervisors	1 2 / 3 4 / 5	
M T / W Th / F S	Review top 5 lean projects. Check for PDCA compliance	1 2 / 3 4 / 5	
M T / W Th / F S	Waste walk with Production supervisors and Supermarket manager	1 2 / 3 4 / 5	
M T / W Th / F S		1 2 / 3 4 / 5	
M T / W Th / F S		1 2 / 3 4 / 5	
M T / W Th / F S		1 2 / 3 4 / 5	

Week Complete / Task / Actions & Follow-Up (right section)

Week Complete	Task	Actions & Follow-Up
1 2 / 3 4 / 5	Audit two work cells per audit schedule	
1 2 / 3 4 / 5	Update Leadership Team on Lean project	
1 2 / 3 4 / 5	Corporate lean monthly report updated	
1 2 / 3 4 / 5	Manufacturing monthly report updated	
1 2 / 3 4 / 5	Waste walk with managers from Leadership Team	

Guidance:
- Always take an opportunity to teach
- Always monitor standardized work
- Make progress to goal(s) visible
- Always monitor for the 3M's (Waste) in your work area (see below)

3 M's

Muda	8 forms of waste
Mura	Tasks performed inconsistently / Things that prevent work from flowing
Muri	Excessive physical stress and strain to perform work

Observations

8 Forms of Waste

1) Over production	5) Excess inventory
2) Waiting (time on your hands not doing anything)	6) Unnecessary Movement
3) Transportation (moving material)	7) Defects
4) Over processing / incorrect process	8) Unused employee creativity

PDCA
Plan
Do
Check
Act

Figure 8.5 Manager's standard work.

you draw a line through the day. (I personally like diagonal lines.) Days the activities do not take place are shaded. You have a column for actions and follow-up notes, plus a section for observations you may want to make note of. The entire back of the page is blank for additional notes. The middle section of the form is for weekly and monthly activities; just note the unshaded weeks, which will tell you how frequently the activity takes place.

We also added a few notes to help the manager remember key Lean terms. Why do this? This was done because any time you work with people, whether in the office or on the production floor, you should always take the opportunity to teach Lean principles. Included in Figure 8.5 are the three Ms of Lean so that we do not forget where to look for waste:

1. Muda: eight forms of waste.
2. Mura: tasks performed inconsistently; things that prevent work from flowing.
3. Mudi: excess physical strain to perform work.

As a manager, you should always be monitoring standard work found in production and the office to ensure that tasks are being performed as prescribed. As you walk through the factory or office, wherever there are productivity measures and goals to be met, you should be monitoring these charts so you know how your company is performing to its planned goals.

Accountability

We use work instructions to hold the operators accountable for assembling the products together properly but now with the use of team leader and manager standard work, we can hold additional staff accountable for doing their work. We all know that each level of staff in the company organization chart is accountable to the next level up. We have always held hourly people responsible but now we have a tool with the standardized work for managers to hold them accountable for their daily work. When done correctly, the process is as follows:

■ The supervisor signs off on team leader's standard work booklet daily.
■ The production manager using their version of standard work approves the supervisor's daily work.
■ The production manager's work is approved by the plant manager daily.

You can see how the system continues up the ladder. There is no need to track down your supervisor to approve your work each day. Have an agreed-upon location to place your standard work every day. Then your supervisor can visit this location and approve it on a daily basis.

Daily Production Meetings

One question I always ask management of the company or factory I am visiting is, "How much time do you spend on the production floor?" If I am performing an audit, I will then ask the production workers how often they see their management staff on the production floor. Many times, the answers are not the same. My question to plant management is, "If you are responsible for the performance of the factory, why are you not on the production floor every day to monitor performance?" I frequently hear, "We have meetings to attend," "That's what my staff is for," or "I'm just too busy" as just a few reasons for not spending time on the production floor.

As the person responsible for the operation of the factory, whether the small business owner or plant manager for a larger company, you should spend at least one hour per day on the production floor. To some this may sound impossible, but you as a leader must be visible in the factory to know what is happening and to take every opportunity to teach Lean concepts. One way to achieve this hour of time is a daily production meeting with your staff on the production floor. This meeting not only gives you time and visibility on the production floor but, more importantly, it provides a daily update on what is happening in production. With daily updates you can quickly respond to issues that need immediate attention to ensure you achieve your daily production and quality goals.

A typical daily meeting represents the following departments: production planning, raw material warehousing, manufacturing engineering, supplier quality engineering, final product testing, production, and purchasing. You may not have all of these areas as separately managed areas, and that is fine.

I like to keep this meeting to five people, typically managers of each area who can update on yesterday's results and address today's issues. These should be manager-level people with the authority to commit resources when a problem arises. The team is kept to five people as this will minimize distractions, side conversations, and extended debate over a particular issue.

Set up glass walls in each department and move through the production floor to visit each glass wall. This is the plant manager or company owner's time to ask questions; follow up on issues and see how their production operations are working. This is "your daily update," so make this a productive time for you and your staff.

Guidance: Daily Production Meetings

 This meeting is a critical part of the daily communication system. The meeting owner is the plant manager, vice president of operations, or company owner. For most of you, this will be the only time you have your entire staff together on the production floor at one time. All of you are responsible for making the factory the most efficient operation possible.

Keeping the meeting focused and to the point with the meeting owner assigning action items will help keep the meeting short. *If team members want to argue about a topic, do not do it on the production floor; people will see your staff arguing and your whole team will lose credibility with the production staff on the floor.*

Schedule the meeting when everyone can be there; for a small company, this is not as big a challenge as it is for a larger one but once the time is set, it is cast in stone and should always happen at that time.

Attendance at the meeting is mandatory; and if someone cannot be there, you must have someone else on the team represent that person. You cannot delegate this responsibility to anyone other than a member of the team, otherwise the whole team will lose effectiveness.

WARNING: If you as the owner of the meeting begin to miss meetings, others will begin to do so and the meeting will be of little value. Worst of all, the people on the production floor will notice your absence, you will lose credibility with them, and they will lose a sense of urgency and commitment. I have seen it happen.

Chapter 9

Work Cell and Factory Layout

One area that is typically addressed during the implementation of Lean manufacturing is the factory layout or, if you are using Lean in the office, it would be the office layout. Because we are focused on production, we will stay with the production floor layout.

Work Cell Layout

Each work cell that is developed for the production of your product should follow some basic rules

1. Safety is number one.
2. Follow good ergonomic practices.
3. Design in mistake proofing.
4. Manual tasks should be close together (limit the steps an operator has to make).
5. Use automated equipment only when it makes good business and economic sense.
6. Automated tasks should be secure and safe.
7. Use auto-load and auto-eject when operator safety is in question.
8. Heavy or awkward parts to handle are good candidates for automation.
9. Use simple one-touch automation whenever possible with automation. The operator pushes a button and walks away.
10. Avoid batching whenever possible. Remember that one-piece flow is the goal.

11. Use visual signals and automated sensors to stop machines if a part fails.
12. Design machine changeovers to be accomplished within one takt time cycle.
13. Design in machine maintenance.

Note: Automation can be as simple as an overhead lifting device or scissor lift table to all-out automated assembly and test.

Ergonomic Design

When designing your work cell, it would be good to consider these recommended dimensions. They are not hard-and-fast rules but the dimensions have been scientifically developed through the study of human anatomy and have been used for years by industrial engineers to design workstations and work cells (Table 9.1).

Why a foot rest when you are standing? By placing your foot on a foot rest while standing, you relieve the pressure on your lower back and, as a result, you can work longer with less fatigue in the standing position. This was discovered many years ago when tavern owners were trying to find ways to keep customers in the tavern longer; the foot rest made the customers more comfortable at the bar and they stayed longer. It has also been noted in past

Table 9.1   Ergonomic Design Chart

	Male	*Female*
Based on average person's height, inches	69	63
Normal workbench height (floor to top of bench), inches	40	37
Normal work area (measured from center of shoulder to in front of person), inches	15½	14
Maximum work area (arc shape from center of shoulder left to right in front of person), inches	26½	23½
Seated chair height, inches	33	29
Foot rest sitting, inches	13	10
Foot rest standing, inches	6–9	6–9

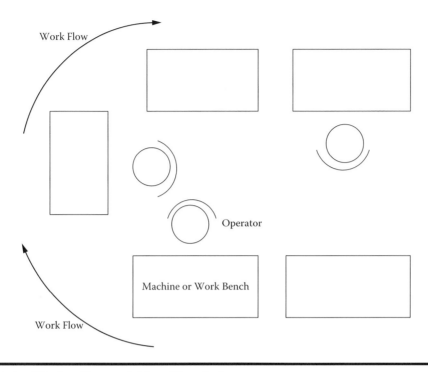

Figure 9.1 Work cell material handling design.

studies that a person can work faster in a standing position unless they are doing fine detail work similar to sewing or working under a microscope.

Work cells are typically designed as "U" shapes to facilitate shorter movements and improve communications between people in the cell (Figure 9.1). This makes it very easy for someone who notices a mistake to tell the person in the cell what happened and they can quickly correct the problem. Work flows in a work cell typically run right to left because most people are right-handed. This allows an individual to move his finished assembly to the next workstation with his right hand while reaching with his left hand to get the next assembly to work on.

Work Cell Material Handling Design

To ensure consistent flow of product to the production line, each work cell needs a consistent flow of raw material. To do this, you can utilize what are known as timed delivery routes, which bring raw material to the work cells on a regular schedule. Machine operators and assemblers do not need to chase parts because they are allowed and expected to stay in the work cell to produce product. Each work cell should try and maintain two hours of raw material inventory or less at any one time. However, this may vary, depending on your type of product. Parts should be placed close enough to the machine or workbench so the operator does not have to leave his work area to get parts. Also, when the material is delivered to the work cell, the delivery should never interrupt the operator or assembler from doing his job. Extra or surplus inventory should not be placed on the production floor or near operators because this promotes the operator leaving the work area to get parts. Use visual kanban signals to replenish parts when parts are needed. When a parts bin is emptied, use it as the kanban signal to refill the bin and work cell. Parts bins are sized to fit the work cell and operator, not for the convenience of the material handler, warehouse, or supplier.

One thing to remember is that machine operators and assemblers add value to the product while material handlers, inspectors, etc. are non-value-added to the product and you never want to interrupt the value-added people.

The material storage racks can be easily made from most materials. For raw materials that have some weight to them, a simple roller conveyor works great (Figure 9.2); for lightweight parts such as you might find in medical or electronic manufacturing, I have found that anything with a smooth, slick surface works well.

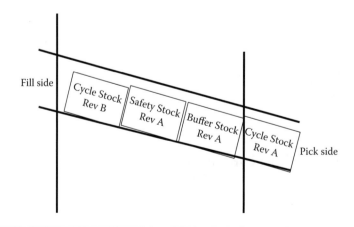

Figure 9.2   Raw material flow rack.

Chapter 10

Creating Your Lean Road Map (Strategy Deployment)

Introduction

You have spent a lot of time learning how to use the tools of Lean; now there is a need to discuss your overall plan for implementation of the tools into your company. Although future state value stream maps provide an excellent way of visualizing your new processes and also include a due date for completion, they do not provide some of the detailed project scheduling or strategic planning that needs to be done; therefore we recommend using this system for a three- to six-year plan. What is good about this system is that you assign, by department, tasks that need to be completed in the first, second, third, fourth, and fifth years. To begin the process, the manager of each department, working with the Lean coach (manager), completes the plan for his or her department and then each department has its staff agree to the plan. Once this is done, the manager approves the plan by signing it. The plan can then be placed on the conference room and departments' glass walls for everyone to see. The plan is updated by the responsible manager on a monthly basis by changing the color of the task from blue to green, signifying that this phase of the project is complete and they are ready for the next phase.

Strategic Lean Manufacturing Plan

To begin constructing your strategic Lean manufacturing road map, you will need a copy of your company's strategic plan. If possible, reconstruct the strategic Lean plan in the same format as your company's Lean plan. This will allow you to easily show how well the Lean plan supports your company's strategic plans. If you can show how the Lean plan supports the goals of the company, it is easier to get higher-level support for Lean.

When discussing Lean production and an implementation timeline, we typically talk about three to six years. This road map has been created as a three- to six-year plan and covers the four basic levels every company experiences when implementing Lean: beginning, improving, succeeding, and leading.

Below are the levels of implementation with examples of what is completed at each level:

- *Beginning:* Focus on initial training of Lean methods, principles, and tools. This training includes the entire staff of the facility. Establish 5S as a foundation for Lean. Create your first value stream maps; learn about and complete your first continuous improvement events. Create your first work cells; begin rearranging the production floor and warehouse. Start creating and populating the PFEP (plan for every part). Establish point-of-use inventory and create standard work for work cells and glass walls; begin focusing on stabilizing processes.
- *Improving:* Continue to expand involvement of people and retrain to reinforce all Lean learning to make it a habit. Implement daily visual management of all key business processes. Implement formal problem-solving procedures and formal total preventive maintenance systems. Provide evidence of growth to other departments of continuous improvement. Expand value stream mapping to other products and have department managers take over leading continuous improvement activities from the Lean coach.
- *Succeeding:* Autonomous cross-functional teams now improving all processes, incorporate finished goods into value stream maps, production floor team leaders take ownership of individual glass walls, significant stability has been achieved in all production processes, product lead times begin to see good results, quality levels have improved significantly, all continuous improvement (kaizen) events are now led by team leaders, problem-solving system is effective in all areas, and A3 reports are used for all problems and projects.

■ *Leading:* Your plant becomes known as the best in the company; people and processes are highly efficient and always use Lean tools. Continuous improvement is the norm rather than the exception and is driven by highly skilled work teams. Value stream maps and management extend beyond the factory and now extend to the customer and your suppliers.

Notice that between the first and third years, you focus on beginning and improving your journey; although you plan your implementation road map for a three- to six-year period, everyone knows that anything beyond one year is only a guess. With Lean implementation, you plan your steps carefully and by looking three to six years out, you know where you are going at all times. Figure 10.1 shows a completed map for a company- or division-level strategic plan for Lean manufacturing. Use the template provided to create individual plans for each department. Keep in mind that each of the individual plans need to feed into and support the next higher-level plan. When complete, there should be a continuous flow from high-level

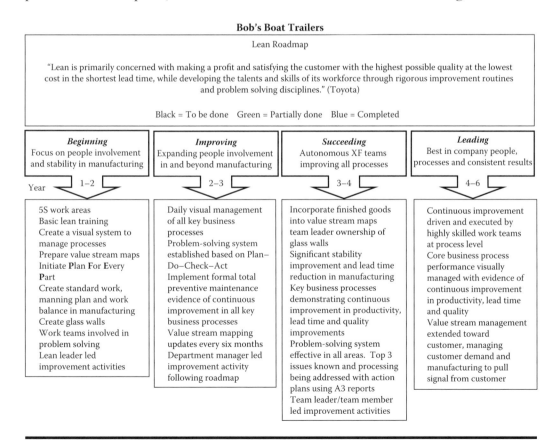

Figure 10.1   Lean roadmap: High-level strategy.

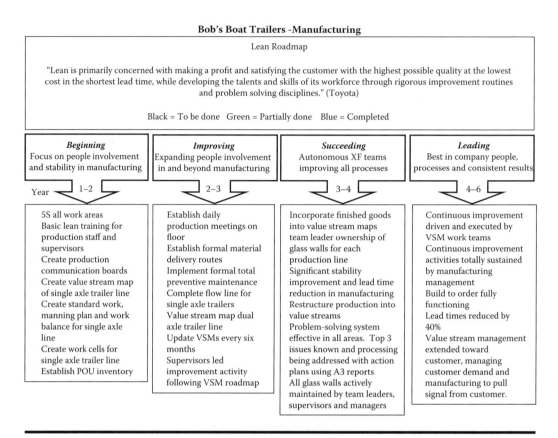

Figure 10.2   Lean road map: Actionable plan.

strategy in Figure 10.1 to an actionable plan in Figure 10.2. Please note that in Figures 10.1 and 10.2 we indicate the completion status of each task by changing its color as indicated in the top box in each figure; however, the version in book is shown only in black and white.

What is good about this planning method is that all the documents are living documents and once you have the system in place, you only need to update it periodically. I would recommend that your plan be reviewed with senior management on a quarterly basis so you have time to adjust the plan based on current business conditions. That said, you do not want to modify your plan very much because the more you modify it, the more apt you are to lose focus on the plan and this will result in losing excitement and drive around Lean, and it will fade into obscurity.

A glass wall (Figure 10.3) is designed to be a central location where you can find all the performance data for each department in one location. The term "glass wall" means that the performance of the business, department, and product line or work cell is transparent: visible and above-board. The

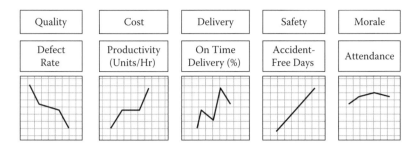

Figure 10.3 Manufacturing glass wall.

progress or lack of progress is there for everyone to see. In a small business that is privately owned, this may be an unfamiliar or even scary idea that you would share this information with lots of people. However, we have seen that the use of proper tracking tools that are displayed graphically and are very visible to everyone is an excellent method of managing changes in behavior. Sometimes this is called "managing by objectives." If we set a goal of 95% on-time delivery to customers and our graph shows that we dropped to 83%, we instantly want to correct the problem. If, however, this drop in customer service is not visible, we may not see the problem quickly enough to respond before we have upset the customers.

I have found that the deeper into an organization the more glass walls are used, the more likely you are to find and correct problems early. So many companies look at performance data on a monthly basis, which in reality is historical data. Who wants to wait for a month to find out that you have not met your goals? You need to find and correct problems quickly to ensure quality product, low cost, and on-time delivery of product to your customers.

On the glass wall you can place any information you might want to track. That said, remember the quality rule: "Measure what you must, not what you can"; so do not go overboard with lots of charts, graphs, and information. Use the most meaningful ones to ensure you can identify and respond to problems quickly and follow the performance of the area so you can adjust production as needed.

For each area such as marketing, sales, finance, engineering, or any other department you may have, you can create a glass wall. In larger companies I have seen glass walls for purchasing, human resources, warehouse, facilities, and many others. The thing to remember is that each of the glass walls allows management to easily see how each area is doing. When work cell glass walls are created, they can be placed on factory walls or free-standing stands next to each work cell.

Table 10.1 Locations of Glass Walls

	Information Required		Suggested Information
Work cell	Quality	Defects or rejects/product per hour	
	Cost	Production/man hour	
	Delivery	Product on time to takt time	
	Safety	Production hours lost to accidents	
	Morale	Attendance	
Production line	Quality	Defects or rejects/product per hour	Vacation plan
	Cost	Production/man hour	Operator training matrix
		Overtime per day	
			Material Inventory—raw and WIP
	Delivery	Product on time to takt time	Current projects
	Safety	Production hours lost to accidents	
	Morale	Attendance	
Factory	Quality	Defects or rejects/product per day	
	Cost	Production/day	
		Overtime/day	
		Inventory turns	
		Finished goods inventory	
	Delivery	Product on time to customer demand	
	Safety	Production hours lost to accidents	
	Morale	Attendance or morale survey	

As you step up to each level within the factory, work cell to production line, to factory, some of the charts change either completely or partially, as you can see in the example (Table 10.1). You can now see how the visual factory becomes even more visible and problems are easily exposed because you have lowered the water in the river and exposed all the dangerous rocks. Pick off each rock (problem), lower the water some more, and pick off another rock.

Visual Controls and Visual Management

Two of the tools of Lean manufacturing are the creation of visual controls and visual displays. These two items, when combined, create a visual management system that provides concise, clear, and timely information about how the factory is operating. As you walk through the factory or even the office, if proper visual controls and displays are used, you can quickly identify how the factory is running. The purpose of visual management is to provide a common and unbiased understanding of goals while aligning actions and decisions with company goals. They create a shared vision that becomes measurable and creates a common visual language that everyone can understand. Most importantly, they make problems visible and allow everyone to see if a condition is in a normal or abnormal state.

The most well-known visual management tool is the sports scoreboard. It tells us what the score is, who is ahead, what half is being played, and other pertinent information regarding the game. Just like that information, you need to know if a factory is running correctly or if you need to make adjustments to the product you are manufacturing.

Visual Management Displays and Controls

Visual displays are such things as

- Street number on a house (Figure 10.4)
- Takt time clock (Figure 10.5)
- Train station boarding gate (Figure 10.6)
- Production tracking chart (Figure 10.7)

Figure 10.4   Street number on a house.

Figure 10.5   Takt time clock.

Figure 10.6   Train station boarding gate.

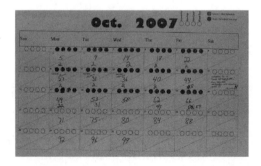

Figure 10.7   Production tracking chart.

Visual controls are such things as

- Gasoline filler tube that is only designed to fit unleaded gas pump nozzle (Figure 10.8)
- Railroad crossing gate (Figure 10.9)
- Stop sign (Figure 10.10)
- Production build schedule board (Figure 10.11)

These items are typically found on the work cell communication center (Figure 10.12).

Figure 10.8   Gasoline filler tube that is only designed to fit unleaded gas pump nozzle.

Figure 10.9   Railroad crossing gate.

Figure 10.10   Stop sign.

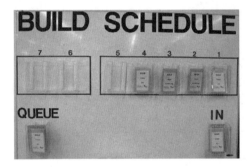

Figure 10.11   Production build schedule board.

Figure 10.12   Work cell communication center.

Andon Display

One of the very first uses by American manufacturers of Andon signals were the familiar stacked lights, usually red, green, and white. These were supposed to be used to signal if a production line or machine tool was in normal production mode, stopped, or needed raw material replenished. Although some companies have successfully used this type of Andon signal, most of the companies that have tried to use them have found that operators and assemblers become desensitized to the lights and do not pay attention to them.

But what is really needed is a way to automatically stop assembly or machine tools when they begin to produce defective product. Many machine tool manufacturers have now included such capabilities; however, the assembly line still lacks a good automatic way to stop should it begin to produce defective product. Should your assembly line have automated test points? These are excellent places to install automated line shut-down systems although the manual assembly line must still rely on humans to catch errors and stop the line when needed. All Toyota manufacturing personnel are trained to stop the line whenever they encounter a problem, which they cannot resolve quickly to keep their section of the assembly line on time and in synchronization with the rest of the line. At the NUMMI plant, a joint venture of Toyota and GM to build new cars, there was a training room that was used to train new and retrain current employees in how to work on the production line. It included when and how to stop the production line. All employees had the power to stop the line should a problem arise. The plant has closed since my last visit, but during my last visit the very large Andon clock in assembly was busy showing the status of the production line and whether or not the line was stopped or running. I was told that the line is stopped for many reasons during a twenty-four-hour shift, sometimes as many as 1000 times per day. Naturally, these delays are of very short time duration but it was living proof to me that Toyota truly does empower its employees and that this is an enormous advantage in helping improve quality. I have visited a number of automotive factories during my career, and Toyota was the only place I have ever seen this done.

I am certain that Toyota has a way of capturing all this downtime and reporting it. I know from discussions with a former assembly plant manager who worked for Toyota that he had to report and justify all the lost production time in a day. He also had to identify what he was doing to resolve the issue.

How can a small company accomplish the same thing? Let us look at a relatively small plant I have worked with. The plant had approximately sixty production floor workers with two supervisors and four lead persons. This plant was set up to assemble two specific electromechanical devices: one was about the size of a typical mechanics floor standing toolbox while the other about the size of a Volkswagen "beetle." However, these products were extremely complex and highly technical. The problem this company had was that the production line kept shutting down and everyone's suspicion was that the availability of parts from the supplier was the problem. How do we use an Andon clock in this situation? It actually was very simple but took a little discipline at the beginning.

First, we installed a large digital clock in the office, one that the plant manager and planning department could see and hear. A second clock was positioned so that manufacturing and quality engineers could see and hear it. This clock had "on" and "reset" buttons. When the production line or a work cell of the line went down for any reason—material, engineering problem, staffing, etc.—the supervisor or lead person would come to the office and start the Andon clock (Figure 10.13). This would start both clocks simultaneously and a large chime would sound.

Next, they would fill out the downtime clock spreadsheet (see Figure 10.14). This would provide information as to which production area

Figure 10.13 Andon clock.

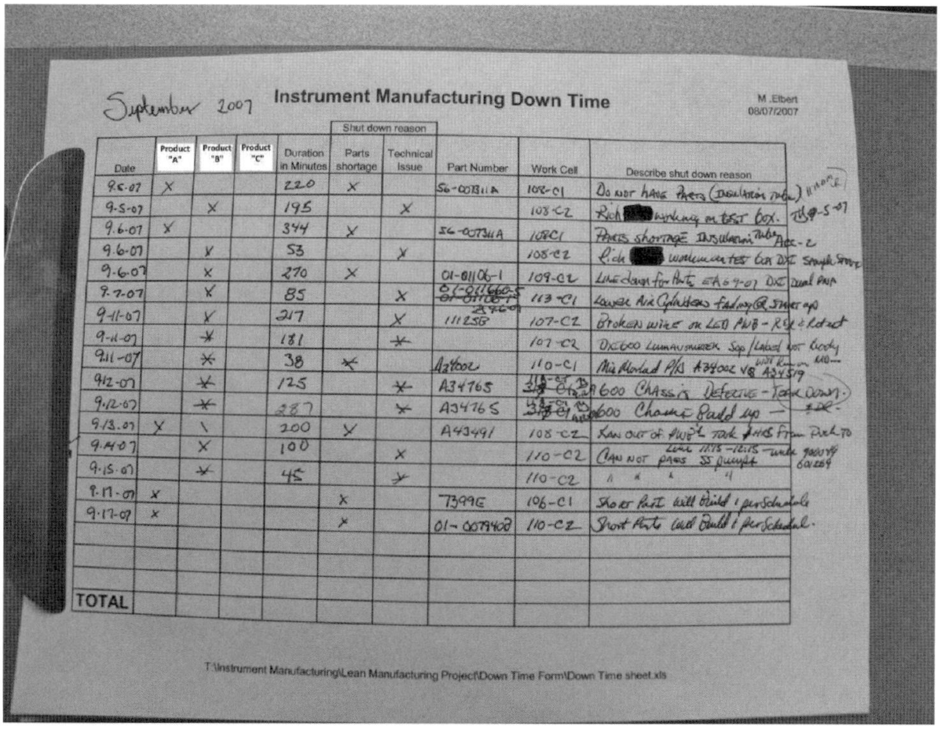

Figure 10.14   Manufacturing downtime chart.

was having a problem. The manufacturing and quality engineers along with a production planner would immediately check the downtime spreadsheet, see where and what the problem was, and then meet on the production line at the site of the problem to resolve the issue. When the production line or work cell was back in production, the supervisor or lead person would reset the clock and complete the spreadsheet showing how long the line was down. There are actually two clocks side by side, one for each product line.

Each day, the production supervisor would compile the downtime data and present the information to the plant manager. He would then have to report to the president of the company the results of the report and the actions to permanently resolve the issues. The company tracked the downtime for one year and found they had more than 2600 hours of lost production due to late delivery of parts and product quality issues. They were surprised to find that three component parts common to both products and used in multiple assemblies caused the largest number of quality problems. From all this data, they were able to create an action plan to solve many of their problems.

Chapter 11

Production Scheduling

Introduction

Production scheduling in a standard Material Requirements Planning (MRP) system is typically based on a weekly production schedule where work orders are cut for each part to be produced. These work orders are then sent to the first work center in the sequence to begin producing the parts. The weekly work-order demand was created by the MRP system based on the forecast that was entered into the MRP system. This forecast typically comes from the marketing department, which for the most part is composed of very optimistic people. Therefore, these forecasts are typically not very accurate. Also, customer demand can be fickle, and the need to constantly adjust the work-order quantity or delivery date makes the production schedule very difficult to achieve. Between inaccurate forecasts and constantly varying customer demand, how do you successfully manage the production floor?

Many years ago when I was in college and first learning about manufacturing, a professor made a statement that all customers and companies had to make a decision based on three criteria. They could have "Price, Quality, or Delivery. Take your pick; you can have two out of the three." Today we know that this is not true; using the lessons and methods learned from Toyota, we can have all three today.

Using Lean planning methods you can ensure that your customers receive the product at the best price with on-time delivery and at the quality they desire. It also allows you to schedule and run the factory in the most efficient manner possible.

MRP and Lean Complement Each Other

Lean planning means neither the elimination of MRP nor that MRP does not have a place in manufacturing. I believe that MRP is an excellent strategic-level planning tool where Lean is an excellent day-to-day operational tool. The two can complement each other nicely; where you can run into trouble is when you have a planning department that is only measured on meeting the "master schedule" from MRP.

For easy comparison, I like to think of MRP as the central planning function of a national government that dictates how much of a given product each factory in that country will produce and when. Although there have been examples of this in modern times with the Soviet Union, we also know that it is highly inefficient. Many times, you have too much of one product or component and not enough of another. How many times have you experienced this in your organization?

Again, MRP has its place. Use it as a high-level planning tool where you input your sales and marketing forecast and then run MRP to see how much of each part you will need for the next twelve months. This makes an excellent negotiation tool with your suppliers. Also, by using this twelve-month forecast, you can create a rough plan for your factory capacity. I call it a *rough* plan because customer demand is fickle, and our plans are only as good as our current knowledge of a situation.

As a small company, you may not use an MRP system; instead, you may use centralized planning. Look at your system and the way you process changes to customer demand, and how you schedule the production floor. Is all of your planning information processed at one central location? If it is, then you have a centralized planning system. To be more flexible and responsive to customer demand, you need to implement a more automatic self-directing scheduling method that can respond quickly to changes in customer demand and at the same time minimize inventory levels.

Before going any further, take a moment to create a box score chart (Table 11.1) for what you would like to achieve when production pull has been implemented. This does not have to be a lengthy list but one with meaningful goals. This box score is very similar to the ones you created when you did your first kaizen events.

You can add anything you like to the box scores; I have seen very short lists and also ones that are an entire page long. I personally would keep it somewhere in between these two lengths.

Table 11.1   Box Score Chart

	Current State	*Future State*	*Actual*
Productivity			
Direct labor (pieces/hour)	50	65	
Downtime			
Work cell 3—Okuma lathe	33%	10%	
On-time delivery			
To shipping	95%	100%	
Lead time			
Production (from order to floor to finished goods)	21 days	11 days	

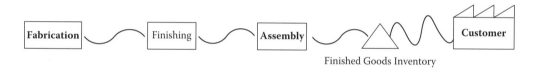

Figure 11.1   Customer demand variation.

What we are trying to do now is to remove customer demand variation from the factory. Customer demand varies from day to day or week to week; it sends ripples through the production floor. Figure 11.1 shows how customer demand varies.

What Finished Goods Inventory Should You Stock?

As a small business, you need to keep a certain amount of inventory for your customers; this is just expected in this day and age. However, you can only afford to keep so much due to cost and space constraints. How do you determine what finished goods to keep and in what quantity?

The typical method is to use an ABC approach to inventory where "A" is the most expensive and "C" is the cheapest cost; thus, you can carry more "C" parts than "A and B" parts. However, this will not work for Lean manufacturing because we need to maintain proper levels of inventory for our customers, no matter what the cost is. Let us use the standard Pareto method for determining inventory levels.

Before you start, I have included a finished goods spreadsheet (Table 11.2) on the CD to help you save time.

Follow these steps to create your own spreadsheet, or fill in the "non-shaded columns" on the included spreadsheet.

1. Make a spreadsheet with all your finished goods part numbers in one column.
2. In the next twelve columns, key in the monthly quantity the customer requested withdrawn from your inventory each month. If you know the daily withdrawal, use it and adjust the spreadsheet accordingly.
3. Total each row.
4. Input the average workdays per year.
5. Calculate the average pieces per day.
6. Input the lead time to replenish one part from start of the first process to final shipping to the customer.
7. Multiply average pieces per day (Step 5) by number of days of lead time in Step 6. This gives you what is known as "cycle stock."
8. Add a reasonable percentage for demand variation and safety stock. This is typically called buffer stock (10% for this example). This gives you your "total finished goods inventory" for each part.

The next steps are optional but I have included them on the spreadsheet because I believe it gives you a more accurate stocking level. All these steps are automatically calculated on the included spreadsheet.

9. Calculate the square root of the total finished goods inventory.
10. Multiply the square root of the total finished goods inventory by 3. This is what is known as the "standard deviation."
11. Now add the answer from Step 8 to the answer from Step 12 and you have your maximum inventory level, which is called the "upper control limit."
12. Subtract the answer in Step 12 from the answer in Step 10 and you have your minimum inventory level, which is called the "lower control limit."
13. Now sort the spreadsheet based on the total in "cycle stock."

You now have a Pareto chart showing you how much inventory to stock for each part you produce, but at some point it does not make economic sense to stock inventory. If the demand is low, you are better off to build whenever you get an actual order.

Note: I have added some additional columns to the spreadsheet in Table 11.2 to calculate the cost of carrying the maximum inventory for each

Table 11.2 Finished Goods PFEP Chart

Customer Part Number	Total	Avg. Workdays/Year	Avg. Pcs/Day	Lead time to Replenish 1 Part (in days)	Cycle Stock	Buffer & Safety Stock Combined (as % of Cycle Stock)	Buffer & Safety Stock Combined (Pcs)	Total Finished Goods Inventory	Std. Deviation	Std. Deviation × 3	UCL (Max. Inv. Level)	LCL (Min. Inv. Level)
8011990	4238	256	16.6	5	83	10.0%	8	104	10.2	30.7	135	74
8012023	5117	256	20.0	4	80	10.0%	8	104	10.2	30.6	135	73
8012034	4402	256	17.2	4	69	10.0%	7	90	9.5	28.5	119	62
8011968	1990	256	7.8	5	39	10.0%	4	52	7.2	21.6	73	30
8011946	1970	256	7.7	5	38	10.0%	4	51	7.2	21.5	73	30
8011957	2185	256	8.5	3	26	10.0%	3	37	6.1	18.3	56	19
8011979	899	256	3.5	5	18	10.0%	2	26	5.1	15.3	42	11
8012100	317	256	1.2	14	17	10.0%	2	33	5.7	17.1	50	16
8012012	477	256	1.9	7	13	10.0%	1	22	4.7	14.1	36	8
8012067	460	256	1.8	5	9	10.0%	1	16	4.0	12.0	28	4
8012056	986	256	3.9	2	8	10.0%	1	14	3.7	11.1	25	3
8012089	131	256	0.5	14	7	10.0%	1	22	4.7	14.0	36	8
8012078	120	256	0.5	14	7	10.0%	1	21	4.6	13.8	35	7
8012001	362	256	1.4	3	4	10.0%	0	9	3.0	8.9	18	0
8012045	362	256	1.4	3	4	10.0%	0	9	3.0	8.9	18	0

part. Also, I have added a column for inventory carrying costs, which you will have to input. I purposely showed in detail the work for calculating your inventory levels so you could see that the program I use is purely simple math—no tricks or black boxes. I did use some statistics to calculate the minimum and maximum levels of inventory but, again, I have included the steps to perform the work. The spreadsheet contains some extra columns because I feel that slightly more information may be helpful to you in making your decisions as to what to stock and what to build-to-order.

Until you have a highly developed Lean production system, you may want to keep additional finished goods inventory even for some low-volume customers just as a safety precaution.

As you build your Lean production system and the predictability of product delivery, machine uptime, and the reliability of each work cell becomes better established, you will begin to reduce the inventory levels that you maintain for your customers. But, you must do this very slowly to ensure that you do not create an out-of-stock situation.

Deciding what to stock versus what to build-to-order is different for each company. You must obviously consider all the various pros and cons for your situation. I suggest you create a decision matrix with the different options for building and holding inventory, that is, hold inventory for A and B parts build to order for C. Hold Cs partially built in WIP (work-in-process), etc.; you will have to determine which is best for your current situation and what is possible in the different phases of implementation ahead.

Types of Pull Systems

In Lean production there are several types of material pull systems that can be used. They are

- Replenishment pull
- Sequential pull
- Mixed pull

Each has its own place and time in which it works best.

Replenishment pull (Figure 11.2) works best when you hold finished goods for each customer and then use the customer withdrawal to trigger production to refill finished goods. The finished goods warehouse would

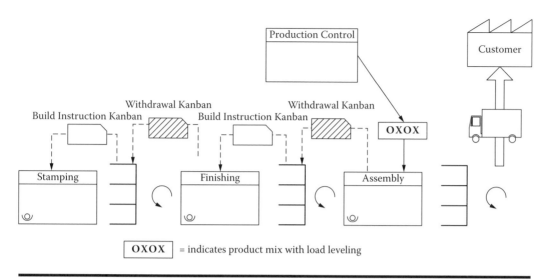

Figure 11.2   Replenishment pull system.

send a signal to the packaging department, which would then trigger
the packaging department to signal production to supply more parts for
packaging. *The whole system works backward from finished goods.* This
system will stock lots of WIP inventory and also have longer lead times
than the other two systems.

Sequential pull (Figure 11.3) is used when you are producing products
to customer orders. Product is built and based on demand from the
customer. The production control department sends build instructions
to the first process step in the build sequence to start to build. This
method is difficult to pace to takt time, and thus makes it difficult to
manage. You would use this method only in special build-to-order
situations that might be required by the customer. This method can

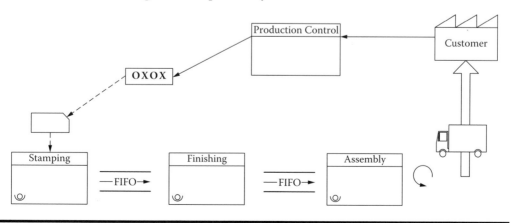

Figure 11.3   Sequential pull system.

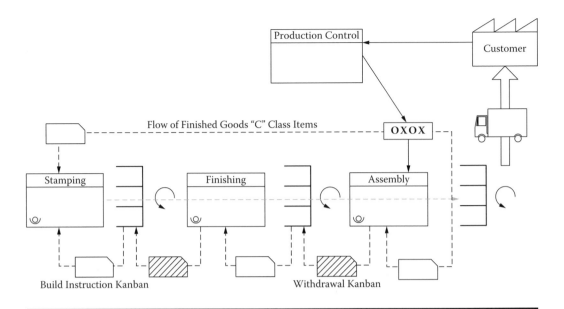

Figure 11.4   Mixed pull system. Flow of finished goods A & B class items. The center dashed line has been added to complete the loop for C parts. This is for information only.

minimize inventory but can really only work if downstream feeder lines can deliver parts without rejects.

Mixed pull (Figure 11.4) is exactly what the name implies: it uses elements from replenishment pull and sequential pull to accomplish production. This method is best used when you have frequent repeat orders for the majority of your customers, while also allowing flexibility to supply infrequent orders without an issue. This method would use a classical pull system to produce "A and B" parts while producing "C" parts when needed. Using this method, the majority of your high-volume parts will require less management oversight and allow you to focus on the "C" parts.

When you begin to create your new finished goods warehouse, you may find you have to work overtime to fill your "A and B" parts, while doing nothing to the "C" parts for quite some time.

Organizing and Controlling Finished Goods Warehouse

There are many ways to organize a finished goods warehouse. You can use the method of random storage by placing product in any location available and then keying the location into the computer. Some companies use the method of placing high-volume product closest to the dock door to be more efficient, while slower-moving product is placed further away. Also, there also are the automated storage and retrieval systems used by very-high-volume distributors. There are many storage methods: pallet racks, flow racks, bins, totes, etc.

The storage of slow-moving and obsolete material is always a cost to the warehouse manager. I have a friend Dennis who runs a large warehouse, and he has what he calls the "dust factor." He says that if you want to find the slow-moving material in a warehouse, just look for the dust on top of the boxes. That is a great idea and could also be used for product that is supposed to be first-in-first-out (FIFO), which turns into last-in-first-out (LIFO) just because the older boxes are on the back of the shelf and difficult to access.

To improve your warehouse operation, keep in mind the idea of visual controls and workplace organization, which are paramount to the success of Lean manufacturing. Applying them to the finished goods warehouse can save time and money when pulling inventory to ship. Using these concepts in a small company can be very satisfying while also being very easy to implement. First, create dedicated locations for each part number in the warehouse. You can even place one customer's product all in the same warehouse area. Next, hang signage over each area that identifies the contents of the area, that is, Mom & Pop Industries, Cyclone Machining, Brown Baby Products, etc. Then, at each storage location, clearly identify the minimum and maximum quantities of product—that is, number of boxes, bags, pieces, whatever works for you—that can be stored in that location. You should also identify buffer and safety stock quantities.

Your warehouse might look similar to that shown in Figure 11.5 when you are finished. As you can see, the method shown would quickly identify if a product were missing or short on parts. You have three rows, with safety, buffer, and cycle stock on different shelves with a standardized work instruction that states the material handler can remove product from the cycle stock locations without approval. As an example, you might set up an approval process where production planning can authorize use of buffer stock, and only the plant manager can authorize the use of safety stock.

The system mentioned above is wonderful because you can easily access material; safety and buffer stock are separated from the normal cycle stock. This way you can see if you start to use up buffer stock due to a

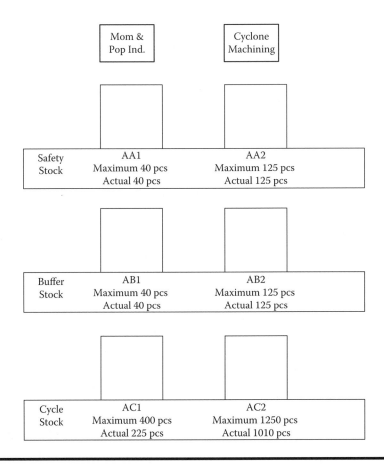

Figure 11.5 Warehouse overview.

quality problem or material delivery issue delaying the production of the parts. However, what if the product is revision controlled? How can you be assured that you will use up existing inventory before moving to the next revision? What do you do with old revisions? The last question is simple if the customer has instructed you to dispose of the old revision. Then all you have to do is scrap them. However, if the customer wants to use up current inventory before moving to the new revision, how can you keep your buffer and safety stock while using up the old material and moving to the new material? How can you keep the visual system going in the warehouse?

If you are using the warehouse method shown in Figure 11.5, you will have to build the new revision while using up all the cycle, buffer, and safety stock and storing the new revision in another area of the warehouse until the entire old inventory is used up. Using two separate locations as far away from each other as possible and directing the material handlers only to use the old material, you will be successful in keeping the material separate.

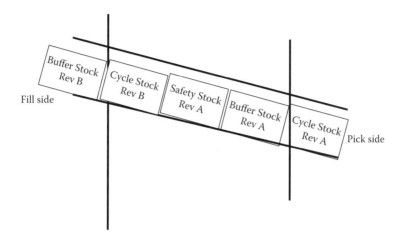

Figure 11.6 Inventory flow rack.

One problem may be that human error can still enter into using the new material. The method I would choose, if possible, would be to use a flow rack; placing the old material to the front while placing the new material to the back. This would look like Figure 11.6.

This is the perfect first-in-first-out (FIFO) inventory method and is the easiest with which to control the use of revision changes. You can keep all three types of inventory on one rack as long as you maintain the proper levels of each type of inventory; the difference is that you stock all the boxes with the same amount of inventory. Box 1, the first box on the pick side, has the same amount of inventory as boxes 2 and 3; if you need a total of 600 pieces to cover finished goods inventory for the cycle, buffer, and safety stock, then you would have all three boxes filled with 200 parts each. When you open the first box, you would send a signal to the production floor to make another 200 parts, and the cycle would continue indefinitely.

Chapter 12

How to Schedule the Production Line (Value Stream)

Introduction

We have now created a number of tools used for inventory flow and control, as well as improved the factory design, creating work cells and laying out the factory for material and product to flow easily through the factory as opposed to moving back and forth across the factory in an inefficient manner. But we still need to schedule the factory more efficiently.

If you go back to your original current state map, remember how all the work centers were scheduled independently with work orders from the planning department. As a result of this type of shop-floor planning and control, each work center worked hard to complete its tasks so that it had 100% efficiency each day while trying to stay on schedule. Have you had planning come running up to the work center and say, "Stop what you are doing. We need to get this order done first because the customer is waiting"? Many times I have heard the following from various workers:

"Planning comes running down every day at the last minute and needs a rush order."—Janie in packaging

"We don't even try to work to the schedule. It's always changing."—Karen in assembly

"Work-order schedule dates don't really mean much. We build what we are told to build."—Clancy in machining

I am sure you have heard many similar comments. Multiple scheduling points, constantly changing priorities from planning, and changing demands from the customer all contribute to the lack of proper use of the work order.

Although some form of MRP (Material Requirements Planning) is almost always used in manufacturing to control and schedule production, it is not necessarily the best tool for the job. The basic problem in trying to schedule the production floor with MRP is that it assumes unlimited capacity for machines and work centers; this alone makes it a less than useful tool for scheduling. There certainly is nothing wrong with MRP, and I do not recommend removing it from use. As stated earlier in this book, it is best used as a higher-level planning tool, one that stores bills of material, production man-hour requirements, and forecast schedules that can be used to create reports showing machine and man-hour requirements used for capacity planning. How then do you schedule the production floor?

Pacemaker Process

In Lean production it is best to schedule the production floor using the pacemaker process. I now provide an in-depth explanation of how the process works.

First, keep in mind that the assembly line is the pacemaker for assembled products. To be more precise, you pick a specific work cell that is as close to the end customer as possible. Work cells such as final packaging, final testing, or final assembly are common pacemaker cells. If you have an assembly line that produces more than one product, you typically move upstream to the work cell that determines the configuration of the product to be made. One example of this might be a lawn mower. The same assembly line produces exactly the same product except for the color of the top cover on the mower: one cover is green for company "A" while another cover is yellow for company "B." The only difference between the two mowers is the color of the covers and the labels that are put on the covers.

Because the work cell where the covers are installed is closest to the customer, you can differentiate which product you have produced, and we will now use this as the pacemaker cell. We place a scheduling board at this cell and place scheduling kanban cards on the board so workers in the cell know which cover to install.

If you have a product that is not assembled, such as machined brackets, molded widgets, or even processed paperwork, you can still have a pacemaker cell. Think about your product: if you are producing machined brackets, they may go through several processing steps before they are complete, such as machining, deburring, painting, and inspection. Which one would you pick as the pacemaker? Probably painting, because each customer may want a different color. We use a scheduling board, but what does it look like?

In the example in Figure 12.1, the dark gray cards indicate green covers, while the white cards indicate yellow covers. Schedule boards can be made in different ways. Figure 12.2 is another example using daily scheduling. This board works by placing all the cards to be produced in one day on a peg. They are placed on the peg in the order in which they are to be produced, with the first one to be produced on top, the next second, and so on. These cards should be placed on the board at least twenty-four hours before the beginning of the first shift so that raw material can be delivered if necessary. If production planning determines that a change to the build sequence must be made, then they only have to go to the board and place a new card on the pin in the order in which they want the work to be completed or rearrange the card sequence. The golden rule is, "If the days' work has already begun, they cannot stop production." The best they can do is place the card on the pin as the next job to be done. However, should

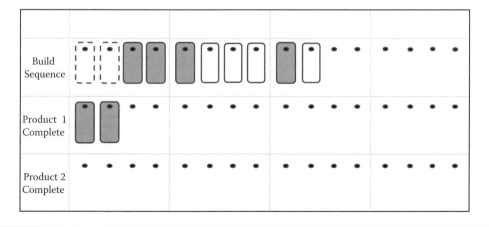

Figure 12.1   Work cell schedule board.

Work Cell Schedule Board							
	Monday	Tuesday	Wednesday	Thursday	Friday	Saturday	Sunday
Build Sequence	⬜	◻	◻	◻	◻	◻	•
Product 1 Complete	◻	•	•	•	•	•	•
Product 2 Complete	•	•	•	•	•	•	•

Figure 12.2 Daily work schedule board.

this be a machining, molding, or some other process where raw material is needed (such as bar stock, plastic resin, paint, aluminum billets, etc.), then production planning should make certain that the required raw material can be delivered to the work cell in time to begin the production run. Should any cards remain on the pin at the end of the day, they must be moved to another pin; typically, this is the next day, either to complete the production run or just to continue the schedule. In most cases, you would do your higher-volume parts first, moving from "A" finished goods parts to "B" and then to "C."

Efficiency versus Changeover

One of the tools of MRP is to calculate economic order quantities (EOQs), with the idea that there is an economic trade-off between process setup cost and the number of parts required to make the setup economically viable to perform. When you follow this methodology, you find that to justify a long setup time, you must produce large batch quantities of parts, which actually in turn increase your WIP (work-in-process) inventory and sometimes finished goods inventory if you are producing component parts for customers. I discuss the efficient changeover of process and machines later in this chapter. But it is important to note here that the shorter the setup time, the lower the cost and the smaller the production batch must be to justify the setup. What you should see here is that quicker setups create smaller batches, which quickly reduces WIP inventory. You will notice this more on your upstream processes where setup of machines can take a significant amount of time. What you are seeing here is what is known as *sub-optimization*. This is where one process or work cell produces at its most efficient point at the expense of other departments—in this case at the expense of inventory. Why do we carry inventory? It is to cover for the variations in production, and one of those variations is setup. If we reduce setup, we can reduce lead time, which will reduce inventory. You can easily see this with a simple experiment with the data in your "Finished Goods Pareto" spreadsheet in Table 12.1. Find the column "Total Finished Goods Inventory" and note the quantity for the first part in the first row; in our example it shows 104 parts with a lead time of 4 days. Now change the lead time to 3 days. What is the new "finished goods inventory" quantity? The change to 69 parts is a savings of 35 parts from the original 104 parts, and we did that just by changing the lead time; thus, you can see the power in short lead times.

The move to level pull is an excellent time to review the work content of parts going through the value stream. Variations in processes should now be more evident now that the push of production is no longer being used.

Table 12.1 shows a finished goods Pareto chart. Create the spreadsheet and sort the results based on the average pieces per day column (Avg. Pcs/Day) to find your "A," "B," and "C" parts. In Table 12.1, "A" parts are equal to 57% of the total daily production.

Supermarket (Warehouse) Location in the Factory

Is there an ideal place for the location of markets? In one word, "No." Several items enter into your selection of the location. Toyota places its markets at the end of its producing processes, which allows the process to see exactly what has been used and what requires replacement. Downstream processes must come and pick up their parts on a regular timed delivery route. This is a great idea but you may not have enough space for such a layout (Smalley, 2004).

If you produce a high volume of parts internally and do not have space for a market at the producing process, your best bet would be a centrally located market. This is probably the most common type of market location.

If your factory does only assembly and your suppliers provide you with all your component parts, you may want to locate the market close to the receiving area; however, this could require longer timed delivery routes.

Table 12.1 Finished Goods Pareto Chart

Finished Goods Demand Category	Customer Part Number	Total Annual Production	Avg. Work Days/Year	Avg. Pcs/Day	Lead Time to Replenish One Part in Days	Cycle Stock	Buffer & Safety Stock Combined as % of Cycle Stock	Buffer & Safety Stock Combined (Pcs)	Total Finished Goods Inventory	Std. Deviation	Std. Deviation x 3	UCL (Max. Inv. Level)	LCL (Min. Inv. Level)	Piece Part Cost	Carrying Cost/Pce	Total Cost/Pce	Total Cost of Max. Inventory
A	8012023	5117	256	20.0	4	80	10.0%	8	104	10.2	30.6	135	73	$8.62	$0.86	$9.48	$1,276
A	8012034	4402	256	17.2	4	69	10.0%	7	90	9.5	28.5	119	62	$9.00	$0.90	$9.90	$1,174
A	8011990	4238	256	16.6	5	83	10.0%	9.5	104	10.2	30.7	135	74	$6.57	$0.65	$7.22	$975
B	8011957	2185	256	8.5	3	26	10.0%	8	37	6.1	18.3	56	19	$7.91	$0.79	$8.70	$483
B	8011968	1990	256	7.8	5	39	10.0%	3	52	7.2	21.6	73	30	$12.84	$0.38	$13.22	$969
B	8011946	1970	256	7.7	5	38	10.0%	6.1	51	7.2	21.5	73	30	$16.23	$0.28	$16.51	$1,201
B	8012056	986	256	3.9	2	8	10.0%	4	14	3.7	11.1	25	3	$17.69	$0.28	$17.97	$445
B	8011979	899	256	3.5	5	18	10.0%	7.2	26	5.1	15.3	42	11	$18.76	$0.65	$19.41	$806

C	8012012	477	256	1.9	7	13	10.0%	4	22	4.7	14.1	36	8	$20.23	$0.65	$20.88	$753
C	8012067	460	256	1.8	5	9	10.0%	7.2	16	4.0	12.0	28	4	$42.00	$0.65	$42.65	$1,187
C	8012001	362	256	1.4	3	4	10.0%	1	9	3.0	8.9	18	0	$60.00	$0.60	$60.60	$1,069
C	8012045	362	256	1.4	3	4	10.0%	3.7	9	3.0	8.9	18	0	$75.00	$0.80	$75.80	$1,337
C	8012100	317	256	1.2	14	17	10.0%	2	33	5.7	17.1	50	16	$126.00	$12.60	$138.60	$6,905
C	8012089	131	256	0.5	14	7	10.0%	5.1	22	4.7	14.0	36	8	$152.00	$15.20	$167.20	$5,982
C	8012078	120	256	0.5	14	7	10.0%	1	21	4.6	13.8	35	7	$125.00	$12.50	$137.50	$4,802

% of Parts

total p/n's

50%	14	C	Total	94
36%	7	B	A	54	0.57
21%	5	A	B	31	0.33
	3			

Which type of location is the most efficient? From my perspective, the Toyota method would be ideal yet it would be difficult to do without a complete redesign of most factories, which would include expensive brick-and-mortar remodeling. I believe you will find that any market location you use, if properly established and run, can be just as efficient as any other.

Signaling Material Withdrawal from the Market

Now you need a method by which you can signal the market to deliver the work cell parts. For this you will use a withdrawal kanban card. This card is designed to supply all the information you need to replenish the raw material for a specific part at the work cell material point-of-use rack. The withdrawal card will have some specific information on it. Figure 12.3 is a relatively simple withdrawal card design. (Note: It includes all the pertinent information needed to stock the point-of-use rack and where to get the parts from in the market. It identifies where the "parts go to," which is the production line number "Line 14" and a description on that production line "Skinning," the work cell [station] number [this is actually the work cell number], and the rack and shelf number that describes the point-of-use rack

Figure 12.3   Production pull card.

location.) The material handler looks for the point-of-use rack labeled number "14"; he sees B05, which tells him the parts should be placed on shelf "B" position number 5. The shelves on the point-of-use rack are lettered from the top shelf to the bottom shelf as "A," "B," "C," etc.; a part number and part name allow the material handler to check the part number on the point-of-use container versus the parts in the container, as well as cross-check the part number located on the fill side of the point-of-use rack in position B05 to make sure he is placing the correct part in the correct location. Next, identify where the parts came from; in this case they are from the market but they could have come from another work cell if the other work cell stocked WIP inventory at the cell. By reading the market area on the card, you can see that these parts are located in row "1"; counting the racks, you go to rack "4" and then to shelf "3" to find the parts in the market. You then count out ten parts and place them in a specially designed container for this part. (Note: The area called "Instructions" in Figure 12.3 is blank. If there are special handling instructions, they would be added here.)

The supplier pull card (Figure 12.4) is very similar to the production material withdrawal card (Figure 12.3). You can see that the supplier pull card also identifies the market location where you can find the material but in this case it is used as a tool to tell the material handler where to replenish

Figure 12.4   Supplier pull card.

the new stock. Again, you find the part number and description. Then you identify who the supplier is, the type of container being used, and the quantity of parts to place in the container.

The company that uses the particular card in Figure 12.4 has color coded them so it is easy to see if a card is being used incorrectly or if it is in the wrong place. They have used hot pink for the production pull cards and white for the supplier pull cards.

Batch Production Signal Kanban

If you are a producer of component parts in your own plant, you will need another signal card. This card will be used to tell a batch process when and how many parts to produce. You can also design these cards similar to the purchasing card because the new batch signal kanban and the supplier pull card function almost identically, except that you are working with an inside producer of parts rather than an outside supplier. You can design your signal card in any configuration you like. The most common is a triangular shape because it is unique and has been used for years by Toyota. There is nothing sacred about the shape or color of the signal card because what you want is to differentiate the signal kanban card from all the other kanban cards. As the story goes, Toyota used a piece of scrap sheet metal that was available and it just happened to be triangular in shape.

The batch pull card was originally designed to hang from a piece of angle iron attached to a bench in the work cell. When the material handlers brought the pull card to the machine to signal the need to replenish the market, they hung the card on the angle iron; the angle iron was sloped slightly so as each order was completed, the next order slid down into the first spot, signaling it was to be produced next. When completed, the signal card was attached to the container, ready for the material handler to take it back to the market. How you design the card and signal which card is next to be produced is entirely up to you. Just remember that this is a visual signal with which to schedule the process work cell (Figure 12.5).

Note in Figure 12.5 that the date and time under "Date Triggered" are handwritten; this allows management to see when the parts were first ordered or how long the parts have been waiting to be produced, and from this they can manage the queue of signal cards more effectively. Because the

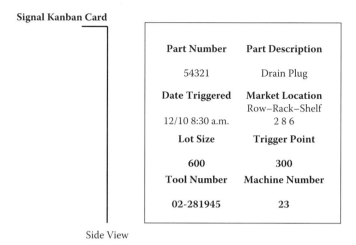

Figure 12.5   Signal kanban card.

date and time are handwritten, I would suggest laminating these cards so you can wipe off the date triggered information and reuse the card.

When the parts container(s) is/are returned to the market and stored, you will need to position the signal card with the container of parts such that when you reach the trigger point, you automatically reorder the parts. If you have three containers with 200 parts each, you would place the signal card on the second container and pull the card when it is half empty.

Production Capacity versus Changeover Time

The chart in Table 12.2 shows how much machine runtime you need to produce three parts in one of your machining centers. Also shown is the average setup time for each part number. Looking at this chart, you can tell what you have:

Total runtime: 744 minutes
Available time per shift: 420 minutes
Total changeover time: 270 minutes
Total required time: 1434 minutes
Number of shifts required: 3.2

Because it is obvious from these numbers that you cannot produce all the required parts in one day, you have a problem. If the number of shifts

Table 12.2 Machine Runtime Chart

Part Number	Average Daily Demand (in pcs)	Average Scrap Rate	Cycle Time/ Piece (in sec)	Runtime/ Day (in min)	Avg. Changeover Time (in min)
8012078	600	2.0%	42	428	60
8012001	410	3.5%	28	198	90
8012045	250	1.0%	28	118	120
Total	**1260**		**98**	**744**	**270**

required was more than 3.5, you would move part of the production to the next day, thus bringing you back to a full three shifts; then again, you are only slightly over a full day's shift. This fraction of a shift is equal to 90 minutes (0.2 × 450 minutes); as a result, you would schedule all this production for one day and consider it the "maximum" number of changeovers you could do.

But there is still a slight problem: if you work at 100% efficiency, you will still need ninety minutes of overtime, and to avoid this you need to look at the amount of waste in processing each of the three part numbers and the waste found in the setup time for the parts.

Determining Production Lot Size

To determine what your product lot size should be using Lean, you need to look at two different methods. The first is known as "fixed-time variable-quantity" and the other is "fixed-quantity per part number." The fixed-quantity per part number is self-evident; you run a fixed quantity of each part, every day, every week, etc. For example, this method would be designed to create one day's worth of production and, as adjustments are needed to compensate for product demand, you would run the part more or less frequently as dictated by demand. This method does cause you to carry more inventories. The fixed-time variable quantity keeps lot sizes closer to customer demand, thus keeping inventories lower. I will not spend time in showing you how to determine lot sizes for both of these methods as it is very easy using the information I have already discussed. (Average daily usage + Buffer+ Safety) × Days between production runs will give you a proper lot size.)

Reorder Trigger Point

Determining your reorder trigger point for signal cards is very simple: use the following equation:

$$\text{Runtime} + \text{Changeover time} + \text{Container-to-market time} = \text{Replenishment time}$$

where

Runtime = Cycle time × Lot size

Changeover time = This includes not only the actual tooling changeover time, but also the average wait time for the previous job to be completed

Container-to-market time = The time it takes for the first container to be picked up at the process and returned to the warehouse and placed on the shelf ready for use

One thing to remember about changeover time is the need to add that little extra amount of waiting time for the previous completion time. Many times, people forget to include this time. Also, people forget to include the time to put away product in the market. (I wish I had a dollar for every time I was told the parts were in the warehouse yet when production needed them, the parts were not there.) Depending on the company, it can take several days from receipt of material at the dock to having the parts in the warehouse ready for production.

Guidance: Pull Cards

You must remember that material withdrawal cards signal the replenishment of raw material inventory at a specific work cell, while pull cards signal the replenishment of raw material from the supplier to the market. When used properly, you will find that the system works very smoothly and significantly reduces inventory costs. It also aids in improving operator efficiency because the operators do not have to leave their workstations to find inventory. The most prevalent cost-saving area of Lean manufacturing is in inventory reduction and control, which dovetails with increased inventory turns and reduced floor space requirements.

To sustain a level pull system, all levels of management must be committed to making it work. If you try to delegate the responsibility of level pull to managers and supervisors below you without your continued commitment, then you can expect the systems to fail. This failure will not be the responsibility of your staff, but rather your own failure because you were not fully engaged and taking responsibility for the success of level pull.

Working without Work Orders

Once you have achieved the level of operating your factory using kanbans, the production pull system, and your pacemaker cell, you can begin to look at why you need production work orders. You no longer use MRP to schedule the work cells or production line, as the visual signals you have installed do the scheduling for you. The only reason you use work orders is to track inventory and labor usage. Some factories use the work order as a tool to track the progress of producing parts through the factory, and typically it is used in batch production, which you no longer use. If you want to know how production is progressing to your schedule, you only need to check your communication boards on the production floor.

As you implement Lean manufacturing and create work cells, you can move from tracking labor and material by process sequence to elimination of labor and material tracking altogether, although the total elimination of the work order is usually not accomplished until you reach a very high level of Lean implementation. Because most MRP systems are not equipped to shut off labor and material tracking for individual work centers, you will have to continue using labor and material tracking until all the new work cells are complete.

Labor and Material Accuracy

Before you can begin to eliminate labor and material tracking, you must be certain that the labor standards on the production routings and quantities of material listed on the bill-of-material are accurate. Because there will be no reporting of variance from either labor or material, it is critical that these items are correct. This sounds like a daunting task but for a small company, this is actually not that bad, having done it myself. Some small companies will hire temporary employees to perform these tasks. The only warning I have here is to have some of your own staff check their work. Although a 100% check would be great, a satisfactory number of random checks that makes you, the owner, feel good is most important. You want an accuracy level of between 85 and 90% because it provides the needed confidence level that the inputted data are correct. Another important point here is that you need to check your bill-of-materials (BOM) and labor standards on an annual basis. Because all the data in the routing and BOM system do not change every year, concentrate the annual checks on the part numbers that have been changed over the past year.

Work-Order Back-Flushing

Now that the labor and material data in the MRP are accurate and all the work cells have been created, you can shut off labor and material reporting; however, if you have overtime labor in a specific work cell, it should be noted on the work order. Once the product listed on the production work order is completed, key the completion information into the MRP system, which then applies the standard cost of labor and material to the product. Any overtime must also be recorded.

Cycle Count Inventory

Sometimes you need to perform a physical count of inventory; this is easy to do in the warehouse but a bit more difficult on the production floor. I have, on occasion, had to include WIP inventory in this count, so this is the method I use.

To the white board:

1. Take a physical count of each raw material part in every kanban bin in each work cell.
2. Calculate the value of inventory in each work cell.
3. Calculate the inventory value of each partially complete product in each work cell.
4. Calculate the inventory value of each product sitting in kanbans ready for the next process step.

5. Now combine the inventory value for all raw material, partially completed product, and WIP inventory in kanbans for the entire product, from the first process to packaging for finished goods.

6. You now have a snapshot in time as to how much inventory **is not** in the raw material supermarket.

Chapter 13

Material Management

Raw Material Inventory Management

To achieve continuous flow in the work cells, it is important to have and maintain a robust material delivery and pickup system. A medical device company was very consistent with the completion of their daily production form, which allowed them to quickly identify critical issues that caused the production line to not flow in a continuous manner. You can see by the production form in Table 13.1 that missing and bad parts were a major problem. One company I was working with used an Andon clock to track, for one year, the amount of time their production line was down. To their surprise, they had over 2200 man-hours of lost time, of which 66% was due to lack of parts on the production line. That meant that 1452 production man-hours were lost due to a lack of usable parts on the production line. So now you can see how important proper flow of materials is. One big question is: How does a Lean material system fit with MRP (Material Requirements Planning)? There are some major changes in the way you will manage your raw material. However, MRP does not go away; instead, it becomes more of a high-level strategic tool used for long-range planning and a tool for purchasing negotiations. For the small company, it may not even have an MRP system and may already be using a spreadsheet or other type of database, or even a manual system to plan material.

If you go back to the plant walk that all your managers participated in and look at the amount of inventory that was in each area of the plant, how

Table 13.1 Production Form

Work Cell Fluidics Control Module				Date 11/11/11	
Takt Time		360 seconds	Team Leader—Scott Wolbers		
Quantity Required		80	Sign-Off		
Time	Plan	Actual	Problems	Team Lead (every hour)	Supervisor (every 4 hours)
7:30–8:30	10	10		SW	
8:30–9:30	10	0	Missing parts	SW	
9:30–9:45		Break			
9:45–10:45	10	10		SW	
10:45–11:45	10	5	Bad parts	SW	DS
11:45–12:30		Lunch			
12:30–1:30	10	0	Bad parts	SW	
1:30–2:30	10	5	Parts missing for half hour	SW	
2:30–2:45		Break			
2:45–3:45	10	10		SW	
3:45–4:15	10	10		SW	DS
Total	80	50	Missing and bad parts		

much was it? Was it all out on the production floor? There was a movement for many years in manufacturing to have what was known as "point-of-use" inventory, and many factories placed a lot of raw material on the production floor. What this did was reduce precious production floor space and create confusion for the materials group, which sometimes could not find material they thought they had. They would then expedite more material into the factory at a high cost.

If you are going to have work cells in manufacturing, you also need very good material flow. The use of Lean material flow and warehousing techniques must also be implemented. This is not an easy task, and some departments will resist the change. From my experience, I would create a

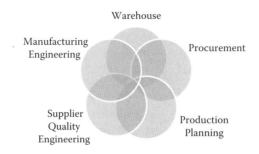

Warehouse

Manufacturing
Engineering

Procurement

Supplier
Quality
Engineering

Production
Planning

Figure 13.1   Material team.

"materials group" responsible for all the procurement, production control, and warehousing of material. I recommend that one person should be head of the materials group, as it will be easier to make the changes needed.

The materials team would consist of those departments shown in Figure 13.1. As a small business, you may not have all these departments, but you probably have some of them with which to set up a team.

To get started with your materials transformation, you must establish five things:

1. A separate warehouse for raw material, which is sometimes called a "purchased part" warehouse.
2. A Plan-for-Every-Part (PFEP). This typically starts as an Excel spreadsheet with all the information pertaining to a given part listed. This is not MRP, but rather a more detailed plan for each part.
3. Set up specific "timed delivery routes" for the movement of material between the warehouse and production work cells.
4. Establish an "inventory pull system" tied in with the timed delivery routes to ensure that only material needed by the work cell is provided in a timely manner.
5. Integrate the use of the inventory pull system with the MRP system so that material accuracy is maintained and material is properly back-flushed from inventory.

At one company I worked with, most of the information needed on the PFEP was located in multiple databases, none of which could communicate with each other—let alone merge the data needed into one database. For this reason, we had to build a completely separate PFEP database. Determining what information needed to be in the database was the first step. Every company is different, and small companies have fewer resources to work with; our example here was created with the most common information required and with a few additions to try and help you with your transition. Also, there is a template on the CD included with this book. Because this will be your PFEP database, you can add any information you like; however, you will need at least the information that is highlighted for you in Table 13.2. Information required in each field is listed below. All areas marked with an asterisk are recommended by Rick Harris in his book *Making Materials Flow* (Harris, Harris, and Wilson, 2003). (Rick and his excellent staff were my teachers [Sensei] for Lean manufacturing based on the Toyota method. Thank you, Rick, Jennifer, and Chuck.)

If you have a complex product to build, I would suggest not including nuts and bolts in the PFEP unless they are specifically unique parts. The use of "free stock" for such parts as nuts, bolts, screws, oil, grease, etc. works well and makes the PFEP easier to manage. Simply determine how much cost is associated with each item used in your product and then take the total amount of all these components and add it to the standard cost of your product as a "plug" number for miscellaneous components.

On the PFEP we have added a section for "buffer stock." Buffer stock includes production delays due to design problems, quality issues, shipping delays, and overtime. Why overtime? If you need to work overtime to complete an order, you may be working Saturday, Sunday, or after hours when parts deliveries are not made. When your material system becomes more efficient and consistent, you may want to remove overtime from the equation by placing a zero in the spreadsheet. Another adjustment that has been added to the PFEP template is one I call "start-up factor." It is difficult to immediately adjust your raw material warehouse to new levels, and in some cases I have seen companies go too Lean too quickly or have other problems as they set up the new purchased parts warehouse. For these reasons I added the start-up factor to the spreadsheet. We use a factor of 2, which in effect doubles "Lean inventory" numbers to provide a cushion until your system works smoothly. You can reduce this number to 1.75, 1.5, or even 0.5 as you become comfortable with the system—eventually reducing it to zero.

Loading the PFEP

Loading the data into the PFEP is without a doubt a somewhat laborious task but it is one well worth doing. You will need to pick or appoint someone to

Table 13.2 Plan-For-Every-Part (PFEP)

Part number*	Specific part number is required for each part. Part numbers do not need to have intelligent meaning, such as 7 means printed circuit board or 5 means baseplate.
Description*	Explains the typical use of part (i.e., gusset, panel, cover, etc.).
Daily usage*	Average number of parts used each day.
Usage per assembly	Describes how many parts are needed for each assembly built.
Hourly usage	The average hourly usage of a part; this is automatically calculated.
Work cell location*	This is the work cell using the part. There may be more than one work cell location. If this happens, you will need a separate line for each work cell location.
Storage location*	Use either the generic word "market," meaning raw material warehouse, or a specific warehouse designator location such as 1B23 where you will actually find the material.
Order frequency*	Order frequency is how often you will order the material from your supplier. Options are daily, 2× per week, weekly, 2× per month, or monthly. When your system is working correctly, it will typically be daily or 2× per week.
Transit time*	The average shipping time for the material to go from your supplier to your dock.
Supplier*	Who you purchase the material from.
City*	Where (name of city) the supplier is located.
State*	Which state your supplier is located in.
Country*	The country in which your supplier is located.
Container type*	What the material is shipped in to you. You will want to store the material in the same box it is shipped in rather than spend the labor to put the material in a new box or bin.
Container dimensions: Length, width, height*	Position the container in front of you with the longest side facing you; this will be the length, narrow end the width, and the height is all that is left.

continued

Table 13.2 (continued)   Work Cell Fluidics Control Module

Container weight	The weight of just the shipping container alone.
Part weight*	Weigh just one part in ounces or pounds, whichever you most commonly use in your plant; but once you pick ounces or pounds, use it throughout the entire spreadsheet.
Standard container quantity*	Typical number of parts supplied in each container; automatically calculated on template.
Total package weight	This is the total weight of the container with the correct number of parts inside and packaging inside; automatically calculated on template.
Container used per hour*	Maximum number of containers used per hour. Automatically calculated on template.
Container usage per day	Maximum number of containers used per day; automatically calculated on template.
Containers to a shipment	Average number of containers in a shipment; automatically calculated on template.
Shipment size*	Size of a standard shipment in days (1 week = 5 days)
Market inventory	The number of days worth of inventory located in the raw material warehouse; automatically calculated on template.
Number of cards in loop*	The number of pull signals that are in the system.
Carrier*	Typical carrier used by the supplier of material.
Supplier performance*	Rate each supplier's performance based on quality, on-time delivery, and support. You will find a dropdown menu on the PFEP template on the CD. Automatically calculated on template.

be the PFEP administrator (manager); this person's responsibility is to see that all the data are entered accurately into the PFEP. This person is also responsible for maintaining the PFEP after it is completed. Because the PFEP is critical to the planning of inventory, the administrator is typically the materials manager or production control manager. Many times, people are not willing to take this role, thinking it will require enormous amounts of time, although at the beginning when you are loading and checking the PFEP, it does take a lot of time; but after it is established, it becomes a simple maintenance plan, making changes only when needed. Some companies use clerks or administrative assistants to input the data but it is ultimately the PFEP administrator's responsibility to ensure its accuracy.

A standard work procedure should be created for the PFEP; it outlines in detail what makes up the PFEP and how to input, update, and maintain the file.

What Data to Input First

The place to start entering data is with the first work cell you are creating. Working together with the people building the cell will help you develop the material timed delivery route as well. Your input into the design of the material delivery system will be of assistance to them when they design and build the flow rack system that will be used to deliver parts to the workbench. Requiring that all new products be placed in the PFEP prior to being placed on the production floor ensures that material is tracked and properly dispensed.

Equations Used with the PFEP

The equations used in the PFEP are relatively simple but can take a little time to get used to.

■ Planned Maximum Level of Inventory in the Warehouse:

Maximum level of inventory = (Daily usage × Shipment size in days) + Buffer stock

Note that shipment size is based on the frequency of delivery from your supplier:
Frequency of Delivery (Table 13.3):

Frequency of delivery = Shipment size in days of production

This is the equation you would use for the "start-up factor" to cushion your change from old inventory processes to your new inventory process. So the equation would look like this:

Maximum level of inventory = ((Daily usage × Shipment size in days) + buffer stock) + Start-up factor

Table 13.3 Frequency of Delivery Chart

Frequency of Deliveries	=	*Shipment Size (in days of production)*
Daily deliveries	=	1 day of production
Twice a week	=	2.5 days of production
Weekly	=	5 days of production
Twice a month	=	10 days of production
Monthly	=	20 days of production

Planning Minimum Inventory Levels

Planning your minimum inventory level is more subjective than using an equation to determine your maximum inventory level. You need to look at a number of things to help you determine the number, including

- Piece part cost
- Carrying cost of inventory
- Cost of lost production if you do not have inventory
- Lost customers if you cannot deliver on time

These are just a few of the items you need to consider when determining your minimum inventory. You may want to think about setting the minimum level of inventory at a point where you know you can expedite material if you need to keep production running.

Value of Frequent Deliveries

Using the PFEP you can easily see the significant savings that can be achieved by increasing the delivery cycle. For this exercise let us assume 325 pieces daily usage of parts with a 5-day lead time from supplier to the warehouse. Next, assume a buffer stock of 600 parts and an overall cost per piece of $5.25. For the sake of argument, assume you have 100 additional parts at the same cost and daily usage rate—just look at the potential material savings!

Daily usage × Shipment size in days (lead time) + Buffer stock =

325 pieces/day × 5 days + 600 pieces of buffer stock = 2225 pieces

325 pieces/day × 1 day + 600 pieces of buffer stock = 925 pieces

Net reduction in raw material inventory = 1300 pieces

1300 pieces × \$5.25/piece = \$6825 material savings

\$6825 annual savings × 100 additional parts = \$682,500 total annual savings

Quantity of Containers Required

You have to size your warehouse for the maximum number of containers needed to support production even if we do not use all of the space. The equation you would use per part number is

$$\frac{\text{Planned maximum inventory level}}{\text{Standard container quantity}} = \text{Maximum quantity of containers}.$$

With the information from this equation, you can now easily calculate the physical size of the warehouse.

Material Reorder Points

Reorder points are simple; whenever you open a box with a purchasing card in it, you place the kanban card on the order board.

Updating and Editing the PFEP

Once the PFEP is determined to be complete, you must maintain it as you make changes to your parts and add new parts to the database. Again, standard work instructions are used detailing this process, or it is a section in the PFEP standard operating procedures that provides a specific method for updating and editing the PFEP.

The PFEP change request form is used for such updating and editing of the PFEP (Figure 13.2).

PFEP Change Request Form

Instructions:
For each item that needs to be changed show the "current data" and the "change to" data.
For a new part, fill in the "Change to" column completely.

Part Data	Current Data	Change To	
Part Number			
Description			
Daily usage			
Usage per assembly			
Work cell location			
Storage location			
Order frequency			
Supplier			
City			
State			
Country			
Transit time			
Container type			
Container dimensions			
Length, width, height			
Container weight			
Part weight			
Standard container quantity			
Containers used per hour			
Shipment size			
Reorder point			
Number of cards in loop			
Carrier			
Supplier performance			

Reason for Change:

Approvals:

Submitted by: _____   Date:_____

Approval required if box is checked

☒	☐	☒	☒	☐	☐
_____	_____	_____	_____	_____	_____
_____	_____	_____	_____	_____	_____
Date	Date	Date	Date	Date	Date
Production Planning	Purchasing	Warehouse	PFEP Manager	Engineering	Production

Figure 13.2   PFEP Change Request Form is used for such updating and editing of the PFEP.

Guidance: PFEP Important Elements

The PFEP is a key element of the material handling and warehouse systems. It also includes purchasing and planning elements. Inventory reduction is one of the major cost-savings elements of Lean manufacturing. The key elements of the PFEP are

1. Use a database that has sorting capabilities.
2. Appoint a PFEP administrator (manager).
3. Create a specific standard operating procedure for creation and use of the PFEP.
4. Establish a documented-controlled method for updating the PFEP.

Creating the Raw Material Market

Finding the proper location for the raw material, "purchased part," market is important because with proper placement you reduce the amount of time a product sits in receiving and you reduce the amount of material handling. Most companies place this market close or next to the receiving department; it is also advantageous for it to be in close proximity to the receiving inspection department. I have seen some companies that cannot place it close to the receiving department due to physical limitations of the building they are in. In one case, a company had receiving on the second floor of a building next to the dock doors, while the purchased part warehouse was in the lower level of the building next to the production floor. Fortunately for this company, the building had a freight elevator nearby, making the situation livable. This company also needed to improve its lead time between the time material was delivered and the time it was available in the warehouse. A Kaizan event was held, and the results are shown in Table 13.4.

Note: The material was handled six times with the possibility of damage and errors at each move. After redesigning the receiving area and placing the material on a short roller conveyor located between receiving and receiving inspection, the number of moves was reduced and the lead time reduced by 58 hours (91%) (Table 13.4).

Table 13.4 Material Handling Chart

Move	Hold Time (hours)	Move	Hold Time (hours)	Hold Time Reduction (hours)
Unload truck and place product in hold area	24	Unload truck and process material immediately	1	23
Move material from hold area to receiving and process	2		0	2
Move material back to hold area waiting for receiving inspection	24	Place material on roller conveyor for receiving inspection	2	22
Move material to receiving inspection and process	2	Move material to receiving inspection and process	2	0
Move material to hold area pending placement in warehouse	12	Move material to transport cart	1	11
Move material to final warehouse location		Move to warehouse every hour		
Total hold (lead) time	64		6	58

Organizing the Warehouse

You have now developed the PFEP and found out how much you can save by increasing the delivery cycle and determining how many containers you need to fill your warehouse. What does the warehouse look like?

In your warehouse you will use the First-In-First-Out (FIFO) method of inventory. This will allow you to more easily control the usage of older parts and make revision changes to parts. You may need to talk with your finance group so they understand the new method of operations for the warehouse, because this may have an impact on how they are currently calculating the cost of inventory.

The best FIFO example I can find is your local supermarket. The stock is continually rotated and the oldest product is at the front of the shelf and in some cases they actually use flow racks to make this job easier. Look in the dairy section and you may find milk products being filled from the back of the shelf; as a result, the older product is always in front.

Let us begin by calling the warehouse a supermarket because we are going to set it up similar to the way a supermarket is set up. We are doing this to make it more efficient and quicker to find the part you are looking for in the supermarket.

Layout of the Supermarket

Lay out the supermarket using any one of a number of different racking and bin systems available today; however, do not forget that you want FIFO inventory flow. This is best achieved using a flow rack system although companies have successfully implemented FIFO using pallet storage racks as well.

The first thing you need to do is create a location system; then you know exactly where everything is located.

In our example in Figure 13.3, we have three levels in our pallet rack storage area. We have labeled them rows A, B, and C. I picked the lower level as "A" although you can label them top to bottom if you wish. Each position on the shelf where we store material is labeled 1 through 6. If we have material located in position B – 2, we can find it on the second pallet rack shelf, second position from the left. However, in most supermarkets, we have more than just one row of racks. We number the racks from the front to the back of the supermarket. If we are looking for a part with a location

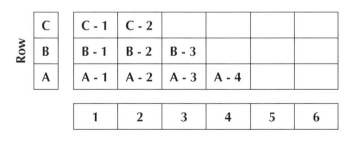

Container Position

Front View of Rack

Figure 13.3 PFEP update form.

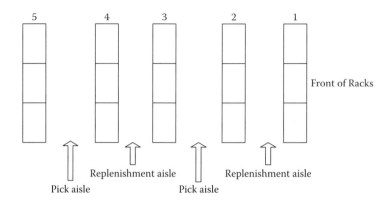

Figure 13.4 Stocking new material on racks.

of 3C2, we would first go to row 3, next to the top row of the pallet rack, and then to the second position from the left.

As you can see in Figure 13.4, we have a slightly different configuration than the normal warehouse. Every other row is slightly narrower than the other; these narrower rows are for the warehouse staff to use when they are stocking new material on the racks. By putting the new material in from the back of a shelf, we maintain our FIFO flow of material as we draw material from the front of the rack.

Creating the Supermarket

The next step is to create the actual supermarket in the warehouse. If you look at the two figures we have just been discussing (Figures 13.2 and 13.3), you can see how the rows and shelves look like a supermarket with canned goods in one aisle, lined up with peas, corn, beans, etc. on each shelf. Now think of your own product; what assemblies do you typically build? Place all the parts for each assembly in one area of the supermarket, preferably on one shelf; in this way it will be very easy to pull all the parts you need for each assembly and you do not have to run all over the warehouse to find parts for a specific work cell.

How Do I Expedite Parts?

We all know that, on occasion, we will need to expedite parts. However, with a properly created and usable supermarket, this should be the exception rather than the rule. If you find yourself in a position where you need to expedite parts because you have reached your minimum level in the supermarket or have found defective parts, you should treat the situation as if you have no parts in the supermarket. You now have a critical situation to deal with. Expedited orders are still acceptable in Lean manufacturing, yet you should not restock with more parts than your normal inventory levels dictate. The person who first discovers the need to expedite parts needs to notify the proper person in production planning or purchasing. The person placing the order should know about the situation within ten minutes of the original discovery of the situation and, if needed, the plant manager or owner of the company should know within fifteen minutes. What we are saying here is that the same urgency that applies to missing a shipment to a customer should apply to expediting a part and it should be just as rare.

Timed Delivery Routes

To deliver material to the work cells, you need to establish specific routes and times that you will deliver the materials; in this way the work cells know when they are going to get parts replenished. This allows the operator in the work cell to continue working, as opposed to filling out material requisition forms or going to the supermarket to pick their own parts.

If you have some familiarity with Lean manufacturing, you may have heard the people who deliver these parts called "water spiders" because they dart around the production floor in short quick runs and then stop. I just call them material handlers.

Think of a timed delivery route like the package delivery company that comes to your company to drop off and pick up packages. They have a predetermined route they drive and make designated stops to drop off and pick up packages. They then take the packages they pick up to a designated central point to be processed. The next day, they return to your company at the same time as yesterday to drop off and pick up packages. This delivery service is so punctual we know when we will get the next delivery and pickup.

The material delivery route is the heartbeat of your material handling system for the production floor; it is so consistent and regular that once established and fully operational you will not even give it a second thought.

Nonetheless, many people and mangers think this is adding a level of complexity to the system that is not needed. In actuality, the timed delivery route

1. Provides better control of inventory
2. Reduces material labor by being more efficient with the delivery of material
3. Frees up production floor space
4. Allows one person to deliver material, pick up empty containers, and move information between work cells plus return empty containers to the supermarket for processing
5. Maximizes the efficiency for the continuous flow of material to the work cells
6. Assures the correct amount and type of material is on hand at the work cell when needed

Basic Material Handling Information

Here are some basic material handling specifications that you may need to use in your factory layout for the timed delivery routes. These are just guidelines and can be adjusted based on your situation (Table 13.5).

Table 13.5 Material Handling Specifications

Standard pallet widths (top 5 in order, in inches)	48 × 40	General use
	42 × 42	Telecommunication and paint
	48 × 48	Drums and barrels
	40 × 48	Military and cement
	48 × 42	Chemicals and beverage
Standard aisle for counterbalanced forklift (sit-down rider, in feet)	12	Two-way aisle
Standard aisle for narrow aisle forklift, powered pallet trucks, pallet jacks, etc. (stand-up rider, in feet)	10	Two-way aisle

When using other material handling devices such as wheeled racks, carts, two-wheeled carts, etc., measure the width of the largest load you are hauling and add two feet to the width.

Creating Your Timed Delivery Routes

Let us assume you have two product lines in your factory and want to deliver material in the most efficient manner; thus you can lay out the factory as shown in Figure 13.5.

The timed delivery route in this example is identified by the solid black arrows. Stop signs indicate where the material handler has to stop to drop off parts and pick up empty containers. We have shown an assembly line in the lower half of the example and machine tools in the upper portion to show you that these routes can be used for any type of production. You will note two stop signs at the office. In this example, we assume that the

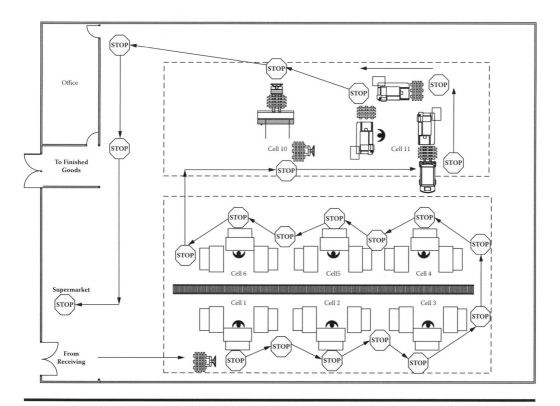

Figure 13.5 Factory layout.

material handler also delivers documents to the office, thus eliminating the need for office personnel to pick up documents on the production floor.

Notice that the material handler uses only one route through the factory and does not backtrack at all. Think of this route as a one-way street that is reserved for timed delivery routes.

Although we show a forklift in our example of a timed delivery route, they should only be used when a full pallet load of material must be delivered. You should strive to keep forklifts off the production floor, using electric pallet jacks instead to carry full pallet loads; however, you must always remain flexible to the needs of the production floor.

The stops on the timed delivery route are placed as close to the material point-of-use as possible. This is to make the material handler's job easier. There is nothing wrong if the stop is a short walk away from the point-of-use material racks. At no time should the material handler go inside the work cell to deliver or pick up parts or empty bins.

If you would like hourly delivery and pick-up of parts, then you need to make sure that the material handler can easily make his rounds within a one-hour time frame. It is important that you follow the material handler on the route, checking how much time it takes to complete one round. A good stopwatch or watch is needed to time the route. Take five measurements and then find the time that repeats most often; this will be how long the route takes. The route will become faster as material handlers become familiar with the routine. If you cannot do the route in the time allotted you will need to establish two separate routes. I have seen situations where the material handler becomes so efficient that he actually has time in the supermarket to load some of his own bins.

Point-of-Use Rack Design

A point-of-use rack is designed to hold and deliver material directly to the work cell. The closer to the work position of the operator that we can deliver material, the easier and quicker it will be to assemble the parts. Empty parts bins should be conveyed away from the workbench and deposited in a location where they can be picked up when parts are delivered. In designing your point-of-use rack, use gravity whenever possible to feed parts or containers to within arm's length of the operator.

How much material should I keep on the point-of-use rack? How big does the point-of-use rack need to be? If it is assumed that the timed delivery route delivers parts once per hour, you would need enough material at the work cell for one hour of production. Check your PFEP for the hourly usage of each part within the cell and then add one additional container for safety. Therefore, if your hourly usage of a piston housing is forty pieces per hour and you place twenty pieces in each part container, then you would need three containers worth of material:

$$\frac{40 \text{ Pieces/hour}}{20 \text{ Pieces/container}} + 1 \text{ Safety container} = 3 \text{ Containers required}$$

You can adjust this equation if you would like more material at the point-of-use rack. I would not exceed more than two hours' worth of material unless you have a strategic reason to do so.

As the operator uses the material in each container, he places the empty container on the empty container chute to be picked up by the material handler on the route. If he is using forty pieces per hour with twenty pieces in each container, then the material handler should find two empty containers each time he stops at the work cell. The empty container return should be sized to match the one-hour timed delivery route so that one hour's worth of containers will fit. If you have a two-hour timed delivery route, you will need the empty container return sized to hold two hours' worth of containers. Now you can adjust your point-of-use racks to size any timed delivery route schedule.

After building and stocking two or three work cells, you should have a good idea of the standard size containers you will need at your point-of-use rack. Pick four to six container sizes and make them your standard size. Remember that these containers are reusable and should be made of a material that can take abuse, such as plastic or metal. Standard sizes make it easy to determine the size of your point-of-use rack. When designing the rack, keep in mind the reach and height of your staff; do not build a rack too tall for them to easily reach the material containers on the top shelf.

Guidance: Point-of-Use Material

Once the point-of-use racks are stocked and operators begin taking material from the containers, some operators will perform what we call "bin dumping." Instead of removing an empty container from the rack and placing it in the return chute, they will take a little inventory from the other containers behind the one they are using because there is a feeling that they will not get parts when they need them. You will need to monitor this closely on a day-to-day basis until they have learned to not bin dump. We do not want them to bin dump because this ruins the inventory count in the racks, and you will run out of material at some point.

Operators may be conditioned to running out of parts and not getting more when they need them. This may find them hiding inventory in their workbench drawers or even their lockers. This is perhaps more prevalent with easily hidden parts. This needs to stop because it is also ruining the inventory count.

Pull Signal for Material

Pull signals are used by the work cell to notify the supermarket that specific material is needed in the work cell. You may use any one of a number of common pull signals but the most common are

- *Colored light towers*: sometimes referred to as Andon lights. These lights are typically used when large bulky items will be delivered to machining centers, lathes, etc. When the light is turned on, it is a signal to the material handler that additional material is needed at the work cell.
- *Kanban cards*: cards that contain all the information needed to fill a container or parts for a work cell. Most cards contain supermarket location, work cell location, part description, part number, quantity of parts per container, and we like to see the container size. Many kanban cards are laminated or placed in some sort of protective covering. Most cards can be affixed to the container holding the parts they describe. The material handlers can pick up a card and go to the supermarket to get the proper container. Then they go to the proper location in the warehouse and fill the container with the appropriate part and quantity all by just looking at the kanban card. This saves a lot of time compared to the traditional method of looking for information in the computer.

Coupled versus Decoupled Routes: What Is the Difference?

In preparing the routes, you need to decide if you want a coupled or decoupled route. The difference between the two lies in who fills the returned containers in the supermarket.

■ *Coupled route:* The material handler (route runner) picks up the empty containers and kanban cards while he delivers new material to the point-of-use racks in each work cell. He then returns to the supermarket where he fills the containers in preparation for the next run.
■ *Decoupled route:* The material handler (route runner) picks up empty containers and kanban cards while he delivers new material to the point-of-use rack in each work cell. When he returns to the supermarket, he hands off the containers and kanban cards to someone in the market who then fills the containers. Then the route runner begins another cycle on his route while the people in the supermarket fill the containers that were dropped off.

In the coupled route, we assume that a one-hour route typically would have 33% of the total route time, as loading time in the supermarket would equal twenty minutes. Travel time for the route would not exceed 33% of the remaining forty minutes of the hour (Harris, Harris, and Wilson, 2003).

Maximum load time = 33% of 60 minutes = 20 minutes
Maximum travel time = 33% of 40 minutes = 13 minutes

Determining the Number of Pull Signals

For each part, you will have to determine how many pull signals you need. This is relatively easy. Heading descriptions for your pull signal chart (Table 13.6) include

■ *Material Being Delivered:* frequency of timed delivery route. In this case, it is one hour or whatever you chose as your delivery frequency.
■ *Material at Work Cell:* amount of production material at work cell point-of-use rack, in this case one hour.

Table 13.6 Pull Signal Chart

Route Type	Material Being Delivered (in hours)	Material at Work Cell (in hours)	Pull Signals Waiting to Be Filled (in hours)	Material Being Filled in Supermarket (in hours)		Frequency Multiplier
Coupled	1	1	0	1	=	3
Decoupled	1	1	1	1	=	4

- *Pull Signals Waiting to Be Filled:* pull signals pending replenishment in the supermarket.
- *Material Being Filled in Supermarket:* pull signals currently being filled in supermarket.

Kanban-in-the-Loop

$$\text{kanban in loop} = \frac{\text{hourly usage} \times \text{frequency multiplier}}{\text{standard container quantity}}.$$

Coupled route:

$$18 \text{ kanban in loop} = \frac{300 \times 3}{50}.$$

Decoupled route:

$$24 \text{ kanban in loop} = \frac{300 \times 4}{50}.$$

As you can see by the numbers, you will need an additional six kanban cards in the loop to support a decoupled route.

Because you are a small manufacturing company, you will most likely not need elaborate calculations to add more work cells to your timed delivery route. Simply keep track of the time the route takes as you add cells. Add the time to fill kanbans in the supermarket to the time it takes to run the route; then add the time for each new cell until you have filled up the material handlers' allotment of one hour (or whatever you decided your frequency of delivery is). When you have reached the maximum time allowed for the route, you will need to consider adding another route and material handler, or switch to a decoupled route.

It is important that you prepare a standardized operating procedure (SOP) for the material handler on the route and for the replenishment of kanban containers in the supermarket. In Lean terms, these SOPs are called "standardized work" and they spell out exactly how to do the job. Why is this necessary? If you have ever had a key person go on vacation or get sick for an extended period of time with no one trained to replace them, you know how inconvenient this can be. Standardized work removes the unknowns from this equation and ensures that if your material handler is gone, someone else—including their boss, plant manager, or even the president of the company—can continue the standardized worksheet and successfully perform the job.

Sustaining the Material Handling System

It is also important to track the success and failures of the supermarket and timed delivery route using simple charts and graphs that show how well the department is doing. Such things as completion of route on time, amount of time each route took per day, number of point-of-use containers filled in each route, and accuracy of container fills are all possible items to track to ensure that the material delivery routes are being sustained and improved.

One area that is very important to audit involves the pull cards for the point-of-use containers. We have determined how many of each card are needed within the system to ensure proper inventory levels. Therefore, on a predetermined cycle, an audit of cards should be made. The material handler for the route is the logical person to do this. With a frequency of no less than every other day, the material handler would pick one part number, then count the number of cards in the system. This would include cards in the supermarket, both filled and unfilled, as well as cards at the point-of-use rack. If you do not have the correct number of cards, then immediate corrective action must be taken. When you first start your timed delivery routes and use of pull cards, you will probably want to audit the system daily until the new methods become routine and your standardized work is well defined.

Remember with your standardized work that each level of management is responsible for checking the work of the next level below them. It is important that people be held accountable in the Lean system for the work they do; thus, without these checks and balances, the system will not be sustainable.

Supplier Replenishment to Your Warehouse

Once you have your PFEP completed and your warehouse set up for pull manufacturing, you need to begin working with suppliers to deliver product, as needed, from them to the warehouse on a pull system. This sounds a little intimidating but really is a very reliable system when implemented. This system will make a significant difference in the amount of material in the warehouse and actually make the purchasing and ordering of parts easier.

The first instinct of people is that you will have an enormous amount of material to receive each day and that, "There is no way we can handle that volume of parts in a day; besides, the suppliers will charge us more freight." What people need to understand is that you are not receiving all the material every day or even every week. Because suppliers have different lead times to deliver parts to you, the volume of receipts per day will vary. Assume that you have 2000 part numbers in your warehouse; with 20 workdays to the month, you would be receiving 100 part numbers per day. But some material you buy may have a two- or three-month lead time, and I have seen longer; so with the varying lead time, the number of receipts per day will typically drop to 50 or less. As for charging higher freight cost, I have found that no one typically raises your freight costs just because of daily deliveries. That is not to say a supplier would not include some type of charge in your next negotiations to cover the extra shipping, but for the most part prices change very little, if any. A good supplier values your business and will not want to lose it over a few pennies of freight cost. Also, you implement the supplier pull systems slowly and carefully so that you do not risk shutting down production.

Getting Started

1. The best choice is to start with local suppliers, and I would start with the ones closest to your plant; that way, if you run into a problem, you can quickly run next door and get some more parts.
2. Pick four or five of your best suppliers and begin working with them. An open discussion between you and the suppliers will let them understand why you want to do this. Very rarely do you have a supplier that is reluctant to try it; and once they do, they are fine with it.
3. You should already have calculated the amount of inventory you need for each part and determined what its reorder point is. Attach a purchasing kanban card to the box that would signal your reorder point. Take a look at the example of the card in Figure 13.6 that shows a typical purchasing kanban card.

Note that the purchasing kanban card has the same information as the other cards in the system except in the "from" row. Here we identify who the

Figure 13.6   Supplier pull card.

supplier is. We can also tell you the name of the part, part number, storage location in the supermarket, the supplier, container type, and container quantity. The container type typically denotes the type of container the product is shipped in from the supplier.

4. Place the box with the card in position on the shelf so it can signal the reorder point and begin using the material on the shelf in the normal manner.
5. When you reach the box with the purchasing card, wait until you open the box to pull out the first piece and at the same time remove the purchasing card.
6. In the warehouse, create a "To-be Ordered board" (see Figure 13.7) and place it in a location in the raw material warehouse.
7. First you place the purchasing pull card in the bin with the buyer's name on it.
8. The buyer then picks up his cards, and orders the part number and quantity of the part called out on the card.

The company in the "Order Board" photograph in Figure 13.7 created twenty plastic pockets under the "Ordered" and "Today" columns on the board. Then they labeled each pocket with the names of their top twenty suppliers.

Figure 13.7 Order board.

9. The buyer then returns the cards to the board in the area marked "Ordered."
10. Warehouse personnel then look at the card to see when the parts are due in. If it is today, they place the card in the supplier's pocket under "Today"; if there is a lead time associated with the part, the cards are placed on the top line, which indicates from today how many days it is before the material is due, i.e., 3 days, 5 days, etc.
11. The cards on the top line are moved daily to show the current expected due date for the part. The cards can move forward and backward, depending on information from the buyer as to the delivery date. All cards eventually end up in the "Today" column.
12. If a card is in the "Today" column and the part does not arrive today, it is moved to the column on the far right of the board, which is the late column, and it stays there until the part arrives. This company has pockets for three days in the "Late" column; in this way, everyone from purchasing to planning to receiving knows when the material will be in.

Once the system has been introduced and is well stabilized, you can move on to the final step of the process, which is having the people in the warehouse order their own material. I can hear the cries from purchasing now as they shake their heads, "No way!" I ask you, "Why not?" The buyers have done their job; they have negotiated the contract, probably set up an annual purchase order if you are buying a lot of material from one supplier, and in the contract agreement it probably states somewhere that the material will be delivered monthly or on a request from purchasing. We have a system of pull in place with kanban cards that tells us who the supplier is and the quantity to order—it is all there on the card. Now let us eliminate one more step in the process at this time. The buyer gets the cards and calls the supplier to order the needed parts. If we create a form that the warehouse staff can input information on for what needs to be ordered and provide them with a fax machine, they can fax the request directly to the supplier and get a confirmation back as to when the parts are due to arrive.

Finished Goods Replacement

As customers pull product from the finished goods warehouse, there is an obvious need to replenish the stock. In a push system, the planning department simply cuts a new work order, usually for the quantity of product the MRP system tells them they need. They feel this is simple and easy because they have done it for so many years and it is automatic to them now. But as discussed in other chapters, this can produce large quantities of product that fill the warehouse and take up valuable real estate in the factory, not to mention the money tied up in inventory and carrying costs.

Now that you have the supermarket in the raw materials warehouse and pull manufacturing on the production floor, you need to join the finished goods warehouse to the remainder of production. Doing this is rather simple but, again, you will get push-back from people saying that it will not work. In my experience, those who have pushed back the most are those in production planning, because they feel they will not be needed and lose their jobs. They will fight back with the arguments that you need MRP to control the factory and warehouses. This simply is not true. Again, let me state that MRP is an excellent strategic planning tool but it is not needed to run the factory.

Tying Finished Goods Warehouse to the Production Floor

If you do not use MRP to replenish the finished goods warehouse, then how do you do it? The process is rather simple but, again, it takes discipline. Once again, we start simple and build upon success. Decide which products you would like to do first. You may decide on two or three if you have a large mix of products, and this is fine.

Packaging Schedule Board

Create a packaging schedule board. In our example, this company called it a "crating board" because their products were placed in crates for shipment. This board is just an example, and you can create your board any way you like. This board is rather simple; when you look at the board, you see two rows of plastic boxes with the numbers 1 through 6 at the top. These numbers for this company represent the number of products one person can crate in one shift. There are two rows: one for today's work and one for tomorrow's work.

How to Use the Packaging Schedule Board

To begin using the packaging schedule board, you need to go to the warehouse and place a kanban tag ovn the materials in stores. The company in the example produces large machines used in the medical field and had about seventy crates in the warehouse, so they placed a kanban card on each one of them (Figure 13.8). Because there were three different product types, they used three different-colored cards. You will find these products labeled on the schedule board. In the bottom-left corner, you find three boxes labeled "A," B," and "C" to indicate the three products this company produced. In the bottom-right corner is another box labeled "Build" (see Figure 13.9).

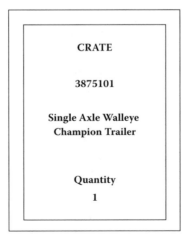

CRATE

3875101

**Single Axle Walleye
Champion Trailer**

**Quantity
1**

Figure 13.8   Crating kanban card.

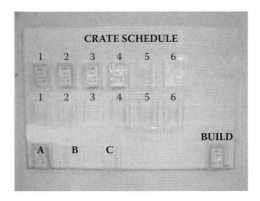

Figure 13.9   Crate Schedule board.

Sequence of Operation

1. When the finished goods warehouse ships a product to the customer, the finished goods material handlers remove the kanban tag.
2. The finished goods material handler places the kanban tag in a designated pick-up location in the warehouse.
3. The material route runner picks up the tags and delivers them to the packaging schedule board and places each card in the corresponding plastic bin for each color. Color coding is used to simplify the process and eliminate mistakes.
4. At the end of the day, you can have the operator in the packaging department, or the planning department, place the cards in the bins numbered 1 through 6 for the next day. The company in the example has a takt rate of ninety minutes per product for product "A"; we should see five cards per day for product "A."
5. The next day, the crating operators complete the packaging of a product by removing the color-coded card from the plastic bins numbered 1 through 6 and place it on the finished product. At the same time, they pick up a build card (Figure 13.10) and place it in the second row of plastic bins directly under the bin that was just emptied so you can see what needs to be built the next day.
6. Planning or a material route runner picks up the build cards (Figure 13.10) at the end of the day and takes them to the Build Schedule board for each product line.
7. On the product lines' Build Schedule board (Figure 13.11) for product "A," they place the cards in the "In" bin.

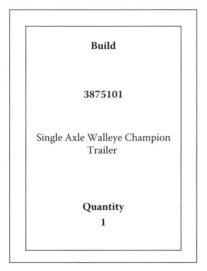

Figure 13.10   Build card.

Figure 13.11   Build Schedule board.

8. Planning, or the production supervisor, then places the cards from the "In" bin into the bins numbered 1 through 5, beginning with bin 1. If there are more cards remaining, they place these in bins 6 and 7; and if there are still cards left over, they are placed in the "Queue" bin.

9. When production begins, the first work cell takes the card out of the furthest left-hand bin with a card in it and places the card with the product to be built. As the day progresses, each time a new product is begun, the kanban card for that product is again removed from the

furthest-left bin, thus moving from left to right all day long until they have finished the required production for the day.

10. Any cards left in the queue bin are placed in the "Build" bins first.
11. The "Build Schedule" board (Figure 13.11) is placed at the pacesetter cell so it can schedule the entire line.
12. When the product reaches the end of the assembly line, it is ready for packaging.
13. When packaging begins to package the product, they remove the production build kanban tag and place it on the packaging schedule board in the "Build" bin.

Before you can proceed, you need to create a build schedule board for each of your production lines. The one shown in Figure 13.11 is an example of what one might look like. In this example, the company builds an average of five products per day, so they have five plastic bins in a black square with each bin numbered 1 through 5. Note that they also have two bins in another square market, number 6 and 7. You cannot see it but the square is red in color, denoting that anything above five products per day is abnormal. Okay, the obvious question then becomes: Why are the bins numbered backward from 7 to 1? The answer: to indicate how many products are left to be built on that day or during a shift.

We have now completed the entire build and packing scheduling route using just kanban cards and no work orders. If you are using work orders to back-flush inventory, then place those with the build card at the pacesetter cell. Then you can begin production and let the work order follow with the card to packing where it can be removed and keyed into the MRP system.

Chapter 14

Standardized Problem-Solving Method

Problem Solving

We find standardization in all areas of Lean manufacturing, so it does not come as a surprise that there is also standardization in problem solving. Common sense is what drives us to do many things, including problem solving. Many times in problem solving we jump to a fix for the problem based on our past experiences, better known as *gut feel*. What we really want is a problem-solving method that will apply logic rather than gut feel to correct the issue. This can be very difficult for some employees to understand. In small companies that have had some of the same employees for many years, it can be traumatic. When introducing the standardized problem-solving method, some employees will feel that you no longer trust their judgment. For these employees, you will have to spend some time working with them to accept the change; their expertise is needed as much now as ever before. They need to understand that you have created a structured approach to problem solving, one that will get to the root cause of the problem and not just patch it to have the problem return at a later time.

You can buy off-the-shelf software to help you with problem solving but it really is a matter of discipline. I have seen large companies go to great lengths to create and document their standard problem-solving methods because the system is neither complex nor difficult—you just need stated roles and discipline to make the system work. You may find that you can fix the problem quickly, while others can take a very long time. The steps are the same in any process:

Recognize You Have a Problem

You have to recognize that you have a nonconforming situation that needs to be correct. Because you have instituted standard work instructions, process cycle times, and other Lean elements, it is easy to see if you cannot meet your production goals or if you are falling behind. Consequently, problems surface quickly. Even without all the Lean elements, some problems are easily recognized. Make certain to identify in writing to the operator at what point he or she needs to escalate an issue.

Elevate to the Next Higher Level

If you are a machine operator or assembler, some problems you may be able to fix yourself—if they are within your control—while others must be elevated to the next-higher level of authority. This is done by activating the Andon device, which signals where the abnormality was found.

Evaluate the Severity of the Problem

The first thing you need to do is determine if this is an isolated problem or a significant issue. If it is an isolated problem within your control, you need only fix the problem and resume production. If the team leader who took over from the machine operator or assembler cannot fix the problem within a predetermined time frame, he or she must elevate the problem to the next level of management and so on until the problem is resolved. Each time the problem is handed off, the previous person trying to resolve the issue leaves and returns to his own work.

Control the Expansion of the Problem

Now that you have discovered the problem and identified its severity, you will want to control the spread of the problem to downstream locations on the production line or—worse—to the customer. In most cases, a stopped production line will eliminate the likelihood that the problem will spread to the customer but to be sure, you should inspect WIP (work-in-process) inventory to ensure the problem has not spread. Stopping the production line typically brings quick response to help solve the problem.

Containing the Problem

You did some containment in the previous step when you inspected WIP inventory downstream from where the problem was found. If you assume that you have now isolated the problem, then you need to investigate and find the root cause of the problem so that you can determine a proper fix. If you need to spend more time determining a permanent fix, a temporary fix may be acceptable but must be approved by management before restarting the line.

Preventing a Recurrence

Now that you have evaluated, controlled, and contained the problem, you need to prevent it from recurring, and an effective permanent fix is required. For those of you in a controlled or ISO certified company, this will mean proper verification and validation of the change to fix the problem. A temporary fix, approved for use by management, is implemented while a permanent solution is found and approved. Temporary fixes are limited to a specific time frame or number of parts.

This type of problem resolution is used for problems found with the product, manufacturing processes, office processes, etc., any place in your organization where a problem is found.

It may sound a little odd but celebrate the fact that a problem was found. I am not saying mistakes are a good thing, and we certainly do not like it when they occur, but the fact that the problem was found before getting to the customer is a terrific thing.

We have a standardized problem-resolution method and that is very good; but what if we could eliminate problems altogether? We could save large amounts of resources—from human resources to cash. In the next section we discuss mistake-proofing, which is a way to ensure that errors are caught early in the process and resolved before moving on to the next production step. If we could successfully implement such a process, we would not have to worry about problem resolution because there would not be any problems. A nice thought, but highly unlikely. But we can do something about improving our quality and catching problems early in the manufacturing process.

Inspect Every Job

As each job is completed in the factory or office, how many times does it get inspected? Quality is everyone's job, and that means everyone is a quality inspector—both of their own work and for the work they are receiving from someone else. Earlier I stated that inspection was non-value-added, but in some cases it is economically viable to do nonstandard work. If the cost of inspection on lower-level parts and assemblies will reduce or eliminate the chances of a more costly problem further downstream, then it makes sense to include the non-value-added cost to the process. This should not be taken as an open invitation to add waste to upstream processes; be very careful when adding waste and make sure it is truly needed.

In many companies both large and small, the responsibility for the inspection of parts was always with the inspection department. Through the years there has been a trend toward having machine operators and assemblers inspect their own work and, even better, let a machine tool do the inspection for them. With a small company we know that some of the automated inspection processes are too expensive.

Each operator in any size company should have the same responsibility for quality:

- Check incoming work to their work area for defects.
- Verify and ensure that the work they do is free from defects.
- *Never knowingly pass on a defective part to the next downstream process.*

Note that the last item is italicized. If an operator finds a problem with the material coming into his work cell or during processing of his work, any defect found must be corrected. His standardized work instructions should clearly state the inspection steps he should follow and, once identified and documented, the operator is held accountable for ensuring that defect-free work is delivered from his workstation and work cell. Whenever possible, inspections should be done internally to other operations, thus resulting in no wasted time between value-added operations.

At Toyota, in-process inspections are normal but are performed while an operator is moving from one workstation to another or is otherwise free to perform additional work. Toyota does do 100% inspection after major processes have been completed, such as unibody welding, painting, chassis assembly, etc. How do you ensure proper inspections are done? During one of my visits to the GM/Toyota Nummi plant, I was watching the assembly of the rear axle to the chassis frame of the car. I watched the operator install all the nuts and washer to hold the axle to the frame. I was then surprised to see him pick up a magic marker highlighter and proceed to touch and mark every single part he had put on the car. I asked what he was doing and was told he was inspecting his work. He knew how many parts he put on the car and was counting to make sure he had installed the correct number of parts. As I thought about it, that inspection process was almost identical to the one my father had taught me when I worked on cars in his auto glass repair business. First I would put all the nuts, bolts, and washers that I had removed from the car into an old ice cube tray. Then as I reassembled the car, if I had parts left over I knew I had missed something. He also taught me to go back and check each part for tightness. Although he did not call it a quality check, that is what is was, a redundant quality check because we checked twice. The Toyota and the auto glass examples show visual ways of completing inspection, and these physical methods help avoid costly mistakes.

Mistake-Proofing

We always endeavor to improve the quality of products because we want to satisfy our customers by providing a high-quality product. This is a very good reason but what if we wanted to improve quality to increase the flow of material through the factory? Is that a reasonable expectation? It certainly is, because if you want to improve the flow of material through the factory, you need to reduce product and process variation, and certainly one way to do this is to improve product quality. We know that the biggest variable in any process, where humans are present, are the human beings themselves. This is not an indictment of the human race but is intended to point out the fact that most errors are human errors; that said, machines can also make mistakes and, if not caught, can produce scrap very quickly. How do we eliminate or minimize the problem?

Poka-Yoke (means mistake-proofing in Japanese) devices are designed to either prevent a mistake from being made or to make the mistake obvious at a glance. If you can prevent workers from making a mistake by discovering and eliminating them before the error turns into a defect, you are far better off.

To aid workers in their efforts to reduce errors, methods and devices are created that attempt to minimize the possibility of ever creating an error. Figure 14.1 is a simple example of mistake-proofing. This example is from a child's toy and solves two possible areas where mistakes can happen. The

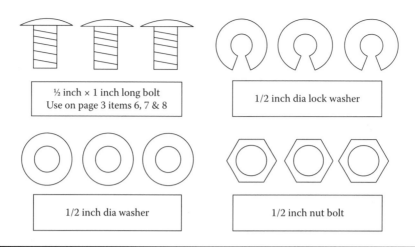

Figure 14.1   Mistake-proof card.

first area prone to errors is packaging, where someone counts out the parts and places them on a card. By showing an image of the parts, the employee can always match the quantity of parts to the quantity on the board, thus eliminating the possibility of missing parts at the customer. The second area prone to errors is when the customer assembles the toy. By adding a description of the parts, the customer knows which part he has.

Error-proofing in manufacturing is just as easy. First, the goal should be zero defects in everything we do. One of the premises of the Toyota system is "Perfection is the primary goal," and you should do anything you can to achieve this goal. Let us base our discussion on the fact that defects are preventable, and one of the ways is to control the process so that defects are impossible and if they do occur you can correct them before they become a bigger problem. Whether a mistake happens on the production floor or in the office, it creates the potential of a defect reaching the customer. Because process variation is the cause of most problems, what causes process variation?

1. *Human error:* Human error is one of the largest areas for process variation and, as a result, errors and defects occur often. We know that many things contribute to why humans cannot avoid making mistakes. Some of those reasons are
   - Distractions: Simple things, such as someone walking by or asking a question can cause you to make a mistake.
   - Mental errors: Simple lapses in memory, causing you to forget what to do next.

- Processes physically difficult to do: Physically tiring due to exertion required to perform the job (e.g., difficult work positions and locations).
- Lack of knowledge or skills: Operators who are not fully trained or lack the ability to do the job.
- Fatigue: Physically being tired due to lack of sleep, long hours of work, etc.

2. *Poor or lack of standardized work:* Experts believe that almost 85% of errors occurring in a work process are due to the tasks within the process:
   - Process steps that are not well defined.
   - Transportation: The movement of material, people, and information during the process of producing the product.
   - Decision making: Clear decision making is essential to good work methods. Every employee should ask who, what, when, and where, also how and why.
   - Inspection activities are prone to errors just like any other process, and for the same reasons.

3. *Machines and tooling:* Machine errors are either predictable or unpredictable. Preventive maintenance can usually take care of predictable errors, while unpredictable errors are caused by such things as tool breakage, sudden machine breakdowns, etc.

4. *Nonconforming material:* Material that does not meet specifications, for example, using the wrong raw material, wrong finish, wrong purchased component, etc. Designed-in errors from product development. Root cause analysis may indicate that the fault lies in manufacturing or material handling.

5. *Measurement:* To be useful, measurements must be accurate, repeatable, and reproducible. However, measuring devices and methods are just as prone to errors as any other processes that you measure.

6. *Environmental:* Many environmental conditions can cause us to make mistakes, things like excessive heat or cold, loud noises, and poor lighting affect the ability of humans to perform their work successfully.

Where Do You Start Error-Proofing?

Here are the four elements that make up mistake (error)-proofing:

1. General inspection
2. 100% inspection
3. Error-proofing devices
4. Immediate feedback

Each one is important in its own right but when put together as a system, they become a powerful tool for the elimination of errors and defects.

General Inspection

Source inspection: The first place to begin your inspection process is at the location where the product is produced. This may be a machine in your own factory or at a supplier. The earlier you catch defects, the cheaper they are to correct. The goal of source inspection is to prevent the occurrence of errors and defects. Another advantage of this type of inspection is that it provides immediate feedback to the producer of the part as to whether it is an operator or an in-house machine error or a supplier error. Some people do not believe source inspection at a supplier is of any value, but I have found having someone from my company in direct face-to-face contact with the inspection department at my supplier helps the communication of information and supplier partnership. If your suppliers are within a 50-mile radius of your plant, source inspection works fine for suppliers. When you have reached a point with your supplier that errors and defects are near zero, then you may want to consider canceling such inspections.

Informative inspections: There are two types of informative inspections: successive inspections and self-inspections.

Successive inspections are performed after each operation in the production process is completed, and the inspections are done by the employees who perform the next operational sequence. This is an excellent method used to check the work of others and provides for very quick feedback on defect information. Many times, the errors are also tracked on paper.

Self-inspections are performed by the operators at their own workstations. If they find a defect, they set aside the affected part and check to make sure that other similar parts have not been passed to the next operation with the same defect. If they find more defects, they set aside the parts and return the parts to determine the root cause of the defect and take action to ensure the problem does not recur. In some cases, they find that putting error-proofing measures and devices in place will help ensure that the problem does not return when another operator performs that particular process.

Self-inspection is the second-most effective type of inspection and is preferred over successive inspection; however, the number of errors found depends on the diligence of the operator. When practical, operators should be empowered to stop the production line to prevent more products from becoming infected with the defect.

Note: Industrial engineering studies have found that human visual inspection is only 85% effective at catching defects. Similar inaccuracies happen when humans measure any physical property. For these reasons, the use of mechanical or electronic inspection devices are recommended to achieve better accuracy (e.g., laser micrometers, go/no-go gauges, noncontact surface finish gauges, etc.).

100% Inspection

This type of inspection is sometimes called an audit check inspection. While this is the most effective type of inspection, it is also the most costly and time consuming unless included within an operation while value-added work is being performed at the same time. Because it is often physically impossible or too time consuming to perform 100% inspection of all products, we can use inexpensive error-proofing devices.

Error-Proofing Devices

Are physical devices used to detect errors? They are typically mechanical or electronic devices that are used to augment or replace the human senses. These devices also use pneumatics to physically operate these devices and fixtures. When used, these devices can achieve 100% detection and prevention of errors. Common error-proofing devices include

- Go/no-go gauges
- Guide pins
- Limit switches
- Contact sensors
- Counters
- Alarms
- Checklists

These devices can detect defects and errors while signaling the operator whether a product is good or bad. Common signaling devices include lights, buzzers, and horns.

Setting functions are incorporated into error-proofing devices when you need to check an attribute of the product, as opposed to a specification of the product. Attributes are physical characteristics of the product that cannot be defined by a specific dimension; an example of an attribute is the shine on the tile floor in your house. We can provide specific dimensions for the length, width, and height of the tile, but for the shine we might state that the floor must look shiny to the average person, *because shininess is a subjective measurement, it becomes an attribute.*

- *Fixed-value setting* inspects for a specific number of tasks, events, or items to be completed. It is common to use this type of inspection to determine if the right number of parts has been used.
- *Motion step setting* inspects a sequence of actions to be sure it was completed in the correct order.
- *Information setting* checks the accuracy of information that will be used later on work schedules, action item lists, etc., and to distribute information accurately across long distances. For example: you place a product into finished goods inventory and record the storage location that must be done accurately. Your sales computer picks up the information that you have a finished product in a specific storage location and saves it. When a customer accesses your sales web page via the Internet, she sees that the product she wants is in stock, she orders that product, and the sales computer tells the finished goods computer to ship the part.

Immediate Feedback

This is the final element used for mistake-proofing. One of the key ingredients in mistake-proofing is to supply immediate feedback to a work cell or person making a mistake so that they can fix the root cause of the problem so it does not reappear. Common feedback methods include lights or sounds to capture the operator's attention. We know that warning methods can be less effective than control methods that actually shut down production until the defect can be corrected. However, warning signals are preferred when the cost of shutting down production is expensive, such as in a processing industry where there are very long lead times and raw material can spoil.

Are zero defects possible? From our perspective, it is a completely achievable goal and many companies have reached it through the use of mistake-proofing methods and tools. The biggest barrier to achieving success in this area is the idea that it is not attainable. Here you have to change the culture and beliefs of your employees that zero defects is possible. You also need to look at this from an economic standpoint and a risk/reward standpoint.

This must be your call because you know your products and what your customers and your company are willing to accept as errors and defects.

Statistical Process Control and Mistake-Proofing

Statistical Process Control (SPC) is based on the use of mathematics and statistics to measure and solve quality problems with your product. SPC is typically used on the production floor to track the quality performance of machines and processes as a product is produced. SPC relies on the product sampling method to gather information so you are only looking at, say, one part out of every twenty produced, as an example; and you only detect errors if they exist on the part you are inspecting. It is a reliable method to indicate errors and also to track machine performance to ensure products coming off the machine are within a specific specification. SPC is a very good tool but cannot predict errors. It can reliably indicate when a machine process is moving out of specification.

Chapter 15

Working with Suppliers and Partners

Introduction

I have discussed how to restructure your company into a Lean-thinking, continuous-improvement manufacturing company, and I am sure you have had great success thus far. But now that you have your plant organized, you need to look beyond the walls of the factory and at your extended value stream, which consists of both suppliers and partners because the value stream does not end at the dock door.

Squeezing the supplier to reduce cost has run its course; you have been asking your suppliers to cut 2%, 3%, 5%, or even 10% off the cost of your products for so many years that it has just become an expectation. But you cannot continue to ask them to do this; yes, they will almost always cut their own profit to save a customer, but at what long-term cost? As your suppliers continue to lose more and more profit, at some point it has to stop and that will be when they go out of business and you, the customer, have to scramble to find a new supplier. The one bright spot in all of this is that the offshore cost savings that many companies thought they achieved by moving to places such as China, India, Vietnam, etc., are now starting to dissipate as their standard of living rises and the demand for higher wages in these countries increases. Also, many companies have found that the hidden costs of off-shoring their products have resulted in no savings at all. For these reasons it is important for small business owners to improve their operations and be in a position of taking back the work to their own country.

As a small business, you have a benefit that mid-sized and larger companies do not: If they are a publicly traded company, they are always under pressure to achieve short-term gains so they look good on the balance sheets for Wall Street every quarter, whereas you have the advantage and only need to look good to yourself and your friendly banker. This allows you to focus as much on long-term goals as it does on short term-goals. Many large companies today want to consolidate suppliers, and there is a logical rationale behind this but you do not want to consolidate suppliers to your own detriment.

Example: A large multinational company with plants on both the East and West coasts as well as in the Midwest embarked on a cost-savings program to consolidate all of its sheet metal work into one supplier on the West coast. There were remarkable savings to be had. But let us think this out: Piece part costs went down most likely due to the high volume of parts, but what about the additional cost to ship parts from California to Florida rather than across town? Also, what about all the engineering time it will take to review all the drawings and reapprove them? And what about all the time taken by the draftsmen to update the drawings? I could go on and on with the list, but you get the idea that when they began to ship parts, there were all kinds of problems on the production floor.

How much did they really save? It looked good on paper and someone's objectives were met for cost savings, but what about the overall cost to the company? Research has shown that only 50% of projects return the savings to the company that were originally protected.

Looking for Suppliers

As a manufacturer, you look for suppliers that can support you; but as a supplier to your customers, you need to support them. In both cases, what type of supplier are "you" looking for? First, you are looking for a quality supplier but there is more to a quality supplier than state-of-the-art equipment. We want to find a company with a compatible culture, one of teaching and training, one whose employees are not afraid to stop the line or raise their hands if they find a quality issue. We want a company that finds and eliminates problems through the use of continuous improvement.

Every company, whether large or small, should be looking for high-quality suppliers for a long-term relationship. If you treat your suppliers as true partners in the business, you can develop a true relationship that will result in high-quality products being produced at a low cost; and as quality improves, your rework and warranty costs go down. You must also keep in mind that the JIT (just-in-time) manufacturing system is fragile in that any weak link in the system can bring it to a stop; thus, you want strong suppliers that are capable of keeping it running. If you have a weak supplier, the health of your company is in jeopardy. The overall strength of the customer–supplier relationship is having good financial health on both sides of the equation.

Asking a supplier for a price cut is never fun but must be done on occasion. What would you do if your customer came in and asked for a 30% price cut? First, there would be shock, then fright wondering what you are going to do. This has happened to Toyota suppliers but with a twist; they are given time to figure out how to achieve their saving before the new product launches. You as a supplier are given several years to bring your costs down and receive help from the Toyota Supplier Support Center, which provides training in the Toyota Production System (TPS). My point here is that you as a user of Lean principles and tools can ask for similar cost reductions but you have to be willing to help achieve the goal. It is important to remember that in order to help your supplier and customers, you must have a true understanding of the TPS. By helping your suppliers and customers learn and use the TPS, they, too, can achieve significant cost savings.

Seven Characteristics of Supplier–Customer Partnering

Toyota has defined what it calls the "seven characteristics of supplier partnering" and from my experience these seven characteristics also apply to your relationship with your customers.

Going from the bottom of the pyramid to the top (Liker and Meir, 2006):

1. *Mutual understanding and trust:* All relationships take time, and they all start with understanding what each member needs out of the relationship. It is important for the upper management of both companies to meet and determine each other's needs. As the customer in most cases, Toyota has found that by going and meeting the supplier at their

location (go see), they can truly understand the suppliers and their capability. For the relationship to get off the ground on the right foot, you need to put in your time and go see your supplier or go see your customer, whichever you are at the time. You want to find honest, reliable suppliers and customers with whom you can build your company.

2. *Interlocking structures:* One thing that has become easier in recent years is the ability to transfer information electronically and to have an interlocking structure with your supplier and customers. As part of an interlocking system that can continually provide you with raw material, you need redundant systems to back up your main supplier of a product. You should never sole-source unless there is a very good reason to do so—and those reasons are very few. Think of sole sourcing similar to investing all your retirement money into one stock; that is taking a lot of risk. Toyota always has two or three suppliers for each part, and each supplier gets the business for a specific car. Suppliers keep the business over the life of the product or until a new version of the car is introduced; then they have to bid for the work all over again.

Be careful with some customers who think they understand Lean because they might try and make you carry large quantities of inventory for them. They should understand that you are a Lean shop and will not carry three, four, or six months' worth of inventory for them. Not only is it costly to you, but it also uses up valuable floor space.

Good customers are always nice to have, especially if they keep your shop busy and pay their bills on time, but you also need to be careful that they do not control your shop. There is the theory that if a customer can control over 50% of your production capacity, they control you and some companies subscribe to this theory. There is nothing wrong with telling the customer that it is company policy to not overload your shop or theirs with only one or two customers.

3. *Control systems:* When you visit your suppliers, ask to see some of their key performance data; things like on-time delivery and quality are two good places to start. The charts should show their performance over a given period of time because you do not want just the information for today.

Have you ever worked with a company that uses target pricing as a way to set the selling price of their product? This is a form of price control and if a company uses it, they will try and dictate the price they will pay you for a given part. They have already determined they need that specific price for that component and that is how they can meet their target selling price for their product. Very few companies have ever developed their ability to predict what you the supplier should charge for a part and still allow you a decent profit. A good customer will understand if you have done everything you can to try and meet your target goal but cannot.

4. *Compatible capabilities:* As you develop your relationship with your supplier or customer, you need to become an integral part of their organization, working in lockstep with them. If you are the customer, you want your supplier to be technically capable of helping you design new product, and the same holds true for you as a supplier to your customers. You need to develop your company with excellent technical staff so you can help you customer; simultaneous engineering will continue to become more and more important as development cycles for you and your customers become shorter and shorter.

5. *Information sharing:* Do not be afraid to share information with your suppliers; the more information you can provide them, the better they can support you in your efforts to produce a quality product. Toyota is at such a high level of information sharing and supplier relationships that they actually have suppliers design parts of the car for them based on their specifications. Developing excellent computer systems that are easily interfaced with most customers and suppliers, along with developing your in-house talent skills, will help make you a better supplier.

6./7. *Joint improvement activities, and Kaizen and learning:* As you move up the hierarchical pyramid and your relationship with your suppliers and customers becomes more trusting, it is a good time to begin joint improvement activities because your supplier has certain skills and you may have slightly different skills, and the combination of the two can make for a potent continuing improvement activity. We are not just talking about the elimination of waste, but also the improvement of quality both for your product and theirs. If there is a problem with a supplier's component, you contact them, tell them the issue, and hope they can fix it. If you are a large enough company, you might send a quality control engineer to visit the company and help them fix it. Have you ever had a custom-designed part that was manufactured by two different companies and both companies had issues with building the part? What do you do? Here is an excellent example of a joint improvement activity.

Example of joint improvement activity: A product was being produced at a large medical device company; the component in question was a very critical but highly complex machined part. The part was machined from a large aluminum ingot with dimensions of about 20 × 12 × 4 inches. This highly complex part took more than three hours to machine completely. Both suppliers had exactly the same machining center, programmed by the same person from the same print revision. The problem was that a lot from supplier A would work and a lot from supplier B would not. Then when supplier A's parts did not work, supplier B's would and we were able to keep production running. But why the difference occurred was the topic of many meetings between the suppliers and us. I asked purchasing to bring in both suppliers at the same time but they refused to do so because it would not be ethical. Eventually, they gave in and the two suppliers arrived to discuss the problem. We spent a long, nine-hour day reviewing and discussing the piece part drawing and machining problems. We were even fortunate to have the creator of geometric tolerancing at the meeting, as one of our engineers knew him. By the end of the day, changes had been made to the drawing and both suppliers went back to update their machines and we have never had a problem with that part again—both suppliers provided it flawlessly. That is an excellent example of joint improvement activities and none of the companies involved found it uncomfortable.

My point here: Do not be afraid to take a risk even if the establishment says it will not work because things are always changing.

Outsourcing Products

Outsourcing a product is more complex than one might think. Over the years, companies have used a variety of ways to determine if outsourcing is a good idea for a component. They always return to the standard make-versus-buy decision analysis, which boils down to, "Can we save money?" Over the years I have been approached by purchasing departments within companies I have worked for and they have wanted to outsource a component or assembly because a supplier said it could save them money. There is no question you could, in most cases, save money but it is important to be careful when outsourcing any part of your product. You have to make a rational decision on what the core competency of your company is, what are the core competencies on your manufacturing floor, and then retain these competencies; you should never transfer a core competency to an outside supplier. The core competency expertise you have is what differentiates you from your competition. If you should decide to transfer some of your knowledge to a supplier, never transfer all the core knowledge or the responsibility for that knowledge outside. If you do not have the competency inside the company to control the technology, a supplier can control you.

Example of outsourcing: One company I worked for had a product that used ultrasonic technology as the key ingredient in its product. They were not experts at ultrasonics and for that reason they farmed out the design and build of the component to an outside supplier that had the technology and skill to produce the product. This supplier was smart enough never to give away all of his knowledge to the company where I worked. In fact, they were the last supplier to sign a release before the company I worked for was sold. The supplier held up the sale for a week while its representatives negotiated with the buyer to sign the release; that is how much power they held over the company.

As a small company, you do not have all the resources it takes to develop a supplier, so it is even more important that you pick good, competent, financially secure suppliers that have a lot of technical expertise and can help you if there is a problem.

I have worked for many companies and with suppliers in many countries, and it has been my experience that chasing the cheap price around the world is never a good idea. The only place I have found where it does work to a large extent is in the toy industry, but even companies in the toy industry maintain offices in or near countries where they are producing product so if there is a problem, they can quickly visit the plant to correct the issue. Also, in most cases, they speak the language of the country, which dramatically aids in communication.

Group Suppliers by Capability

One of the things Toyota does is to group its suppliers by capability. This is very similar to a process called "group technology," which was developed in the 1950s. The system works as follows: First, determine the skill level and capability of the suppliers you would like to use. Look at types of material, typically processes, tolerances they can hold, and finishes they can produce. Is the supplier more capable at producing round parts with a lathe or square blocks with a machining center? What is the supplier's core competency— turning, machining, working with castings, etc.? A lot of this information can be gathered on a plant visit to the supplier. Next, group your parts by drawings based on geometric shape, material, tightest tolerances, surface finish, and coating. Now, cross-reference the suppliers and the part groups to see which parts should be with which suppliers. You will most likely have to move around parts between suppliers but in the end you will have your parts with suppliers that have the core competency to produce them very successfully. You will find that the quality of the parts will go up, thereby reducing problems and scrap and increasing product quality.

Chapter 16

Lean Accounting

Show Me the Money

One of the areas of business that always seems to be one of the last to implement Lean principles is the accounting and finance area. I have tried to determine why this is by discussing it with people I know in finance and even my own son-in-law, who is a CPA and an assistant controller for a very large corporation. The most common theme I hear is that, "We have to conform to the accounting rules set forth by GAAP (General Accepted Accounting Principles)." I may take a simplistic approach to this thought process but to me the requirements set forth in GAAP are similar in nature to those set forth by the ISO, the FDA, and other controlling and regulatory bodies. There is nothing in Lean management accounting that would violate any of these principles. In an effort to remove waste from your company, I want to discuss a company I know and have read about. The company is Lantech, Inc., and they produce automated packaging machines. I have purchased equipment from them and was intrigued by their approach to "leaning out" their accounting and finance departments.

The book *Real Numbers* by Jean Cunningham and Orest Fiume presents a new model for managerial accounting. The old model, which has been in place for some seventy years, has needed a facelift for many years, just like most old houses. It is time to modernize the accounting function, a function that makes managerial accounting a partner in business rather than just a scorekeeper. Cunningham and Fiume (2003) present a model that provides timely information that is easily understood and assimilated to quickly make decisions in this ever-changing world of business. As more and more companies become intertwined due to shorter supply chains and quicker turnaround of material, the need to make quick, well-informed decisions becomes more critical. They suggest that "what accounting should do is produce an unadulterated mirror of the business—an uncompromised truth on which everyone can rely." In their book they offer a reason why managerial accounting must change and a guide by which to change it.

Performance Goals

You establish performance goals so that you can track whether you are gaining or losing ground to your objectives; therefore, the goals and tracking measures should be very carefully selected to clearly reflect what is critical to your success. Many of you may have been taught management by objectives (or MBO). This form of performance goal tends to make you focus on what you as individuals need to accomplish for self-satisfaction and survival within the company. These types of goals make you silo thinkers, thinking only about your own goals and thus creating sub-optimization within companies.

What is sub-optimization? "Sub-optimization occurs when different subunits (department) each attempt to reach a solution that is optimal for that unit, but that may not be optimum for the organization as a whole" (Siegel and Shim, 2005)

For example, a purchasing department has a goal of reducing material costs by 10%, this being accomplished by buying large quantities of material all at one time to obtain a price break. This goal is directly opposite to the production and warehouse managers' goals to reduce inventory and floor space by 5%. The warehouse cannot meet its goal; in fact, the warehouse incurs more cost to inventory and more physical material, thus offsetting the purchasing department's goals.

A disconnect between objective goals and strategic goals is common when the two are not directly tied to each other. An objective goal is an actionable goal, one that you would find on the department-level Lean road map, whereas a strategic goal is the next higher-level goal and would be found on the plant- or division-level Lean roadmap.

We know that people will strive to achieve a goal when it is presented to them, especially if it is tied to their annual performance review. Therefore, if an objective goal is well established and linked correctly to strategic goals without conflicting goals between departments, then your success rate at accomplishing Lean will be very high.

If Lean systems and methodology are used in your company correctly, then the "make-the-month" mentality will be eliminated. How can you tell if you have a "make-the-month" mentality? Look at your shipments; if 25% or more of your shipments fall within the last week of the month, then you have a "make-the-month" mentality. When you use continuous improvement to investigate why this happens, you will find that delays in manufacturing with material availability, quality problems, equipment availability, etc. have contributed to delays. As a result, many times overtime is paid in the last half of the month to meet shipping or master scheduling numbers.

If your CEO or plant manager can use customer service levels and inventory turns as the only two metrics they watch, then you have achieved a high level of success with Lean production. Why? Because if you have reached this level, you have attained a very high level of customer satisfaction and high inventory turnover rates. This indicates that you have eliminated a lot of waste in your systems and created high velocity through your production areas, which allow for on-time delivery of product to the customer. Because you have high velocity through production, you must have improved your quality significantly, which also adds to customer satisfaction.

Box Scores

Similar to a baseball or football game, you can use the "box score method" for tracking your progress to goals. And like these scores, they are after the fact, after the run is scored and the touchdown made, so these are called visual measures and, in accounting terms, "lagging indicators." They are lagging indicators because they show what has happened and not what is expected to happen. Ideally, you will have both lagging and leading indicators in your measures. A leading indicator is one that allows you to more easily predict the future and adjust quickly to resolve issues.

Table 16.1 shows the difference between leading and lagging indicators, and their relationship to each other. You can see that if you have an hourly production report showing results to your daily production plan, you can adjust quickly if you see a problem that endangers meeting the daily production goal. The same holds true for the daily-versus-weekly report and the weekly-versus-monthly report. See Chapter 10 for visual controls and visual measures.

Table 16.1   Leading and Lagging Indicator Chart

Leading Indicator	Lagging Indicator
Hourly production report	End-of-day production report
Daily production report	End-of-week production report
Weekly production report	End-of-month production report

There are several things to consider when developing your goals:

1. Is visually simple to understand
2. Shows a trend line
3. Is easy to update
4. Measure results to your goal
5. Measure the process, not people
6. Measure what you must, not what you can (this means you should not spend your time measuring what is irrelevant but measure what is important)
7. Goals must be motivational in nature
8. Mostly nonfinancial in nature (most people in production do not find financial goals relevant)

When creating goals, you must be careful to structure the goal so that it is clear, understandable, and cannot be manipulated.

Example of setting goals: The raw material warehouse has a goal to process and place on the shelf any material that arrives. Their goal is to have the material on the shelf within one hour of arrival, and the goal states first-to-arrive, first-on-the-shelf. This is a clear goal. On the other hand, the shipping department has a goal to ship 100 boxes per day. This is not a clear goal because it allows the people in shipping to decide between many small shipments or one large shipment. What will they do? You are right: many small shipments so their numbers look good and their productivity is artificially inflated, while some orders get delayed because they are in large boxes.

Three basic cost formulae used in accounting are

1. Price − Cost = Profit
2. Profit = Price − Cost
3. Price = Cost + Profit

From a mathematical standpoint, all three formulae are used to calculate the profit you need in your company and are mathematically correct; nonetheless, each has a somewhat different meaning when it comes to how you look at cost and profit.

Let us assume that your accountant says that profit is price minus cost, which is the most common statement. This means he is looking at cost as a variable; and if we can reduce cost by eliminating waste, we will create more profit for the company. A product costing $50 with a price of $100 gives us a profit of $50; but if we can reduce the cost by 10%, we can have an additional profit of $5, thus making our profit $55 while not increasing our sales price. The first place companies look to reduce cost is labor, and it seems like they always attack production labor costs first, as it is obviously directly tied to product cost. But because most of the cost of any product is material, typically 60 to 80%, this leaves very little cost to save in labor. If we look again at our product cost of $50, and we take an estimate of 70% material cost, that leaves us with 30% in other cost. Therefore, we have only $15 of cost to work with. Let us assume that the typical product has 12% labor cost and this amounts to $1.80 of cost, leaving $13.20 of fixed and variable costs. If a typical variable cost is 40% of cost, that equals $6; then $7.20 is fixed cost. If we look at it another way: 88% of a product's "cost" is not related to direct product labor costs. This shows that most of the available wasted cost that can be removed will be found somewhere other than direct labor and material. We can attack material costs, but close to 90% of material cost is "designed in by the development engineers," and we also know this is very difficult to change.

$35.00 material cost
 $6.00 variable cost
 $7.20 fixed cost
 $1.80 labor cost
$50.00 product cost

However, as you can see by this example, focusing on material and variable and fixed costs should provide the most optimized cost-savings approach, and by utilizing Lean manufacturing principles you can effectively reduce all these costs over time. Look at your labor and variable costs and consider what you have learned in this book about value-added and non-value-added costs. If you can reduce your labor and variable costs by 50%, then you can save $3.90, which is the result of removing non-value-added waste from the system.

What You Get for Your Effort

Let us assume that you have worked hard using Lean to reduce your costs. What benefit is it financially to you and the business? I remember talking to a friend of mine who was consulting with a small company when he told the owner of the company that he would forgo his consulting fee if he did not save the company twice his weekly fee for a kaizen event, which was focused on material reduction. When the week was over, his fee was $12,000; he had saved the company over $38,000 just in one week. The owner of the company was amazed and stated that the money saved would go directly to profit for his company, plus he saved interest costs on the money he would have had to borrow to cover the inventory carrying cost.

Another example is Wiremold Corporation, which in less than two years of Lean implementation had freed up over $11 million in cash. The company used the money to fund growth through acquisitions rather than needing to fund inventory. For you the small business owner in a tight money market, this can be an excellent way to internally finance growth.

Profit and Loss (Income) Statements

When using Lean systems, you need an accounting tool that can easily show the effects of your efforts with Lean. For the small business, where the owner is heavily involved, it may be easy to see the effects of the changes, whereas with a slightly larger company, it becomes somewhat more difficult. Simply presenting your financial information in a different way can provide meaningful data that can show where the waste is present and must be reduced. The profit-and-loss statement (P&L statement) in Table 16.2 has been redone to provide ease of reading and understanding.

In this example we have assumed that the factory has been restructured into "value streams," which is the desired way to structure a Lean factory, but you could create your P&L statement using product lines, customers, or any other method you feel allows you to easily understand the location of waste within your system. Lean manufacturing is about making waste visible, and restructuring the P&L statement, as we have done, is designed to do the same. We all know accountants and CPAs understand what goes into each element of a financial report. We as laymen sometimes forget what is included in the elements because we may only look at them once a month. In an effort to

Table 16.2 Profit and Loss Statement for Value Stream Product Line "1"

	This Year	*Last Year*	*% Change*
Net Sales	**$550,000**	**500,000**	**9.1%**
Cost of Sales			
Purchases: raw material	$31,500	42,500	
Inventory material increase (decrease)	$7,200	(8,000)	
Total Material Costs	**$38,700**	**34,500**	**10.9%**
Production Costs			
Hourly wages	$20,200	20,000	1.0%
Salaried wages	$12,000	10,000	16.7%
Benefits (hourly and salaried personnel)	$12,880	9,900	23.1%
Operating supplies	$6,100	6,000	1.6%
Material Scrap:			
Raw material	$1,500	2,500	−66.7%
WIP material	$1,575	3,200	−103.2%
Finished goods	$250	2,000	−700.0%
Total Production Costs	**$54,505**	**53,600**	**1.7%**
Building and Equipment Usage Cost			
Building Services (utilities + taxes)	$3,800	3,500	7.9%
Building Depreciation	$1,000	1,000	0.0%
Equipment Depreciation	$2,300	2,200	4.3%
Total Building and Equipment Usage Cost	**$7,100**	**6,700**	**5.6%**
Total Manufacturing Cost - Value Stream "1"	**$100,305**	**94,800**	**5.5%**
Inventory Carryover from Last Reporting Period	**$6,000**	**(6,000)**	
Cost of Sales	**$106,305**	**88,800**	**16.5%**
Gross Profit	**$443,695**	**411,200**	
Gross Profit %	**19.3%**	**0**	
Accounting Notes: Inventory carryover accounts for inventory built in the last reporting period but not sold during that period.			

help those of us who are not fluent in accounting jargon, I have tried to make the document easier to read by adding some additional information. (I should note here that I am not an accountant but do have some knowledge of financial accounting practices. That said, to the best of my ability I have tried to conform to GAAP requirements for this form. Data used in an official form for your company should meet all GAAP requirements.)

First, we constructed our P&L statement to reflect the performance of one product value stream. We did this to separate the costs directly associated with product "1"; in this way we get a very clear picture of what it costs to make the product. It also allows us to reflect on the wasteful areas this product may have. Anyone who works in or directly supports the value stream for product "1" is accounted for here. I would suggest a separate sheet for each product you build. You should have already done a current value stream map and by looking at it and the P&L statement together, you will have an excellent idea of the status and health of the value stream for that product. Let us break down the profit and loss:

- Cost of sales: This section remains the same as a standard P&L statement, except we add clarification as to what the *purchases* are (i.e., raw material).
- Production costs: This section refers to what it has actually cost us to process raw material into a finished product. Each line item below this is more definitive than what you would find in a standard report.
- Hourly wages: Anyone who is direct or indirect labor, needed to run the production floor, warehouse, quality inspection, planning, purchasing, technicians, and draftsman; include office personnel supporting the value stream, etc.
- Salaried wages: Anyone who is exempt (e.g., managers, engineers, purchasing, etc.).
- Benefits: These are the combined health, vacation, life insurance, etc., benefits for both hourly and salaried personnel.
- Operating supplies: Costs associated with expendable material used on the production floor (e.g., cutting oils, glues, hand wipes, uniform cleaning, etc.).
- Material scrap:
  - Raw material: any raw material scrapped before being used.
  - WIP material: any material that is currently in the process of transformation from raw material to finished product.
  - Finished goods material: any material that has been placed in the finished goods warehouse.

■ Building and equipment usage costs: These are costs typically allocated to the value stream based on square footage of factory space used. I like to include office space as well, which is directly attributed to the value stream.
  – Building services: utilities, maintenance department, computer services, taxes, etc.
  – Building depreciation: this is self-explanatory.
  – Equipment depreciation: any capital equipment used to produce the products in value stream product "1."
■ Total carryover from last reporting period: This is the cost of inventory that was produced in the last reported period shown on the P&L statement but not sold. This cost of product must be transferred to the current reporting period.
■ Cost of sales: This is the "Total manufacturing cost + Total carryover from last report."
■ Gross profit: This is "Net sales – Cost of sales."
■ Gross profit %: This is " 1 – (Net sales/Cost of sales)."

As we look at the P&L statement in Table 16.2, we can easily see that first sales are up by 9.1% and we have had good growth in sales. When we look at total material cost, it is obvious that an additional 10.9% of material was purchased and carried at the end of the year in support of the sales growth shown for the year.

Processing costs show some very interesting changes (Table 16.2). Hourly wages have stayed consistent from last year even though sales are up, which indicates that the hourly staff has been more productive this year than last, which is a result of efforts at leaning out the factory. We see a jump of 16.7% for the salaried wages, which is most likely due to a new person we added. If we examine further, we know that the typical raise at the beginning of the year was 3.5%; part of the increase is due to raises given to current employees and the remainder must be the new person we hired. But is that extra percentage difference reasonable? Go ahead and talk with accounting to see if that makes sense. If it does not, we need to look at what has caused the extra cost: Is it waste we can eliminate? The benefits line item shows a very large increase from last year at 23.1% and is a warning signal for us to check with the human resources department to see why this has taken such a jump. Is there an opportunity to perform a continuous improvement kaizen event here? The line item for service and supplies has stayed relatively constant with last year; as a result, there is no need to look further here.

The material scrap section of the P&L statement (Table 16.2) shows some very significant changes from last year in each of the scrap areas. Our efforts at implementing Lean practices on the production floor are beginning to pay off. We see very nice reductions in raw and WIP inventory scrap, and we suspect that is due to fewer mistakes by our operators. If we compare it to the increased productivity shown in our "Hourly wages" line item, we can assume the following: better standardized work instructions have led to reduced assembly errors, which in turn led to improved productivity because we do not need to stop the production line as often to handle mistakes. The very significant reduction in finished goods scrap is also tied to our productivity and quality improvements because we have not scrapped finished goods due to product quality issues. We have not had to scrap as much finished goods due to product obsolescence because we build and ship product quicker than we did last year, thanks to the Lean manufacturing ability to reduce product lead times.

When we look at building and equipment usage costs, we see that there has been a slight (5.6%) increase but we know building taxes and utility costs have gone up, and that we are on an accelerated depreciation plan for our equipment, and we expected that cost to go up as well—thus no surprises here.

We have a good understanding of our value stream costs and areas to look at for continuous improvement but we saw a 9.1% growth in sales and a 1.1% drop in profit. The company owner has just called us. He said, "This Lean thing is not working. You told me it would save money, improve operations, make us more competitive, and increase profits, but profits have dropped. I don't know what has happened but I need to get rid of that Lean stuff because it is costing us too much money."

What is the problem here? Production is doing fine, costs have been held the same even with an increase in production demand, inventory turns are up and scrap from poor quality has taken a wonderful downturn, productivity is up, and we generated more cash because gross profit is up. In an old-style P&L statement, our answer to the question would be hidden somewhere deep in the numbers and would take the accounting department days to find if it were a large complex company. But with the use of the simpler P&L statement, the answer is visible but probably needs to be explained to laymen.

Look at the line item in Table 16.2 called "Inventory Carryover from Last Reporting Period"; notice that last year we saw an increase of $6000 in inventory and this year we show a decrease in inventory of $6000. Follow this through carefully, as it can be confusing:

- Last year we were building inventory.
- The inventory left over from last year was capitalized and placed on this year's P&L statement as an asset. This we have to do to satisfy GAAP.
- The left-over inventory from last year is expensed as it is sold during the current year.
- "In years when inventory is increased, that period's profits are enhanced by moving costs out of the profit and loss statement and on to the balance sheet" (Cunningham and Fiume, 2003, p. 113).
- "In a year when inventory is decreased, which happens rapidly during the Lean transformation, those periods are penalized by having to recognize this charge for past years' expenses in addition to the current ones" (Cunningham and Fiume, 2003, p. 113).

If the company management is still using financial reports based on the standard cost formats, they will have problems understanding that you are truly succeeding in improving costs. Until the accounting department changes these reports to truly reflect the impact of Lean, you will have to explain things many times until people truly understand the results.

Cash-to-Cash Cycle

Lean looks at all manufacturing and business processes as a combination of value-adding flows and activities comprised of people, material, and information. In the case of accounting, we are working mostly with the flow of information. In all cases, the value-adding activities culminate when the customer's needs are satisfied. There are many things that make the stream work, such as machines, material, people, and *cash*. Cash is used to support and enable production; and if cash is in short supply, just like machines without sufficient capacity, it will be difficult to meet the customer's needs.

We know how to measure whether people, material, and equipment are operating Lean and the methods used to measure this success are well known and documented, but how to measure whether your cash-to-cash cycle is operating *Lean* is not as well known. We need to answer two questions:

1. How do you measure if you are operating Lean with regard to cash?
2. How does implementing Lean improvements on the production floor free cash so it is value adding?

Before going any further, let us define what the cash-to-cash cycle is:

The cash-to-cash cycle is a financial ratio that shows how long a company has to finance its own inventory. It measures the number of days between the time the company pays its suppliers and the time it receives cash from its customers.

There have been some studies that indicate good performance on the cash-to-cash ratio has been associated with improved earnings per share. Some people refer to this cycle saying, "Your cash is out of reach," which means that cash is not available to expand the business in any way.

One way to keep this idea in your mind is to think of inventory as a sponge; and just as a sponge absorbs water, inventory absorbs cash.

Calculate Cash-to-Cash Cycle

First, calculate the components of the equation. (Note: The inventory and receivables equation results refer to "days cash is locked up" and unpaid bills refer to "days cash is free because the business has not paid its bills." Due to space limitations on this page, we have had to remove this information from the right-hand side of the equation.)

$$\frac{\text{Average dollar value of inventory during reporting period}}{\dfrac{\text{Cost of goods sold}}{\text{Number of days in reporting period}}} = \text{Inventory}.$$

$$\frac{\text{Average dollar value of accounts receivable during reporting period}}{\dfrac{\text{Sales}}{\text{Number of days in reporting period}}} = \text{Receivables}.$$

$$\frac{\text{Average dollar value of accounts payable during reporting period}}{\dfrac{\text{Sales}}{\text{Number of days in reporting period}}} = \text{Unpaid bills}.$$

Example: Table 16.3 provides balance sheet data to be used in the example; we have shown the dollar amounts in "hundreds" for easy calculation.

Table 16.3   Balance Sheet

Balance Sheet			Profit and Loss Statement	
	November 1	November 30		
Accounts receivable	$800	$1,200	Sales	$2,000
Raw and finished goods inventory	$1,000	$600	Cost of goods sold	−$1,400
Accounts payable	−$600	−$200	Gross margins	$600

$$\text{Inventory} - \text{Average number days} = \frac{(\$1000 + \$600)/2}{\dfrac{\$1400}{30}} = \frac{\$800}{46.67} = 17.14 \text{ days.}$$

$$\text{Receivables} - \text{Average number days uncollected} = \frac{(\$800 + \$1200)/2}{\dfrac{\$2000}{30}}$$

$$= \frac{\$1000}{66.67} = 14.99 \text{ days.}$$

$$\text{Days cash is free*} = \frac{(-\$600 + -\$200)/2}{\dfrac{\$2000}{30}} = \frac{-\$400}{66.67} = -5.99 \text{ days.}$$

* Days cash is free because the business has not paid bills.

Review the calculations shown and note which values came from the balance sheet (Table 16.3) and which came from the P&L statement (Table 16.2). Also note that we used thirty (30) days for our time period on the balance sheet, and in the receivables and days cash is free equations; we divided the upper half of the equation by 2 because we were looking for the average between the two numbers. Now all we need to do is total the answer in days to find our cash-to-cash cycle (Table 16.4).

The final analysis of the data (see Table 16.4) shows us that we have 26.14 days in our cash-to-cash cycle. In Table 16.4 we add inventory and receivables then minus days cash is free to get the best cash-to-cash cycle, which means we have our operating capital unavailable for 26 days because it is tied up in inventory and accounts receivable. If we can reduce the

Table 16.4 Cash-to-Cash Cycle

Inventory – average number of days	17.14 days
Receivables – average number of days uncollected	14.99 days
Days cash is free because the business has not paid its bills	−5.99 days
Cash-to-cash cycle	26.14 days

number of days our cash is tied up, we will have more money to grow the company.

In a true Lean system there is no waste at all in the value stream. Goods and services are not produced or shipped until the customer demand is activated by purchasing the product. It should be noted that you can even have a negative cash-to-cash cycle time, but that would mean the company is doing something with the customers or suppliers that is inconsistent with Lean principles.

A proper evaluation of your cash-to-cash cycle time ratio is important, and the numbers we have just calculated are only part of the information needed to determine how Lean and successful your company is. Knowing whether you are doing better or worse with your cash-to-cycle time as compared to other companies in your industry is vital information. Financial ratios are available from companies such as Dun and Bradstreet, Standard and Poor's Corporation, RMA Risk Management, and the Federal Trade Commission. Looking at multiple cycles of your data is better than just one point; that is, month to month, quarter to quarter, and year to year are all standard ways to look at financial data. Get a copy of your accounts payable aging report from your accounting department. It shows the distribution of payables based on different time intervals, that is, 31 to 45 days, 46 days to 60 days, etc. In almost all situations, there should not be any unpaid bills for longer than 45 days; if there are, you can consider that you are using your supplier's cash to help augment your operating capital.

To improve your cash-to-cash cycle time, begin by reducing inventory and increasing inventory turns while at the same time holding a continuous improvement (kaizen) event to find the hidden waste in the order-to-cash cycle. The more you can do to improve the cycle, the more cash you will have to grow the business. Lean business and manufacturing systems and principles will lead to a more efficient and growing company.

Chapter 17

Achieving a Higher Level of Lean

Culture Change: Learning to Stop and Fix the Problem

Is Lean transformation a cultural change? Yes! You will have to deal with lots of politics as you move through your transformation. The dissension level you go through will be directly related to how much politics there are in your organization. We hope your company is one in which reason rules and a common goal is shared by everyone, and they are all working toward that goal. However, in reality, that is rarely the case. The more irrational the methods of management, the more politics you must deal with.

Politics happen when you have different people with differing views, values, and agendas in your life. This can be found in the workplace, at church, and in organizations to which you belong. If a person has his own view of a situation, particularly in an organization, we call it vision. Vision in most cases refers to what you want something to look like in the future. When you have people who embrace your vision, you are in harmony with them and they will support your actions to achieve that vision. On the other hand, when people have varying views on a subject, opposition can arise in the form of roadblocks, either physical or political in nature. How much support or push-back you get for your vision really depends on how open your organization is to accepting new ideas and the change that goes with them.

Politics is all about power and the ability to get things done even against the wills of others. But what we need to facilitate change in a company is "leadership." We have many managers who do things right, but a true leader does the right thing for their organization and employees. True leadership can energize an organization to do great Lean improvements. At Toyota, they say, "We do great things with ordinary people," as opposed to the General Electric approach of "top grading," where they keep only the best and the brightest in the company. Although both companies are excellent examples of their own philosophy, I tend to like Toyota's idea better, as I believe there are a lot more "ordinary people" in this world than there are high achievers. Why not use a system in your company that allows you to become a highly efficient learning company, willing to listen to and implement the ideas of the ordinary people who have excellent ideas? Let's face it, ordinary people came up with the paper clip, typing correction fluid, and toy dogs called "Pound Puppies," out of the need to correct a problem. In some cases it was a business need and in the case of the Pound Puppies, it was a personal need to supply a child with a dog to play with because they could not have a dog in their apartment. All of these ideas from ordinary people went on to become huge successes and generate a lot of money for people. I have personally seen a small team of people change a business process and save the company more than $200,000 in less than a week.

All of that said, we still need leadership with vision to steer businesses in the right direction. There are two types of power: legitimate and perceived. A manager may have power legitimized by his position, but many people other than managers have perceived power. These are the people in the line organization to whom people go to get things done, to bounce ideas off of, or just to get advice. They may be a co-worker, a team leader, a supervisor, or even a manager, but these are the people who are your rising stars. You can easily see who they are by watching and listening to what people say about them. They may not always be the ones with the most technical skills in their area, but they are the ones with charisma and political connections to get things done. You probably already know who some of these people are.

Changing the Cultural Change

Changing the culture of a company or any organization begins with you, the manager, making changes. If you are a manager who only looks at the numbers and tells your supervisors and employees that they did not meet the performance goals for the month, then next month everyone will try and make the numbers even if it means running a machine longer to increase machine efficiency. This creates excess inventory or sales numbers that look like they are going to be short for the month. Your sales manager ships product to a customer before they want it so he can count it as monthly sales even though the customer does not want the product until the middle of the month. These are just a couple of examples employees will use to try and meet "the numbers."

When changing your culture from a numbers-driven system to a Lean system, you yourself need to change your focus. People notice what drives you; if it is numbers, they will give you the numbers or if it is quality and following the Lean system, then that is what they will give you—quality and a Lean system. You as the manager or owner are still the key element of success for Lean. *You need to change the culture of your company.* You as the CEO or owner of the company need to visibly and actively support and drive Lean or it will fail within your company.

Key Ingredients in Cultural Change

- *Change people's behavior, not how they think.* You cannot change the way people think, but you can change the way they behave and, as this becomes the normal way of doing work, it becomes the new culture. If you focus on meeting the goals of the customer and shipping their product on time with few if any errors, the employees will follow— rather than focus on stocking the warehouse with what sales predicts they will sell to the customer. Do you always hit your sales numbers?
- *Respect for people.* This does not just mean being nice to people or respecting their feelings. What it means is that people are the only resource you have that can think and solve problems; machines cannot. They can only remove monotonous, strenuous work from humans. Use machines where you can to allow your people to put their knowledge, skills, and talents to better use by adding value to the product for the customer. This means listening to what employees have to say and supporting them in solving problems they have with their jobs. It means showing how much you respect them—not only as people, but also for their knowledge and skills. Keep in mind that everyone—from the office to the production floor to the warehouse to the janitorial staff—has a right to be successful. Every time they do their job, we as

managers have an obligation to provide our employees with the tools to find those problems and make improvements.

■ *Give employees the obligation to stop production whenever they find a problem; this enables them to work in a way that builds in quality.* This is where you will really change the way you do business. In the employee's job design, state that you give them the obligation to stop production if a problem is found. This is a major shift in cultural ideas in America. This is great but you must be able to respond and help correct these problems as quickly as possible. Any "Andon" system you install to signal problems must have audible and visual indications of the exact location on the production line where the problem has occurred. Forget pagers, cell phones, panic emergency phone numbers, etc.; make the audible signal loud, and annoying if you like. I heard of one company that used an old submarine dive alarm bell. Now that is annoying! Toyota uses different musical melodies to indicate which area is having a problem. Make it visual so everyone can see it. There is nothing wrong with flashing red or blue lights. Now the big problem is getting people to respond quickly. Again, this is management's responsibility, and management should put reasonable punishments in place if you do not respond quickly to a line shutdown. Time is money, and you must also keep the customer happy. I was taking a plant tour at a large computer manufacturer one day and an alarm went off; the vice president giving the tour excused himself, said his production line was down, and that he had to go. He did not apologize for his abrupt departure, and I do not think anyone on the tour expected him to; they were all amazed at how quickly he knew and responded to the problem. He even rejoined the tour later. That is what you want to see in your own plant; not just the vice president or plant manager responding, but engineering, planning, production supervision, materials, and anyone who can help resolve this issue needs to be there. I would rather have more people than not enough to solve the problem.

 – Hold your people accountable for responding. You can do this in a nice way but you need to be firm and *"you" and your staff need to set the example.*
 – Make sure you have designated people to respond when a work cell or production line goes down. Define each person's roles so there is no misunderstanding as to who is to do what.

For many of us in manufacturing, when we build a batch of parts, put them in a container, and send them to the warehouse, of the 250 pieces we sent, we know statistically that 3% are bad (nonconforming) and that seven or eight parts will be defective and most likely create a problem on the production line. What we want is to enable our employees to build in quality; we want them to stop the machining center, stop the lathe if a part is nonconforming, find out why it is not conforming, and then correct the problem before any more nonconforming parts are made. We want them to stop the production assembly line for the same reason, and we want to teach them that this is a completely acceptable way to do their jobs at our company. Some of you have heard that there is a "cost for quality" and that you "cannot build in quality." I believe there is a cost associated with quality and that you can build in quality. There is a definite cost for quality as we teach our employees to stop the production of nonconforming parts. Due to the downtime involved in dealing with the problem, we may not make our daily production goal; however, this cost is dramatically reduced as we correct quality issues so they do not reoccur. The same holds true for the assembly line. When operators on the assembly line find a problem that they cannot resolve within their work cycle (the time allotted for them to do their job), they can stop the production line. In most cases, these stoppages take very little time but each stoppage adds up and before you know it, you have lost production time. But there is an upside because the product going out the door to the customer is built correctly to their accepted specifications; and when the product is delivered on time with no quality issues, the customer is happy and you get repeat business.

What have we done here? We have given employees the tools to build in quality and made them responsible for using them.

■ *Guarantee to your employees that if they have a problem completing their standardized work instruction, their team leader will come to their aid within their job cycle time.* To get your employees to use the tools you have given them to build in quality, they must know and feel secure in knowing that if they stop the production line, there will be no repercussions to them. To do this, you will need a system that provides for them to contact their team leader if there is a problem. The team leader must respond within the operator's job cycle time to help resolve the problem; if it cannot be resolved in that time, then the line is stopped. This means the team leader must be on the production floor at all times and not running around looking for parts or doing the supervisor's job.

Figure 17.1   Good job design.

Take a look at Figure 17.1 and you can see all the elements of good job design. It is not a mistake that two of the circles—*management support* and *employee ownership*—are larger than the others. We go back to the premise that it is management's responsibility to change the culture. By providing new specific guidelines for job design with guaranteed support for the employee, it would be expected that, in return, the employee would take ownership and responsibility for the obligations of tasks listed in the job design such that product quality is significantly improved.

Team Leader and Stopping the Production Line

In some companies where employees are not empowered to stop the production line, they have to wait for their supervisor to come and approve the shutdown. At Toyota, it is a little different. We have talked about employees stopping the production line when a quality problem is found. At Toyota, if employees installing lug nuts find a problem starting a nut properly due to a burr on the thread, they may decide they need help. They call their team leader over and the team leader will try to fix the problem; but if they cannot resolve it before the cycle time runs out, they will need to stop the production line so it can be fixed. In most cases, the operator and the team leader make the decision to stop the line. Once the problem is fixed, the line is restarted.

But if I am busy working, how do I know I have reached the limit of my work cycle? At Toyota, which has a moving assembly line, there are marks on the floor to indicate to the worker how much time they have (Figure 17.2).

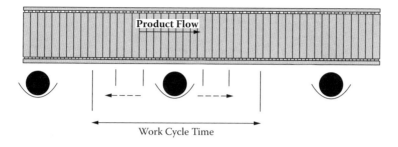

Figure 17.2   Work cycle time.

Notice in Figure 17.2 that you have one operator inside two vertical lines. These lines represent the work cycle time "box." With a moving conveyor, the operator has to complete his work within the confines of the box, working in the direction of the powered conveyor flow. If the operator goes outside the box, the powered line has to stop so he can complete his work. The line restarts and the operator returns to his starting point at the left side of the cycle time box. This will be quite a cultural change for some people.

Creating a Culture That Will Stop and Fix Problems (Get Out of Fire Fighting)

How many times have you been in the production area and observed even a simple problem, such as the paint on the exterior cover of the microwave oven is scratched? You decide to bring this to your production line supervisor and you say, "Look, the cover is scratched. What should we do?" The line supervisor responds, "Oh, don't worry about it. I'm sure someone knows about it and is taking care of it." Ever had something like that happen? It happens all the time and is a result of a lack of interest in correcting a problem, laziness on the part of the supervisor, or even an in-bred culture that "Marion in the repair shop will fix it. She is awesome, we can count on her to fix anything." I have heard something like this many times during my career, and each time I wondered if it ever was fixed.

We discussed in the previous section about stopping the production line to resolve problems. This idea, this change in culture, will help get us out of our fire-fighting mode. If we continue not resolving problems when we find them, then we will always be urgently running to fix them further down the production line so we can expedite the shipment to the customer on time.

Using Metrics to Track Change

I recently was cleaning out my desk in the office (5S was what it needed!) and in the process, I picked up an old monthly report from a company I once worked for. As I looked through it, I could not help but notice how thick it was. The company was not small; it had about 700 employees and was doing very well in sales. But as I looked through the booklet of thirty-two pages printed front and back, I could not find one metric concerning how we were doing against our goals for change implementation. There were charts and graphs for all sorts of items, such as direct versus indirect cost, overtime costs, product cost variances, sales per employee, cost ratio charts, and absorption numbers—I always wondered if anyone ever looked at all of the numbers. I know we never talked about them in staff meetings with the upper management. When we started our Lean journey, we constructed our glass wall to have the five main metrics all Lean factories should have: quality, cost, delivery, safety, and morale. Talk about cutting waste? We cut the report by 50% just for production! Yet we could tell what was happening with the factory: if the quality chart went up, it meant we had fewer quality problems; if costs went up, that meant labor or material costs had risen; if safety went up, we were having too many lost time accidents; and if morale went down, we could usually see the effect with quality numbers going down because people were not as careful with their work.

We still had goals on the charts, which in most cases were tied to changes in product and processes that had to be done. We were to improve quality by 20%, which meant that we had to improve the product or processes to eliminate errors and variation. The delivery goal was to improve by 15% and this meant we had to deliver product to the warehouse on time; thus we needed better throughput through the factory and to do this we needed to use pull manufacturing and eliminate the waste in process steps to reduce lead time. I could go on here but you can see from these examples that these five charts could tell us if we were succeeding at meeting our goals for change. We did end up creating a graph for lead time reduction and one for production space saved, but those were extra graphs that were nice to have but not really needed to tell us how well we were doing. Remember that if you look at a graph and you see a change for the worse, quickly investigate the problem and correct it to get back on track.

To Change a Culture, Change a Behavior

Many scholarly papers, books, and research projects have shown that to change a culture, you need to change the behavior of people. While we as leaders of Lean cannot change deeply rooted ideas that individuals have about such things as likes and dislikes of food, their feelings about minorities, or even their religion, to name a few, what we can do is change their approach and attitude about how they work and how they interact within the confines of the "company." Sometimes, we do see changes in attitude when we change behavior; if it is for the good of the team in the company, then all the better.

If you want people to enjoy change, then you need to make it as fun and interesting as possible. I discovered many years ago that if I listened to the operators and assemblers on the production floor and incorporated some of their ideas into the changes we needed to make, they accepted the changes more readily and the changes were more sustainable. If you want people to accept and change their attitudes about Lean manufacturing, then you need to let them experience it first-hand. This is why you want to try to move relatively fast while implementing changes on the production floor such as work cells, timed delivery routes, flow manufacturing, etc. By incorporating the production staff into the planning and implementation phases of Lean, you slowly change their attitude, which ultimately changes the culture of the company. This is not a quick process. In one company, it took us a year to change the attitude of the hourly workers on the production floor; they were convinced that Lean manufacturing would eliminate their jobs. It did not and as a result of Lean manufacturing, we did not have to hire any more people even though the production volume went up. The resulting attitude change was that Lean manufacturing made their jobs more secure, and they became even more interested in making Lean a success. Another reason their attitudes changed was because of the way work was now accomplished and how raw material was delivered, which made their lives less stressful.

Earlier in the book we spent quite some time discussing how to hold and perform a kaizen event. Although kaizen events are a great way to get people involved, they will not necessarily change the culture you are trying to effect. A kaizen event is typically a week long and when it is over, everyone on the team will go their own way. The facilitator who is usually the

Lean coach will move on to another event with a different team, although while the facilitator is with the team, he can create an atmosphere of cooperation and team spirit while the team members discover they can also actually effect change in areas they want to. At best, people who did not know each other very well will have a better understanding of the new people they have met. "The real value of the event is not in the money saved that week but in the potential for learning and cultural change which is often not realized (Liker and Meier, 2006)."

It has been suggested that if you create a cultural change in one area of the company, you can then transfer that culture change to another area. This suggestion is true based on my experience. While working with a medical device manufacturer that manufactured diagnostic equipment for medical laboratories, we first focused on what we will call product line "A." We restructured the entire value stream, which existed on the production floor and warehouse. We saw a significant change in the attitude of the people working in the value stream. As each work cell was created, we included the assemblers by giving them an opportunity to provide input into the flow and layout of the work cells. They reviewed work instructions and incorporated necessary changes to provide better flow; once completed, these documents were formalized. Assemblers working with a material handler created the locations on the point-of-use racks for all raw materials. Typical rack flow was from left to right in order of assembly. After using these new work cells and pull inventory from station 1 to station 2 and so forth to the end of the production line, they had become believers in the value of Lean manufacturing. When we started work on the next product line, product "B," we simply had people from product "A" help people on product "B" create their work cells and value stream flow. From the experiences learned by the people of product line "A" and taught to the "B" line, the entire restructuring of the value stream actually took less time. When completed, everyone on the production floor agreed that Lean manufacturing did deliver the expected results.

How do you know when the culture is changed? You will know you have reached a true learning culture when you believe, and believe in each other, to a level where you are consistently seeing continuous improvement in your organization—and when your employees consistently deliver changes they would like to make or have done without being asked. But do not forget that changing culture takes time and patience.

Chapter 18

Final Thoughts

What Have We Learned?

One thing we have learned is that we do not always see the problems and opportunities that are in our midst. Remember when I talked about my sensei (teacher) telling the story about sitting in the circle and seeing nothing to fix? When he reported back to his sensei, the sensei told him, "No problem is a big problem," which means we have a much bigger problem because your mind is blocking out what needs to be seen. I have been in manufacturing all my life and thought I could see problems where they existed…that was, until I sat down in the circle and observed the people on the production floor and even in the office at work.

You will get lots of questions about what you are doing when you are observing, but no one will really bother you. After you sit there for a while, people will get used to you observing their activities and they will go back to their normal routine. Then watch with a critical eye and see how many things you can find that need to be corrected. Count them, write them down, and then create a plan to implement the changes.

We have learned about kaizens and what a wonderful tool they are to help us implement change and to eliminate waste in the system. Kaizens alone cannot change the culture. In fact, you should not use kaizens as your main method to implement change, but rather as a way to cultivate and grow your employees to continuously look for areas that need improvement.

Use kaizens to facilitate breakthrough change when you need to fix a cross-functional problem.

What we have learned from the value stream map is that there is an enormous amount of waste in our systems and that we have a powerful tool here. If we did a value stream map for the office, it would show as much waste if not more than the production floor. You have learned how to build and read a VSM (value stream map) and you have been shown how to determine what areas you should attack in order to reduce inventory, production complexity, and wasteful steps. When identified on a VSM, it is easy to plot a course to correct these issues. Another thing about knowing how to read a VSM is that if you visit a supplier or customer who has them posted on the wall, you can easily see how much waste there is in their system. Whenever you begin to analyze a new production workflow, you always begin with the VSM.

The PFEP (Plan-For-Every-Part) is the elephant in the room that no one really wants to try and tackle. It is big, it is tough, and it has the potential for causing great damage if handled incorrectly. You have learned how to create a system that looks at all of the attributes of a part and its packaging that comes from a supplier, and how to use that information to build a supplier network for the replenishment of your supermarket and the production floor. Remember to properly maintain this system so that you will benefit from its ability to reduce and maintain inventory.

Another culture change to employees in small companies is that there is a predetermined time to complete a task. In some small companies, you have a work order with stated production times. When the employees complete a task, oftentimes they just write down the stated production time even if it took a few minutes longer or they put down the actual time it took on the work order. In the Lean factory, they no longer have to do this.

In teaching the American worker that it is OK to shut down a production line to fix a problem is a huge cultural shift and one that takes time to instill in everyone.

Sustaining Lean Conversion

Many times, I find myself asking the question, "How do you sustain Lean conversion?" When you ask other people in the Lean field the same question, you get plenty of different answers. Sustaining Lean improvements that have been completed is not difficult, but sustaining the Lean movement and continuous improvement is very difficult. The real and only way to sustain Lean manufacturing is to change the culture, which as we have discussed can be difficult but completely achievable with the commitment of the owners and senior management of your company. The people in your company need to know that Lean is not a way of thinking but rather a new way of doing business. Without this commitment and a show of support from management, you may end up implementing some of the tools of Lean but not put into action the constant learning culture, which is being free to stop the production line whenever there is a problem and challenge the status quo with continuous improvement. At one company, all of the senior management, from the CEO on down, meet for one week at one of their factories and hold a kaizen event for themselves; they do this for a couple or reasons. First, it shows the rest of the company that even the high-level managers are using and supporting the tools and processes; and secondly, it allows them time to focus on one problem each year that they would like to resolve.

If you believe in Lean manufacturing, you need to believe in a self-directed workforce and supervisors who are coaches and facilitators—and not the old hard-line supervisor.

At some companies, all supervisors and managers are required to complete a specified number of Lean activities, such as kaizen events, which are tied to their annual performance review and compensation. I have seen this method of holding people responsible used successfully in many companies but each company is different, so determine a method of holding people accountable that works for your organization. I do believe there must be some form of accountability for Lean implementation tied to a person's annual performance review that will help to ensure the implementation of Lean.

The use of audits and reports helps the sustainment effort but nothing works as well as having management show itself on the production floor; this shows they are committed to watching and listening to what people have to say. The more management and the office staff use and support Lean, the more readily the factory staff will too. Many of the factory staff look at the initiatives of management and think of them as just another flavor-of-the-month campaign that will be gone before you know it; and if it is one that only focuses on the production floor, you will continue to enlarge any gap in trust that there might have been between you and the production floor. That is one of the good things about Lean manufacturing: its tools and principles can be used in the office as well as the production floor, thereby making everyone equal.

Sustaining Lean also has marketing and salesmanship included in the effort. We all know that restaurants update and refresh their menus, and companies are always refreshing their commercials to peak people's interest in their products. Lean manufacturing is the product you are trying to sell to your employees so you need to "freshen up" the message and signs on occasion just to garner new enthusiasm. You need to revitalize some of the materials used for training and updating, or reassign responsibilities whenever you can to keep the product "Lean" and selling well.

The top five reasons that Lean implementation fails (Schlicting, 2009):

1. Missing management support
2. Lack of employee involvement
3. Lack of customer focus
4. Operational instability
5. Lack of money

Most companies focus on implementing only two areas of Lean. First is *just-in-time production* (single unit pull) and second is *building in quality*. In this book I have attempted to teach you how to implement a solid basis for your house of quality by emphasizing operational stability and employee involvement, in addition to just-in-time and by achieving built-in quality with error-proofing using the 5 whys, etc.

There are three major wastes: "muda," which means waste and which we have discussed in detail, overburdening ("muri") and unevenness ("mura"). Overburdening is pushing a machine or person too far, and mura is unevenness of demand for the product, which hides waste.

Missing management support: This is when one person in the company is assigned the job of implementing Lean but gets no support from upper management in the form of money, people, or equipment.

Lack of employee involvement: This happens when information about Lean is not communicated to all the employees in a timely manner and when employees are not trained in Lean principles and ideas.

Lack of customer focus: This happens when your employees and management forget that they need to look at the company in a different way, through the eyes of the customer.

Operational instability: This happens when you have not created the proper foundation to build Lean upon.

Lack of money: Management does not supply the necessary funds to buy the material to implement and sustain Lean.

You need a focused and sustained effort to ensure that the top five reasons for failure do not exist or your results with Lean will not be as successful as you would like.

The Human Factor

You need to continually reinforce the idea that Lean manufacturing will not eliminate anyone's job. If you have a situation where, as a result of Lean, you need to reassign human resources because the extra manpower was no longer needed in a given area, it must be made very clear to the people involved that they have not lost their jobs and are merely being reassigned to better utilize their skills or to expand their skills. If they leave the company because they do not like their new position, it becomes even more important to let people know why they left. The hourly staff will understand if you have cultivated and achieved a good level of trust with them.

Goals and Measurements

One of the biggest problems I have found in any business is the lack of goals and objectives that are linked and support each other. If you have a company that has competing goals between departments, you will never succeed in implementing Lean. All goals in the company must support each other and the implementation of Lean; you cannot have a cost reduction goal for purchasing without a supporting goal in engineering. Also, you cannot have a goal for the warehouse to reduce space without a supporting goal for purchasing to reduce the amount of inventory they bring in. One company created a team called the Global Metrics Team, and their job was to develop metrics for the entire company; when a department made a goal for themselves, it had to be approved by the Global Metrics Team so that all goals were interdependent of each other. This is an excellent idea.

Rewards Help

I have accumulated a number of ideas for cost reduction programs during my years in industry and have found one method that paid dividends with little outlay of cash. We had about 350 employees in the plant and this was before Lean manufacturing and continuous improvement were well known in the United States. For each suggestion an employee turned in, we gave them 500 Gold Bond stamps. For my younger readers, a specific number of these stamps were given to you when you purchased gasoline, food, hotel rooms, etc., at participating stores. They were similar to frequent flyer miles today, with one exception: as you collected more and more stamps, you would trade them for goods found in the Gold Bond Merchandise Catalog. You might need 2000 stamps for a small suitcase or 500,000 stamps for a television. Because of the popularity of such stamps back in the 1960s and 1970s, we received as many as 200 suggestions a month. Then if your suggestion was implemented, we documented the actual savings and you received a specified number of stamps for each $1000 saved.

I give you this example to show you that simple incentives, even today, can work wonders. Although we want continuous improvement to be a way of life in your company, there is no reason you cannot have incentives to get ideas. It is also critical to the success of your program that you celebrate each successful improvement that is implemented. This can be as simple as a free lunch in the cafeteria, a gasoline gift card, a department store gift card, or even donuts and pizza. Do something to show your appreciation for what your employees have accomplished because for each continuous improvement idea implemented and wasteful steps or processes corrected, it will provide more profit to the company. But do not overdo it! You need to keep it as a reward and not let it become an expectation of your employees that Friday is pizza day. Until the culture of continuous improvement becomes second nature to your employees, you may need to use incentives to keep the ideas coming. Even today, Toyota pays cash rewards for some of the ideas employees submit.

Where Do You Find People with Lean Business Knowledge?

Many people are unaware of one of the smallest and least-tapped resources in the engineering profession. Everyone has heard of mechanical, electrical, and chemical engineers. You may have even heard of a manufacturing engineer, but what is an industrial engineer? As a small company, you may not have heard of such a career specialty; however, if there is one engineering and business profession that encompasses the goals and ideas of the Toyota Production System, it is that of the industrial engineer.

An industrial engineer is one who is concerned with the design, installation and improvement of integrated systems of people, material, information, equipment, and energy by drawing upon specialized knowledge and skills in the mathematical, physical, and social sciences, together with the principles and methods of engineering analysis and design to specify, predict and evaluate the results to be obtained from such systems (Salvendy, 2001, p. 1).

Taiichi Ohno calls industrial engineering "a total manufacturing technology reaching the whole business organization" (Ohno, 1988). Ohno believes that the industrial engineer should be a profit center; in other words, the industrial engineer needs to produce cost savings that increase profits. And I agree completely with this idea. Based on my own experience and Ohno's, we would recommend at least one industrial engineer on staff to promote and champion continuous improvement. This will provide a continuous flow of change ideas, which provide continuous profit from operations. Some of the industrial engineer's other areas of responsibility are work simplification and justifying large-scale capital projects. Performing time studies is an old standard job requirement of the industrial engineer, one that has now been transferred to technicians. However, a well-trained industrial engineer can do time studies very well.

Conclusion

Changing the culture of a company to be one of continuous learning, continuous improvement, and building trust and respect is a very challenging task. Lean manufacturing is a never-ending quest; I like the word "quest" better than "journey" because I think it truly says what we are doing to the company and ourselves as we move forward with Lean. The *Encarta Dictionary* defines quest as "a search for something, especially a long or difficult one." No one has said that the journey to implementing Lean will be an easy one; it is full of roadblocks, politics, concrete heads (people who will not change), not to mention complacency and passive resistive rejection. But through all of this you can find a way to truly change and improve the company you work for. You need to find in yourselves the desire to change and make things better in the workplace even if it means giving up part of the department you worked so hard to build. It can be tough to accept these changes, especially if you are not the type of person who readily accepts change, but this goes back to the quest: it is a long and tough road but you can be successful and when you do, you are all the better for making the quest.

As the owners of small- and mid-sized companies, some of which you have started and grown yourself, you are not unaccustomed to a quest. You were on a quest when you discovered that you wanted to start that bakery or manufacture bicycles, or the quest to improve human life with new and innovative medical devices and equipment. Getting to the point you are at today was a difficult journey, one filled with risks, danger, and strife; and for these same reasons you are a risk taker in your organization, someone who likes to change the way the world does things, and this is why you are willing to take on the challenge of implementing Lean manufacturing.

If you are a perfectionist or someone who believes the only way to do something is to follow verbatim the book you just read, then you may find the quest to Lean difficult. The quest to Lean is one of trial-and-error experimentation with changes and a willingness to make changes even if you do not have all the information you need. We say that if you believe you are 50% correct on the way you want to do something, then go do it, try it, see if it works. If it does not, then come back, look at the results, change your plan, and try again—for without risk there is no reward.

Run on the edge of being out of control: in other words, do not be afraid to take risks.

Good luck on your quest.

Glossary

This glossary is not intended as a comprehensive list of words used in Lean manufacturing or the Toyota Production System, but rather as an attempt to cover the important words found in this book.

5S: Five words beginning with the letter "S" that describe the workplace practices that are conducive to visual control and Lean manufacturing. 5S is one of the foundations of Lean manufacturing. The 5Ss are

1. Sort: Remove all unneeded items from your workplace.
2. Straighten: Neatly organize with a place for everything and everything in its place.
3. Shine: Clean your work area, sweep, wash the desk or workbench, throw away the trash, etc.
4. Standardize: Standardize the process of the first three steps by adding it to your standard workplan.
5. Sustain: Discipline yourself to perform all four previous activities on a regular basis.

A3 report: A report developed by Toyota that gathers all the information for a problem on a single sheet of paper. This includes the problem statement, analysis, corrective actions, and action plan, which many times include graphics. A3 is an international standard for a specific size of paper, the equivalent United States size is 11 × 17 inches.

ABC production analysis: Separates part numbers into groups based on product demand. Lean practitioners use the process to decide how much inventory to hold for each product, with "A" items being high runners, "B" items medium runners, and 'C" items low runners.

Andon: Is a visible lighted management tool that indicates the status of operations in a given area. It signals when an abnormality occurs, usually with a light and sound signal. It is typically hung from the ceiling in a position that is easily seen by everyone. The most common design is two or more rows of numbers corresponding to work cell numbers, with the numbers lighting up when a problem is found. An operator or machine sends a signal to the sign to turn on the appropriate light. You can use other forms of signaling but they should include some form of visual and sound signal.

Batch-and-queue production: A typical mass production method common in many companies where large lots of material are produced in one process and then moved to the next process, whether or not it is ready for the product. The material then sits in a queue, known as work-in-process inventory, until it is ready to be used.

Build-to-order: A condition that exists when the production and order lead times are less than the time the customer is willing to wait for the product and the producer builds only to a confirmed order rather than to a forecast.

Change agent: A person who is responsible for converting a company to Lean manufacturing. He or she has the willpower and drive to initiate the changes needed and to make them sustainable.

Changeover: The process in manufacturing where you switch from one product or part number to another. Usually refers to the switching of tooling or material to produce the new product or part number.

Continuous flow: Producing and moving one piece of product through the manufacturing process continuously without stopping or being held between processes as a WIP.

Cycle time: The time it takes to successfully complete the tasks required for a given work process. An example of cycle time:

Step	Process	Time	Internal time
1	Get raw material	5 seconds	
2	Place part in machine	7 seconds	
3	Tighten machine chuck	7 seconds	
4	Machine part	104 seconds	
5	Remove part from machine	14 seconds	
6	Inspect part		30 seconds
7	Place part in container		10 seconds
	Total cycle time	137 seconds	40 seconds (this time is internal to the 137 seconds)

You can see from this example that the inspection process and placing the finished part into a container is done while another part is being machined. Is there waste in this process? The answer is "yes" if we assume the operator is only performing the tasks shown. How do we determine the amount of wasted time?

Steps 1–3   =   19 seconds

Step 5   =   14 seconds

Total of   33 seconds (this is actual hands on time to get and place material in the machine and remove it)

Step 4   = 104 seconds (to machine the part)

Total cycle time = 137 seconds

Step 4   = 104 seconds (to machine the part)

Steps 6 & 7   = –40 seconds (these steps are done internal to step 4)

Total   =   64 seconds (operator wasted time, "idle" waiting on process to complete)

If we assume we can do 26 parts per hour, then 26 × 54 seconds = 1404 seconds lost operator time, or 23.4 minutes per hour. Assume a 7½-hour workday × 23.4 minutes/hour, and your operator has lost 175.5 minutes, or 2.9 hours. If we assume this is a skilled operator at $18/hour × 256 work days/year, we have just lost $13,363 for the year.

Downtime: Production time lost due to planned or unplanned stoppages.

Error-Proofing (mistake-proofing): A method that helps operators and assemblers avoid making mistakes when they produce product. Methods and tools are designed to reduce or eliminate the possibility of choosing the wrong part, assembling the wrong part, leaving out a part, etc.

Every-Part-Every-Interval (EPEI): The frequency with which a given product is produced within the production system. If a part number is produced every other day, its frequency would be every two days.

Gemba: The term for "actual place," typically used in conjunction with the production floor, that is, "go see the process in work cell 3 so you can write the standard work process." The term is often used to stress the importance going to see the process or problem in person so you can make a good decision.

Just-in-Time (JIT) production: JIT is the delivery of product to the customer when the customers need it and only when they need it. This does not only mean the end user of the product produced, but also the next distributor, warehouse, department, or work cell that is next in line. The theoretical goal is to produce and deliver one product or part at a time.

Kaizen: The Japanese word for "improvement." Kaizen's goal is to improve standardized processes and activities by eliminating the waste found within the process or activity.

Kanban: A signaling device that indicates a product is ready to move on to the next process, or withdrawal from the previous process. It can also be a signal card showing how much of a product to make.

Non-value-added time: Any activity that adds cost but no value to the product from the customer's viewpoint.

Operator balance chart: A tool used to assist in the analysis and distribution of work to create a balanced continuous flow of product from a multi-step and multi-operator process, while keeping the work elements below the work cell's takt time.

Overproduction: Producing more products sooner or faster than is required by the next process. It is the most grievous waste a company can have.

Pacemaker cell, or pacemaker process: A process located along a value stream that acts as the scheduling and pace-setting control point. The pacesetter is not a bottleneck on the value stream because it does not constrain the flow of product.

Pitch: The amount of time it takes to create or pack-out one container of product. The formula for pitch:

$$\text{Takt time} \times \text{Pack-out quantity} = \text{Pitch}$$

Plan-Do-Check-Act (PDCA): An improvement cycle that is based on a scientific method of proposing a change to a process and then implementing the change, measuring the results of the change, and then taking the appropriate action. PDCA definitions follow:
- Plan: Determine the process you want to change and the goals you want to see when the change is complete.
- Do: Implement the change.
- Check: Compare the goals against the final results to see if you accomplished your goals.
- Act: Stabilize and standardize the change or reevaluate your plan and try again.

Plan-For-Every-Part (PFEP): A detailed plan for every part in a product that includes the part number, dimensions, amount of usage, and many other attributes that provide for specific handling and use of every part.

Seven Wastes: The seven major wastes typically found in mass production and identified by Toyota Corporation are listed below:

1. Overproduction: Producing more product than is needed by the next process. This is the worst of the seven wastes because it contributes to all the others.
2. Waiting: Operators standing, waiting for machines to cycle, or waiting for parts.
3. Conveyance: Moving parts and product unnecessarily from a process to a warehouse or between processes.
4. Processing: Performing unnecessary or incorrect work to a document, part, or product.
5. Inventory: Any extra material that is above the minimum required to maintain precise control of the pull system.
6. Motion: Operators taking unnecessary moves, reaches, stretches, steps, etc., that are not needed.
7. Correction: Rework, scrap, and inspection.

Standardized work: The instructions created for a given process when you take small elements of any process and combine them into one process and document the process on paper. It is then a requirement of the people doing the process to perform it in the manner described in the process.

Supermarket: Our new name for the raw materials warehouse. The old warehouse is restructured to resemble a modern supermarket with components for each assembly next to each other, rather than varying locations within the old warehouse.

Takt Time: How often you should produce a product to match the demand of your customer. What does the word "takt" mean? It is a German word meaning rhythm or meter. Example: Your customer pulls from your inventory a specific product at the rate of 200 parts per day, so your "takt" rate:

$$\text{Takt time} = \frac{\text{Average working time/day}}{\text{Customer demand/day}}.$$

Therefore, we need to deliver product from the production line to the finished goods warehouse every 2.25 minutes for a takt rate of one part every 2.3 minutes.

Value-added time: Any activity that adds cost and value to the product that the customer is willing to pay for. This is the same as "cycle time."

Value Stream: All of the actions, both value added and non-value added, that are required to bring a product from concept to customer order. This includes all the support activities needed to transform the product from concept to finished product. Value stream typically refers to the operations organization and the use of one value stream manager to oversee an entire product line from purchasing to the finished goods warehouse.

Value Stream Map (VSM): This is a relatively simple diagram showing every step in moving material and information from raw material in the door to finished product to the customer, and then showing new orders back to production planning and on to the raw material suppliers. This is a closed-loop diagram that also shows the amount of waste held in the system.

Water spider: A water spider is also known as a material handler or timed delivery route runner: the person who runs material through the factory at designated times. This is a very important job and it should be considered a special advantage to hold this position because the person gets to see everything going on in the factory and is responsible for delivering material and information on time to all work cells.

WIP: Work-in-process.

Work instruction: A work instruction is a detailed description of how to produce a part or assembly for a given product. Work instructions include detailed information such as torque requirements, quality checks, labor standards, and other fine details needed to create a quality product. It is different from standard work due to its fine detail. Standard work is more macro in nature and typically is placed above a work cell to let management know what activity is being done at that workstation.

References

Aberdeen Group. *The Lean Strategies Benchmark Report.* Accessed May 15, 2011, Aberdeen Group 2004.

Cunningham, Jean E., and Orest J. Fiume. *Real Numbers: Management Accounting in a Lean Organization.* Durham, NC: Managing Times Press, 2003.

Dennis, Pascal. *Getting the Right Things Done.* The Lean Enterprise Institute, Brookline, MA, 2006.

Harris, Rick, Chris Harris, and Chuck Streeter. *Lean Supplier Development: Establishing Partnerships and True Costs Throughout the Supply Chain,* Productivity Press. New York: CRC Press, 2011.

Harris, Rick, Chris Harris, and Earl Wilson. *Making Material Flow: A Lean Material-Handling Guide for Production Control, Operations, and Engineering Professionals.* Brookline, MA: Lean Enterprise Institute, 2003.

Jones, Dan and Jim Womack. *Seeing the Whole: Mapping the Extended Value Stream.* Brookline, MA: The Lean Enterprise Institute, 2003.

Liker, Jeffery K. *The Toyota Way: 14 Management Principles from the World's Greatest Manufacturer.* New York: McGraw-Hill, 2004.

Liker, Jeffery K. and David Meier. *The Toyota Way Fieldbook: A Practical guide for Implementing Toyota's 4P's.* New York: McGraw-Hill, 2006.

Ohno, Taiichi. *Toyota Production System: Beyond Large-Scale Production.* New York: Productivity Press, 1988.

Rother, Mike and Rick Harris. *Creating Continuous Flow: An Action Guide for Managers, Engineers, and Production Associates.* Brookline, MA: The Lean Enterprise Institute, 2001.

Rother, Mike and John Shook. *Learning to See: Value Stream Mapping to Create Value and Eliminate Muda.* Brookline, MA: The Lean Enterprise Institute, 2003.

Salvendy, Gavriel. *Handbook of Industrial Engineering: Technology and Operations Management.* New York: John Wiley and Sons, 2001.

Schlichting, C. *Sustaining Lean Improvement.* Master's Thesis, Worcester, MA: Worcester Poly Tech Institute, 2009.

Siegel, Joel G. and Jae K Shim. *Dictionary of Accounting Terms,* 5th ed. Hauppauge, NY: Barren's Educational Series, Inc., 2010.

Smalley, Art. *Creating Level Pull: A Lean Production-System Improvement Guide for Production-Control, Operations, and Engineering Professionals.* Brookline, MA: Lean Enterprise Institute, 2004.

Index

Page numbers followed by f indicate figure
Page numbers followed by t indicate table